Bin Laden in the suburbs

criminalising the Arab Other

Scott Poynting, Greg Noble, Paul Tabar
& Jock Collins

Sydney Institute of Criminology Series
Sydney 2004

Sydney Institute of Criminology Series No 18

Series Editors: Chris Cunneen, Mark Findlay, Julie Stubbs
University of Sydney Law School

Other titles in the Series

Aboriginal Perspectives on Criminal Justice, Chris Cunneen (out of print)
Doing Less Time: Penal Reform in Crisis, Janet Chan
Psychiatry in Court, Peter Shea
The Man in White is Always Right: Cricket and the Law, David Fraser (out of print)
The Prison and the Home, Ann Aungles
Women, Male Violence and the Law, Julie Stubbs (ed)
Fault in Homicide, Stanley Yeo
Anatomy of a French Murder Case, Bron McKillop
Gender, Race & International Relations, Chris Cunneen & Julie Stubbs
Reform in Policing: Lessons from the Whitrod Era, Jill Bolen
A Culture of Corruption: Changing an Australian Police Service, David Dixon (ed)
Defining Madness, Peter Shea
Developing Cultural Criminology, Cyndi Banks (ed)
Indigenous Human Rights, Garkawe, Kelly & Fisher (eds)
When Police Unionise: the politics of law and order in Australia, Mark Finnane
Regulating Racism: Racial Vilification Laws in Australia, Luke McNamara
A History of Criminal Law in New South Wales, G D Woods

Published by:
The Sydney Institute of Criminology
University of Sydney Faculty of Law
173–175 Phillip Street
Sydney NSW 2000
Ph 61 2 9351 0239

Distributed by:
Federation Press
PO Box 45 Annandale
71 John Street
Leichhardt NSW 2040
Ph 61 2 9552 2200

National Library of Australia Cataloguing-in-Publication data
Bin Laden in the suburbs : criminalising the Arab other.
Bibliography. Includes index. ISBN 0 9751967 0 7.
1. Minorities - Press coverage - Australia. 2. Arabs -Australia - Public opinion. 3. Muslims - Australia -Public opinion. 4. Discrimination - Australia. 5. Multiculturalism - Australia. I. Poynting, Scott. II. Title.

Cover Design by Pro Bono Publico P/L
Photograph of Arab Rd by Scott Poynting
Printed by Southwood Press
Typeset by the Institute of Criminology
Index by Glenda Browne

Contents

List of figures

Foreword

The anatomy of anti-Arab racism

An 'interesting' conspiracy tale circulated in the aftermath of September 11. It went like this: Arab Muslims are too dumb to plan something like the terrorist attack on the towers; it was really Mossad that was behind the attack.

The story is interesting because it combines two racial stereotypes in one: the anti-Semitic stereotype of the conspiratorial Jew and the typical colonial stereotype of the dumb, inferior, 'third world looking' colonised. The fact that these two racisms are combined in trying to come to terms with an action initiated by Arab Muslims is not a coincidence. The latter has always had an ambivalent position within the spectrum of European otherness.

This spectrum is structured by a polarity between what we might call 'the other of the will' and 'the other of the body'. The other of the will is the cunning other, the competitive other, the manipulative other, the conspiratorial other, the other that can thwart my plans and undermine me, the other who, deep down, I fear might be superior to me ... at least with regards to intelligence. The epitome of this other is of course the anti-Semitic figure of the Jew. It is also the product of a racism very specific to it, the racism of extermination.

The other of the body, on the other hand, is an unambiguously inferior other, inferior in terms of intelligence, inferior in terms technical know-how, inferior in terms of capacity to be productive (e.g., the category of 'the lazy other'). The epitome of this other was the colonial portrayal of the black African. Likewise, it is also the product of a very specific type of racism, the racism of exploitation.

Paradoxically, it was his or her supposed inferiority and lack of intelligence that made the lazy other of colonisation, the other that is all body, exploitable. The other of the mind, the cunning other, was by definition un-exploitable, for if anything, such an other had the potential to himself or herself exploit the European colonisers, manipulate them and use them against their will. By definition such an other could only be exterminated.

This does not mean, of course, that the other of the body was never exterminated. The history of colonial extermination in the process of territorial and political domination is well established. Yet, what is interesting about such processes of extermination is that within them the colonised other was much less and on fewer occasions *essentialised* as an object of extermination. The European colonisers, like everybody else in this world, try to exterminate what they classify as a threat, not what they classify as inferior. And once the colonised other are eliminated as a threat, once they have been reduced in number, once their political will has been eradicated, once their capacity for resistance has been squashed, that is, once they have been 'killed' politically and socially as a group, then, most often than not, begins a period where a substantial number of people among the colonisers begin to 'love the socio-politically dead other', and yearn to 'preserve' its culture. One can see this, in an anthropological spirit, as a kind of 'political necrophilia' specific to the evolution of colonial culture. Perhaps it is best exemplified by those European settlers or their descendants who, once the natives have been politically smashed, but only then, not only express their love of 'native cultures' (like the European 'appreciation' of Indigenous desert paintings in Australia) but manage to express outrage at their 'living conditions', at 'the death rate among them' and even courageously celebrate their 'resistance'. All is done for as long as it is subliminally well-known that it is a resistance of the politically dead, doomed to have no effect on the quality of life they, as colonisers or descendant of colonisers, have acquired from being 'well positioned' in this cumulative process of resource appropriation and theft. It is this necrophilic appreciation of the politically dead other that characterises the racism of exploitation. Practically, it means that the other has been subjugated, pacified and tamed enough to become classified as 'valuable', either aesthetically or for labouring purposes.

This necrophilic dimension is totally absent in the racism of extermination. For the Nazis, no matter how many Jews have been exterminated, the Jew was still a threat. The capacity of the cunning, manipulative other to be a threat is not dependent on numbers as is the case with the colonised. One manipulative Jew can do as much harm as ten, or a thousand, or a million. One cannot imagine a situation where a Nazi says, 'we have this Jewish family in our neighbourhood, they have such an interesting culture' while another says 'we have too many'. For the Nazi, one Jew is always already too many.

It is from within the field constituted by the polarity between the racism of exploitation and the racism of extermination, and their imaginary others, that we can appreciate the 'ambiguous categorisation' of the Arab by the European colonisers. For the Arab is at the same time, a hybrid that is both a 'Jew' and a 'black African' and an in-between that is neither. He is an other of the will and the body, and neither. She is both cunning, and too dumb to be cunning. Even in phenotypical terms, the Arab is neither a 'Jewish type' nor a 'black type' but an in-between, or a 'both'. The Arab is both an uncivilised other like the black African but also, like the Jew, belonging to an early modern civilisation that has shaped European civilisation. The Arab is a monotheist like the Jewish other but with an 'inferior' religious imagination (e.g., the paradise as full of virgins) akin to more primitive religious forms. And while the dangerous Jew of the anti-Semitic imagination is categorised as a snake, a hyena, or a vermin, and the exploitable black as a domesticated animal, the Arab is neither. The Arab seems to be for the European coloniser what the pig is for Jewish and Muslim cultures, a polluting non-exploitable (i.e., not good for consumption) creature, and yet unlike the 'Jewish snake' not so much of a threat that it must be exterminated at all cost.

Today's racialised Arab, the bin Laden-like figure of the scheming international terrorist, is a continuation within a global context of this racialising dichotomy. For is not the imaginary bin Laden an in-between figure, hybridising the two key figures of otherness in the era of globalisation: the superior, manipulative, scheming (Jewish) international banker and the miserable, inferior, exploitable (third world looking) migrant labourer?

And here again, the post-colonial state is ambivalent about the Arab within the metropolis in much the same way as the colonial state was ambivalent about him or her in the colony. It continually asks itself the same question: Is the Arab a migrant 'black African' bodily other, or a 'Jewish' subversive scheming will?

Like every bodily migrant other, the Arab migrant smells (his or her house, kids, clothes, cars and cooking smells and pollutes the neighbourhood), his or her way of life and place of worship is an eyesore that needs to be contained. Within this 'bodily register', one or two Arabs might be tolerable but when there are 'too many' it becomes unbearable.

But, unlike most migrants, the Arab migrant is a subversive will. He or she is not only interested in opening a restaurant and offering exotic food. He or she (especially, she, the veiled one) embodies the will of the other, the one who can subvert the European national/patriarchal order by speaking and acting in the name of another, Arab Muslim, supranational patriarchal order. They invade our shores, take over our neighbourhood and rape our women. They are all little bin Ladens and they are everywhere: explicit bin Ladens and closet bin Ladens; conscious bin Ladens and un-conscious bin Ladens; bin Ladens on the beach and bin Ladens in the suburbs, as this book is aptly titled. Within this register, the Arab, like the Jew of the Nazis, is intolerable as such. Even a single Arab is a threat.

Contain the Arab, or exterminate the Arab? A 'tolerable' presence in the suburbs, or caged in a concentration camp? Exterminate their political will or remove them physically, in their totality, will and body? The politics of the Western post-colonial state is constantly and dangerously oscillating between these two tendencies today. It is this dangerous oscillation that is so lucidly exposed in this book, a book written by veteran anti-racists as it were.

When I first arrived in Australia in 1976, I was an anti-Muslim racist. Born and raised in a staunchly Christian Lebanese environment, leaving Lebanon in the midst of a civil war I clearly perceived as 'backward Muslims hordes out to destroy civilised Europeanised Christians', I embodied and felt most of the racist categorisations I am critically reflecting upon today.

In my first year at Macquarie University, I encountered another Christian Lebanese who was giving a talk on the Lebanese civil war. He spoke against the confessionalist Christian versus Muslim conception of Lebanon and I thought he was just a misguided idiot. His name was Paul Tabar. I later discovered that he was married to a Shi'a Muslim woman, which confirmed to me that he was an idiot. But in the end, he was offering a version of human relations that was very far from, and I un-hesitantly say ethically and practically far superior to my world outlook at the time. As I thought things through, which is what a university allows you to do — despite what some simplistic anti-university journalists want people to believe today —, it did not take me much time before I was won over.

In the meantime, I was in the company of more and more students who had an anti-racist ethical and practical view of what human relations ought to be about. A handful of those became long term friends and a major influence on me. Among them were Greg Noble and Scott Poynting. Together as postgraduate students we debated the early writing of Jock Collins on migration and labour market segmentation as part of our anti-racist abc.

So, the reader can imagine how grateful I am to be given the opportunity to write the Foreword to a book on anti-Arab racism authored by the very four people that contributed to cure my anti-Arab racism. I like to think that they are the people through whom the Australian society of the seventies made me a better person. They represented some of what was best about that society. And so, today, as I see Australian society moving towards the very 'Christian versus Muslim outlook' that it has so successfully rid me of, I experience puzzlement, pain, and a sense of dread. On one hand, I can see in the new 'Christian versus Muslim' zealots a part of me, and as such, I understand how good people can come to think in such ugly ways. I have no desire to diabolise racists just as I don't diabolise my early self. But on the other, I cannot but feel that such people, in the name of being part of an advanced civilisation, are taking Australian society backward in the direction of the ignorant, arrogant and prejudiced Lebanese culture of the 1970s promoted by a substantial number of Christian chauvinists at the time. And so I have to tell such people, even if part of me thinks that it is useless to preach, I have to tell them: You never go forward by thinking of yourself as protecting Western Christian civilisation against Muslim hordes. You only go backward. This has been proven historically again and again if you care to learn and listen.

Ghassan Hage
Anthropology, University of Sydney

Introduction

'TERROR AUSTRALIS: Bin Laden groups in our suburbs', shrilled the front-page tabloid headline in October 2001 (Miranda 12/10/01b:1). The Australian Federal Police, the Australian Security Intelligence Organisation (ASIO) and 'other agencies' had allegedly 'found sham charities linked directly to terrorist work'. The *Daily Telegraph* editorial of the same day asserted that such 'intelligence ... has identified up to 100 operatives in Sydney suspected of this activity', and urged that 'immediate action' be taken (*Daily Telegraph* 12/10/01:20).

In fact, the 'immediate action' had already begun. In September 2001, ASIO, along with the Federal police, was raiding at gunpoint the homes of Muslim, mainly Arabic-speaking immigrant citizens, amid paper-talk of Al Qaeda 'sleeper cells' in Australia's suburbia. A year later, the papers had the terror in our 'backyard' or on our 'doorstep' in Bali, and 'we' were not sure whether it had a Middle Eastern appearance or a defiant, evil South-East Asian smile. ASIO then raided Indonesian immigrants. No suspects — Arab, Indonesian or other — were charged with terrorist-related offences, after either security swoop. Yet in the panic which ensued, sheikhs of any sort became suspect, turbans of any type were terrifying, and mosques menacing. Numerous letters to the editor and radio talkers-back echoed these concerns, which in many cases vilified people of Arabic-speaking background and in some instances gave rise to acts of racial violence against them.

How could such hysteria be so commonly shared in contemporary Australia? What was in the cultural background that made an alarmist headline like 'Bin Laden groups in our suburbs' resonate with readers? This book looks for answers to these questions: answers — or at least the search for them — that might tell us something about ourselves.

This monograph is not about 'ethnic crime' in the manner of our earlier effort, *Kebabs, Kids, Cops and Crime* (Collins, Noble, Poynting & Tabar 2000). This present work is rather about what public worrying over 'ethnic crime' tells us about Australian society at the beginning of the twenty-first century. Why is it, for example, that culpability for several horrific gang rapes in Sydney in 2000 can be attributed so widely to whole ethnic communities? And under what conditions does, say, a minor incident such as a 'good news story' on the operation of a halal hamburger shop become an occasion for a moral panic about the failures of multiculturalism? How is it that the arrival off Christmas Island in August 2001 of a foundering boatload of emaciated people seeking asylum, mostly from despotic regimes in 'the Middle East', can be manipulated to characterise complete cohorts of applicants for refuge — and their immigrant countryfolk — as dangerous, dishonest, criminally inclined and inhuman? All this, recall, was before 11 September 2001. How did the terrorist attacks of that day in the USA exacerbate existing tendencies in Australia to stereotype Arabs and Muslims as backward, inassimilable, without respect for Western laws and values, and sympathetic to, or complicit with, barbarism and terrorism?

Moral panics usually entail diagnoses of a society's ills, and prescriptions for remedy from both the pundits and the punters. What makes the diagnoses 'ring true' is that they strike a chord with people's experiences; those suffering from particular anxieties about, say, the direction or extent of social change, can identify elements of their worries in the acceleratingly generalised, shared sense of a social ailment. 'Explanations' offered by the 'experts' take up their inchoate concerns, render them more articulate, plausible, and scientific-sounding, and deliver them back to the anxious audiences in a feedback loop which works to the extent that it reverberates with popular anxieties. 'Folk Devils' serve as simple, readily digestible apparent causes of the problem, which is invariably presented as straightforward and without complexity, and a range of simplistic 'solutions' are accordingly proposed. Thus, the examination of a series of moral panics about the 'Arab Other' which we undertake in the chapters that follow, is intended to throw light on what relevant popular anxieties are arising in contemporary Australian society, among whom, how they are taken up, how they are elaborated, how they are circulated, by whom, with what effect, in (or against) whose interests, how the folk devil is 'assembled', even how (some of) the diabolised people themselves (some of the time) are drawn into this construction.

This book addresses some of these questions, and others. It argues that in contemporary Australia we are witnessing the emergence of the 'Arab Other' as the pre-eminent 'folk devil' of our time. This Arab Other functions not only in terms of the specific concerns embedded in fear of crime; it also functions in the national imaginary to prop up the project of national belonging. We show that the concern with 'ethnic crime' and 'Lebanese gangs' meshes with national and international politics in forming an image of a violent and criminal Arab Other, a process in which community leaders often unwittingly participate. This mythic Other has little to do with the lived experience of those of Arab or Middle Eastern or Muslim origin, and everything to do with a host of social anxieties which overlap and feed upon each other in a series of moral panics. This is not simply a process of ideological representation by media and politicians, but impacts upon policing, the judicial system and social policy. This manipulation of the politics of fear ultimately undermines rather than produces social cohesion in a culturally diverse society like Australia, bringing forth a decisive moment in the existence of multiculturalism.

Consider some 'snapshots' of us. The Mufti of Australia, well-known religious leader of this country's Islamic community, is allegedly seen driving in a Sydney suburb with a piece of plastic (or might it be metal?) protruding from the vehicle. Sheikh Al Hilaly is pulled over by police, manhandled, body-searched in his religious robes. Careful, he might be carrying a firearm! Purported, unconfirmed security reports, four years old and unacted upon in the meantime, supposedly suggest the Sheikh may have a gun. He doesn't; but he does object to the treatment. The car is found to be some days out of registration. The Sheikh is arrested, handcuffed and charged with assault and resisting arrest, as well as driving an unregistered and uninsured vehicle. It is page one news. The controversy reverberates for a week in the letters pages and opinion columns — not to mention talkback radio. Most are condemnatory. His 'chequered history' is listed by the *Daily Telegraph*, beginning with the statement that he doesn't speak English in public after twenty years in Australia, although 'critics claim he is fluent' (Morris & English 7/1/03:1,4). The non-traffic charges are dropped before the trial proceeds, some seven months later. Police admit they could not sustain the charges, as they had no lawful reasons to subject him to the search.

Here is one more snapshot. A man who 'loves cricket, voted for John Howard, admires Liberal Party values, and owns a computer hardware company' (Cameron 28/11/02:2) applies to build a Muslim prayer centre in middle-class, semi-rural Annangrove, in Sydney's north-western 'Hills' District where the white-thinking majority likes its fundamentalism Christian. The local council receives thousands of objections and complaints, and the applicant, Australian-born Mr Abbas Aly, receives racial vilification in a poster campaign, a brick through his office window, arson at his home, and eventual smashing of the property in contention, marked with obscene graffiti. The Council, despite the recommendations of its own planning experts, rejects the development application as out of keeping with 'the shared beliefs, customs and values of the local community' (Morris 19/12/02:4). This decision was to be eventually overturned in the Land and Environment Court. There, according to the *Sydney Morning Herald*, Mrs White, secretary of the Annangrove Progress Association, told the court that she was 'unaware of the origin of those putting forward the centre and did not know they were of Australian-Indian background'. She was quoted as saying, 'All I can say is that a jihad has been placed on

Annangrove ... and that creates some fear' (O'Rourke 14/5/03:9). There was fear among the locals of sexual violence, as well as of jihad, from the outsiders. Senator George Campbell cited Baulkham Hills Mayor, lay preacher John Griffith, as 'suggesting the safety of "girls and ladies" is at risk if the mosque is built' (Cameron 28/11/02:2). Irene Buckler, of Glenwood, wrote to the *Daily Telegraph*:

> By surrounding themselves with the trappings of their traditional cultures, the newcomers gradually ousted mine. Like many traditional Australians living in south-western Sydney, I had no choice ... but to move on. The residents of Annangrove have a right to protect their patch without being vilified as racist rednecks (Buckler, 1/8/03: 26).

The next day the *Telegraph* printed the result of its 'Voteline', canvassed on the same day as Buckler's letter. 'A court has overturned a council decision that prevented the building of a mosque at Annangrove. Was it right to do so?' Some 90% of voting readers (616 of them) recorded a 'No' answer; only 10% (or 66) responded 'Yes'.

How do we go about investigating the common sense of 'race', nation, fear and criminality? What are the 'data' of our research; what are our 'methods' for gathering, recording and analysing these? How can we observe and grasp such ideology? Many of our sources are media extracts, garnered from an exhausting but not exhaustive monitoring of the major print media (and to a minor extent, because of costs, the electronic media) in Sydney concentrating around November 1998 to early 2000, and August 2001 to September 2003. There is also some material from national media and other (mainly capital) cities, but Sydney is the major destination for Arabic-speaking immigrants and has the highest population of this cultural and linguistic background — especially concentrated in certain suburbs which have drawn considerable media attention. Nevertheless, the book moves between global, national, state, city and local events to show how these levels are imbricated in moments of moral panic.

The media material is not the only source for our analysis. We also try to grasp how people make sense of their everyday lives by using open-ended, conversation-like recorded interviews and (to a much lesser extent) participant observation. The interviews which we draw upon from various projects over the last six years are more with people on the less powerful side of 'ethnic relations', and we try to incorporate their standpoint(s) in our interpretations.

Thus, in various chapters of the book, there is a mix of media and interview sources. The binding and connecting arguments throughout the book unfold as follows.

Chapter One describes a series of events or issues over the last few years which have been the subject of much media coverage and public debate — 'ethnic crime gangs', 'race rapes', the 'Tampa crisis', the terrorist attacks in the USA on 11 September 2001 and in Bali in October 2002, as well as a series of minor incidents — that reveal social perceptions of the Arab Other. The links that are made between these events and the 'perpetrators' involved, however problematic, constitute a homogenised category of those of Arabic-speaking background, Middle Eastern appearance or Muslim faith. They are seen as a 'dangerous other', radically different from an implicit Australian norm. The racialised 'frame' at work here naturalises cultural explanations of criminal and terrorist activities.

Chapter Two picks up this argument and shows how military metaphors in the representations of these events form a crucial link, positing an equivalence between rowdy young men of Middle Eastern appearance, criminal gangs, pack rapists, people-smugglers and queue-jumpers and terrorists, and casting all their offences as a generalised threat. Two narratives employ the metaphor of war in describing these events, but both attempt to recuperate a morally innocent position of the 'ordinary Australian'.

Chapter Three critiques the oft-repeated claim that the young men who are seen to be at the heart of key social problems are 'lost between two cultures'. It demonstrates that this discourse is ethnocentric, inaccurate and part of the repertoire of social control.

The chapter uses interview material to show, rather than a 'loss' of culture or a failure to integrate, the complex and 'hybrid' cultural resources which second-generation Lebanese immigrant young men deploy strategically in their everyday lives. We suggest here that even the 'sympathetic' and well-meaning liberal way of framing the culture of the 'lost' young men of the second generation of immigrants, fails to capture the conscious creativity of their everyday life. Moreover, such framing takes for granted the culturalist 'explanations' critiqued in Chapters One and Two (and later in Chapter Six), and problematically assumes an essential conflict between 'Australian' and 'Middle Eastern' cultures.

Chapter Four traces the Western Sydney 'ethnic gang rape' moral panic of 2001–02, showing how this horrendous crime was racialised and ideologically associated with the masculinity of Muslim culture and the failure to assimilate. (It should not be necessary to point out that to sustain this argument is *not* tantamount to condoning the crime or diminishing the suffering of the victims, as some media columnists have accused.) Not only did the media and populist political representation of these crimes involve racialisation, they also became interwoven with the contemporaneous 'othering' of Arab and other Middle Eastern immigrants and asylum seekers and also Muslim Australians, discussed in Chapter One, as: illegal immigrants, people-smugglers, criminal gangs, terrorists, rapists. The interconnected threads involve common-sense 'orientalism' of the Arab/Muslim Other's masculinity as deviant, immoral and dangerous: racialised and criminalised. These contradictory racist themes include: Lebanese/Muslim men's purported disrespect of women in general; Lebanese/Muslim men being allegedly brought up to regard 'White', 'Western', 'Caucasian', women as 'sluts' and thus 'fair game'; 'ethnic gang rape' as an expression of anti-'Aussie', anti-White, anti-Western hatred which is supposedly encouraged in Muslim communities at large; Muslim and 'Third-World' cultures as barbaric, uncivilised, violent and misogynistic in their law and their morality; condemnation of laxity and indulgence in the Australian legal and political system towards 'unAustralian' transgressors. The chapter further shows how the justice system responded to the moral panic in the context of a political 'law and order' auction.

Chapter Five argues that the construction of the Arab Other has facilitated the emergence of 'dog-whistle politics' in Australia, where politicians and media talk about certain events in nuanced or coded ways, which speak to pervasive fears and prejudices of the Australian population towards people of Arab background, and especially towards those of Muslim faith. These everyday fears can be found in discussion of such supposedly mundane and non-criminal issues such as the opening of a halal Macdonald's, the creation of a specific classes for Muslim women at a local gymnasium, and the case of the Muslim man threatened with dismissal for continuing to pray at work. This form of politics licenses appalling acts of racial vilification that have been on the rise during the moral panics, and increasingly aggressive forms of state repression.

Chapter Six details the ways in which Arab and Muslim community leaders have been drawn into complicity with the pathologising and criminalising of those of Arabic-speaking background, through accepting a discourse which explains criminal behaviour in terms of cultural attributes and through being incorporated in a multiculturalism based on an 'ethnic politics' of party patronage and beholdenness to the state.

Chapter Seven returns to the theme of everyday fears in Australian national life, and details the underlying aspects of Australia's paranoid nationalism. It argues that fear of crime has become increasingly meshed with a range of social anxieties in a climate of panic; anxieties which are projected onto those of Arab or Muslim ancestry and onto multiculturalism generally. These are managed by the State and media organisations in such a way as to promote rather than diminish fear.

The conclusion considers the perilous existence of multiculturalism in the current climate but construes it as a fateful moment full of possibility despite the dominance of 'penal populism'. Rather than witnessing the death of multiculturalism, we are faced with an opportunity to reflect upon the nature of community, cultural diversity and national belonging.

A comment about referencing is called for here. Because we are presenting a considerable amount of media extracts, and because many are written by the same authors on several different days of the same year, the standard author/year referencing method will not suffice. We have used author and date (dd/mm/yy) for media references and the usual author and year for books and scholarly journal articles. Letters to the editor are identified in the text, referenced by name of the letter's author, and indicated as such in the reference list at the end of the book. Newspaper editorials are referenced by the name of the newspaper, as is conventional, with 'editorial' noted in the reference list; newspaper articles without by-lines are also referenced by the name of the newspaper. The press sources referred to in this book may be found in full in the archive editions of the publications that are referenced in the reference list.

Finally, it remains to record our thanks to those who in various ways have contributed to the collective labour of the book. We thank Ghassan Hage not only for his kind Foreword, but for encouraging us to write the book. To Chris Cunneen and the Institute of Criminology, go our thanks for welcoming the idea of the monograph and supporting its production. To Tessa Boyd-Caine in the early stages, to Jocelyn Luff and especially Nina Ralph in the text-editing and production stages, we owe a special thanks. We would like to thank Rob White and Trevor Batrouney for their helpful comments.

We are grateful to Bruno di Biase, Yama Farid, Randa Kattan, Michael Kennedy, Jillanne Martin, Richard Martino, Helen Masterman-Smith, Vicki Mau, Ruth McCausland, Cristina Pebaque,

Frances Simmons, Michael Strutt, Keysar Trad, and the many others — especially our anonymous interviewees and informants — who gave their time, trust, material, ideas and myriad other contributions to the book.

We also thank the Centre for Cultural Research at the University of Western Sydney for helping with the cost of the indexing, ably undertaken by Glenda Browne.

We wish to acknowledge that some chapters and parts of chapters of the book have been reworked from previous publications: parts of Chapter One appear in *Current Issues in Criminal Justice*, vol 14, no 1, pp 43–64; Chapter Two has appeared in an earlier form in *Media International Australia: Culture and Politics*, no 106, pp 110–123; a version of Chapter Three appears in *Palma Journal: An interdisciplinary research publication* vol 9, no 1, pp 93–114; parts of Chapter Four are published in proceedings of the Annual Conference of the Australian Sociological Association, University of New England, Armidale, 4–6 December, 2003. Parts of Chapter Five appear in *Media International Australia: Culture and Politics*, no 109, pp 41–49.

1

The Arab Other

Over the last decade, and intensifying in the late 1990s, there has been a series of events which have been subject to much media coverage and public debate in Australia — 'ethnic crime gangs', 'race rapes', 'invasions' of asylum-seeking 'boat people', the terrorist attacks in the USA on 11 September 2001 and the terrorist bomb blasts in Bali in October 2002. Because of the perception that these events have in common the presence of people from what might be broadly identified as a 'Middle Eastern' ancestry, these events have formed the basis of a series of cycles of moral panic which have centred around those of Arabic-speaking background and especially, but not exclusively, those of Muslim faith. Such waves of panic have recurred over a much longer time span, but we have seen an intensification of these waves since the late 1990s. They have been whipped up by the tabloid press, talkback radio and opportunist politicians, with a subsequent increase in racial attacks in public places across Australia. The second half of 2001 saw one such crescendo, leading up to the federal election in November, during which both the refugee crisis and the insecurities caused by international terrorism were exploited by the Liberal-National Coalition government in their successful bid to return to office, against earlier expectations.

A 'moral panic', in the now oft-repeated formula of Stanley Cohen (1973:9), is a period during which a particular social threat — whether it be a 'condition', a crime or a social group — is identified and made subject to public debate and sustained media coverage. A number of social actors — including politicians, journalists, experts and a range of 'moral entrepreneurs', articulate and evaluate the social threat and its consequences for moral and social order, and offer 'solutions' which may form the basis of governmental responses to the condition. Cohen's model described the processual nature of panic — the stages of its unfolding and the ebb and flow of social concern, and he emphasised the role of the media in symbolising and amplifying the problem in shaping it as deviance and hence a wider *social* threat. Hall et al (1978) famously extended this model by providing a more nuanced account of the role of the media and their interaction with politicians in what they termed the 'signification spiral' endemic to amplification, and the way this was framed in populist rhetoric. They also reshaped the focus on social and moral order to show how this related to the role of the state in maintaining hegemony amidst a sense of crisis.

Cohen suggested that central to moments of moral panic was the creation of a folk devil, an object of hostility that could bear the brunt of social anger and be seen as the wrongdoer or cause of the social condition (1973). Critcher has recently suggested that the folk devil is not necessary to the existence of a moral panic (2003:177), but it is clear from the analysis of moral panics that the creation of a folk devil is a key way of focusing the moral and social anxieties embedded in the moment of panic, and providing an object of hostility which concretises and focuses those anxieties. Critcher has also pointed out that there is little elaboration of the moral dimensions of moral panics (2003:144), so it may be useful to give the function of the folk devil more attention than is often provided.

In the last ten years or so, and quickening since 1998 because of the concerns over 'ethnic gangs', 'race rapes', the asylum-seekers and the terrorist attacks, we have seen the emergence of a significant folk devil in contemporary Australia. The links that are made between these events, the 'perpetrators' involved and their perceived communities, however problematic, rest on the identification of what we might call 'the Arab Other', a supposedly homogenous category which includes those of Arab or Middle Eastern or Muslim background. This is not a singular category, of course — it includes people from quite diverse ancestries and with quite distinct histories — but it is seen to be a singular category. A commonality is found not just in behaviour which is unarguably criminal, but also in actions which become perceived as 'deviant' — such as seeking asylum — and also in a range of other practices whose key feature is their visible and threatening difference — such as the building of a prayer centre. This chapter will recount these events and begin to explore the ways they are seen to feature the figure of the Arab Other, homogenising a diverse group of people and putting them in opposition to some cultural norm. Certain key ideological elements recur in the formation of this figure — images of violence, barbarism and animality, the contravention of social rules and the exhibition of 'offensive' behaviour. This chapter will draw on detailed discussions of media commentary and political debate to explore the formation of this folk devil.

It is important to stress, of course, that 'the media' are not a single entity that promotes a single ideological version of the world; nor, therefore, are they in any simple sense 'racist', as Hartley and McKee (2000:6,242) point out. The media, they argue, are 'dialogic', providing a variety of stories, often from conflicting perspectives. Yet these stories, especially in news production, function according to certain techniques and values — narratives of battlers and leaders, conflict and sensation, structures of opposition, attraction to the anomalous — which shape the ways stories are told. These individual stories produce what Hartley and McKee call, following Attwood, 'narrative accrual', ongoing myths or histories that shape our perceptions of the world (2000:275,76). They constitute what other scholars refer to as 'discourse frames', which, rather than predetermining single messages, set the terms in which conflicting perspectives can be communicated. Thus it is not simply the case that sensationalist media coverage delivers simple ideological messages (Tulloch 1999), but that media narratives, and particularly the 'moral tales' through which the 'drama of crime' is played out, make sense to us because these frames give order to our perceptions of social reality (Sparks 1992). The media is also a set of organisations functioning amidst a broader array of institutions (Chan 1995) but, as both a network of powerful if competing organisations with vested interests in connecting with and shaping social values, and as a network of conduits through which conflicting perspectives get played out, the media remain a primary cultural device for defining social order and deviance (Ericson, Baranek & Chan 1989). The media, in ordering our perceptions of the social world, are central in reproducing dominant cultural frames, connecting the mundane to the wider world and generating a kind of 'common sense' of the world which naturalises that reality and the relations of power which structure it (Couldry 2000:12–15,45).

We have seen the emergence in recent years of a highly racialised framing of current events, around crime and terrorism, on a local, national and international level. 'Racialisation' here is understood as the ways in which complex social phenomena are refracted through and become explained primarily in terms of ethnic and racial categories of social perception (Miles 1982). This framing works to marginalise certain groups because crime images are typically structured via oppositions of us and them, good and bad, victim and villain, right and wrong (Young 1996:1), oppositions which are then understood in racialised terms. While criminological studies have explored in detail the 'demonology' of the criminal in news media (Ericson, Baranek & Chan 1991) and the constitution of an 'unpredictable stranger' upon whom we project our fears and anxieties (Lupton 1999a), much less attention has been given to examining the racialised dimensions of these discourses. The centrality of the Arab Other to our current frames around crime and terrorism has the effect of not only 'ethnicising' or racialising certain criminal practices; it also produced the 'criminalising' of a range of cultural practices whose only offence is their perceived difference. The effects of this figure are not purely symbolic for, as we shall explore later, they license an amplification of racial violence and repressive measures across all levels of state organisation, cementing a neo-assimilationist ethic of social exclusion.

'Gangland'

In *Kebabs, Kids, Cops and Crime* (Collins, Noble, Poynting & Tabar 2000), we dealt in detail with the moral panic around 'ethnic' and especially 'Lebanese' gangs that escalated after the stabbing of Edward Lee and the shooting up of the Lakemba police station in south-western Sydney in late 1998. We don't want to go over that ground again in detail, especially since we will revisit the representations of gangs in Chapter Two, but we do want to reiterate the salient points for this study. We showed in *Kebabs* that the spiralling moral panic around ethnic gangs involved a number of social assumptions about the links between criminal behaviour and young men of certain non-English speaking backgrounds in Australia — particularly those of Middle Eastern ancestry. After de-mythologising some of those assumptions, we argued that what this moral panic engendered was a *racialisation* of criminal and especially gang activity, whereby the causes of crime and social incivility were seen to be related pathologically to the culture and ethnicity of those involved. Not only did this ignore the complex relations between ethnicity, peer group formation and criminal and 'anti-social' practices, it had consequences for policing methods, government policies and Australian multiculturalism as a whole, as well as shifting blame for these events onto whole communities.

Since the publication of *Kebabs*, the theme of a rampant 'crime wave' — especially in Sydney — continues to feature in the media and in the rhetoric of politicians (Devine & Skelsey 10/7/03:1). There is regular coverage of the availability of illegal firearms (the 'handgun epidemic') and knives, car 'rebirthing rackets', drugs and violence in schools, drive-by shootings, and so on. Young men of Arabic-speaking backgrounds seem to feature frequently in this coverage. The anxieties unleashed by the ethnic gangs panic have by no means diminished; indeed, they have been exacerbated by various events involving young men of 'Middle Eastern appearance' in Sydney. Apart from the 'ethnic gang rapes', to which we will turn in due course, during the last two years we have seen concerns expressed over: 'teenage drug "hot spots"' operating around railway stations and schools on Sydney's north shore, which the *Daily Telegraph* editorialised as 'Community fighting for our children' (*Daily Telegraph* 6/11/00:20); triad extortion rackets targeting high school students, again on Sydney's north shore (Kidman 7/12/00:3); a shooting in Kathleen St, Lakemba, (Kennedy & O'Malley 25/11/00:9); forty 'gangs' battling for control of 'our streets' in wars over drugs, extortion and prostitution (Miranda 8/1/01:4); a 'crisis of violence among Lebanese Australian youths' (Sutton 25/2/01:10), requiring new initiatives to target 'Arab gangs' (Kerr 11/7/01:4); the exploits of criminal Michael Kanaan and the death of 'drug lord' Danny Karam (Knowles 16/4/02:11); and the stabbing of an Asian 'family man' by men of 'Middle Eastern appearance' in a 'road rage' incident in Hurstville (Lawrence 22/4/02:4).

The themes we identified in *Kebabs* — the racialisation of crime and the criminalisation of Arabic-speaking youth — can be retraced here, but the most significant point to emerge out of the more recent coverage is the perception that Sydney's south-west was not just a dangerous area, but central to the creation of what the media dubbed 'Gangland'. Gangland was a place ruled by 'organised ethnic gangs' (of Arab, Asian and other backgrounds) who had 'secret signs such as sucking on coloured straws or wearing red necklaces — signatures of the new criminal fraternity' which was increasingly occupying territory across Sydney, even infiltrating parts of the prestigious north shore (McDougall et al. 6/8/01:1,4–5). This imagining of a place called Gangland provided a tangible entity on to which we could project our anxieties, giving them a concrete, spatial character as a place to avoid. This spatialisation of our anxieties helps produce 'landscapes of fear': landscapes which are constituted largely by media representations rather than personal experience of crime (Tulloch 1992:55). These landscapes are now being 'mapped' by police, identifying the 'meanest streets in town' (Lewis 18/8/03:5). The identification of Gangland also provided a set of descriptions of people who might harm us and a 'six-point checklist' for spotting them — much more than a simple ethnic profile. The *Daily Telegraph* gave us suburb by suburb details of the gangs' locations, their ethnic affiliations, the secret symbols that identified them, their methods of recruitment, and so on, construing their existence as an 'ethnic problem' and hence blaming 'Sydney's community leaders' for being 'too timid to confront' their problem (McDougall et al. 6/8/01:1,4–5).

Of course there have been and continue to be parallel concerns about 'Asian gangs'. As well as the focus on men of Middle Eastern appearance, there has also been wider and ongoing coverage of 'ethnic crime' and gangs: concern that 'crime and fear still rule' the streets of Cabramatta, a key centre of Sydney's Asian populations (Sofios & Skelsey 18/2/03:10). In April, 2003, the *Telegraph* repeated its 2002 catalogue of ethnic gangs, announcing that the 'Boys are back in town: 10 gangs spreading fear and violence' (Miranda 28/4/03:5). While this list contains young people of Asian, Islander and Aboriginal background, and even 'North Shore schoolboys', the emphasis has shifted over the last decade towards young men of Arabic-speaking background as a major threat to public safety. The 'Middle Eastern appearance' of such young men is usually still identified even when, as in the case of a 'Lebanese-born youth from Merrylands' apprehended for sexual assault, this information is not needed for help from the public in identifying suspects (Kidman 18/5/03:34).

We will return to some aspects of the ethnic gangs panic and the creation of 'Gangland' in the following chapter, but we want to shift the focus to specific events which have been most significant in constituting the Arab Other in recent years; events which augment the processes of racialisation and criminalisation we outlined in *Kebabs*.

'Ethnic gang rapes'

From August 2000 to August 2001, there were eight serious group sexual assaults in the Bankstown area of south-west Sydney, according to the Bankstown Police Local Area Commander (cited by Bankstown City Council 2001; *Bankstown-Canterbury Torch* 22/8/01:1). This is an area with one of the highest concentrations of Arabic-speaking background immigrants in Australia, and the centre of the virulent moral panic over 'ethnic crime gangs' in previous years. Police informants fed the story to the tabloid press that there was a racial motivation involved in these instances:

> Almost one year ago, when the youths were first charged with this crime, a *Daily Telegraph* court reporter was telephoned by police contacts and told of their upcoming court appearance.
>
> She was told that the rapes were being perpetrated on Australian women and the victims were asked if they had Arabic blood or Arabic boyfriends and that this was part of an increasing trend (Wockner 25/8/01:4).

The ethnic dimension changed these brutal attacks into something with much wider, and more dire consequences, producing a spiral of hysteria and hyperbole in which the number of alleged assaults rapidly escalated. The *Sun-Herald* warned about this 'new race crime': '70 girls attacked by rape gangs' (29/7/01:1). 'Caucasian' women and girls were being 'lured' by 'race gangs' into meeting them, it was claimed, and then brutally assaulted (Kidman 29/7/01:4–5). Commercial radio compere Philip Clark mentioned an alleged 30 such offences, and broadcast an interview with the purported father of a victim, who asserted that his daughter was raped by a refugee (Clark 30/9/01). The *Daily Telegraph* emblazoned its front page for August 15 with a large, menacing image of a man of 'Middle Eastern appearance' and described it as the 'Face of a rapist' (Birch 15/8/01:1). As the investigations, arrests and trials for these offences ensued, there were increasing reports that 'racially motivated attacks could be spreading throughout Sydney' (Downie 29/8/01:3). Amidst the ensuing panic, intense debates took place regarding the use of ethnic descriptors by the police, over whose culture was to blame for the incidents of sexual assault, and over 'soft' sentencing.

The NSW Bureau of Crime Statistics and Research (BOC-SAR) issued a press release to counter this panic, informing that:

> ... the recorded rate of sexual assault in Bankstown has remained stable since 1995, mostly remaining under 10 offences per month.
>
> The only change to this pattern occurred in the month of June 1999, when 70 incidents of sexual assault were recorded by Bankstown police.
>
> These offences were not committed by members of a gang. Police advise ... that they were mainly committed by a single individual (Lesley Ketteringham) who has since been charged, convicted and imprisoned for committing a number of willful and obscene exposure offences (Weatherburn 2001).

Bureau Director, Don Weatherburn, pointed out that the rate of sexual assault was nearly twice as high in the state's Northern, and over twice as high in its North Western, Statistical Division. Very few Arab-background or Muslim people live in these areas. Weatherburn (2001) also recognised that many sexual assaults are not reported to the police, but stated, 'There is no reason to believe ... that victims of sexual violence are any more reluctant to report that violence to police in Bankstown than they are in any other area of the State'. Despite these attempts, the reportage and political commentary on these incidents made it very clear who was the problem. The *Daily Telegraph* had already reported that police were concerned that 'race rape' was 'culturally institutionalised' (Kidman 29/7/01:4).

We do not dispute that these were brutal assaults, during which the perpetrators may have made derogatory comments about the victims' 'Aussie' backgrounds. What was problematic in the media coverage and the political utterances that ensued was the assumption that Sydney was experiencing an epidemic of 'race rape' and that these incidents were endemic to Lebanese or Arab or Muslim culture.

Pauline Hanson, then leader of the anti-immigration party, One Nation, opted to 'wade into the ethnic crime debate' with a call for rapists to be flogged (Doherty & Jacobsen 23/8/01:7):

> You can't have gangs going around and committing these of-
> fences. And especially what's happening of raping of women
> — white women on the streets — because, in their opinion,
> white women are worth absolutely nothing to them, to their
> race, their cultural background (*Insight* 23/8/01).

She 'blamed the problem on a lack of respect for Australian culture', according to the *Sydney Morning Herald*, which quoted her as saying, 'A lot of these people are Muslims, and they have no respect for the Christian way of life that this country's based on'. Hanson boasted: 'Before I came on the scene, this was all politically incorrect'. She called for stricter sentences by judges (Doherty & Jacobsen 23/8/01:7). The *Daily Telegraph* and *Sun-Herald* and many of their opinion-writers subsequently campaigned for such changes, and NSW Labor Premier Bob Carr made significant concessions to these demands (Wainwright 31/8/01:9; *Daily Telegraph* 31/8/02:6; *Daily Telegraph* 1/9/01:22; *Australian* 20/9/01:8, *Express* 13/9/02:19; Ackland 8/9/01:8). 'True justice', trumpeted the front page of the *Sunday Telegraph*, celebrating that 'The NSW Government has bowed to public pressure by increasing the maximum sentence for gang rape to life' (Vass 26/8/01:1). Its editorial on the same day, headed 'Our community demands justice', referred to 'community concerns' including 'the vexed question of the relationship between crime and ethnicity; the terrifying stories of gangs of youth pack-raping Sydney teenagers; and lenient sentences being dished out for a range of serious crimes' (*Sunday Telegraph* 26/8/01:87).

A clear opposition between 'our community' and the 'ethnic' criminal underlay these statements. Journalist Paul Sheehan, well known as a critic of multiculturalism, claimed that ethnic gang rape emanates from Muslim and Arab culture and showed that it was a global phenomenon, because it had been perpetrated earlier in the year in France by 'urban immigrant poor' from these backgrounds (Sheehan 29/8/01:20). The *Australian* made clear where the problem came from in its front-page headline, 'Rape menace from the melting pot': NSW Police Commissioner Peter Ryan stated that 'a particularly defined cultural group of attackers' was attacking 'a very clearly defined cultural group of victims'. Premier Bob Carr was adamant in rejecting any 'paroxysm of political correctness' which objected to such definition (Chulov 18–19/8/01:1).

Yet such clear ethnic identification of victims and perpetrators, and public apportionment of blame by political leaders, police spokespeople and media opinion-makers did not apply to 'retributive' attacks on Muslim and Arab immigrants, including reported sexual assaults. Muslim community leaders reported that 'after Mr Carr had blamed Lebanese gangs for a series of rapes there had been an increasing number of attacks on Muslim women' including the rape of an 18-year-old Muslim girl (Walker 26/8/01:10). Numerous other reports followed, but none referred to the ethnicity of the attackers.

The degree of public anxiety was maintained throughout 2002 as the *Daily Telegraph*, for example, gave detailed and lengthy accounts of the trials of the men arrested for the rapes, in a specially presented section on almost a daily basis, written by Cindy Wockner. The panic became so great that Judge Finnane had to remind jurors in one trial that:

> You have to put aside any view that you might have … about Muslims, either favourable or unfavourable because this court is not concerned with a political trial.
>
> We are not trying a class of persons or a race (quoted in Wockner 4/6/02:11).

The judge's caution is contradicted only two months later in his assertion, echoed by the *Telegraph*, that 'the rapists had injected racism into the crimes' (Wockner 16/8/02:4). This claim shifts the blame for any prejudiced take on these events to the youths themselves and ignores the already racialised context in which these events and their reportage occur. Politicians and journalists echoed the judge's claim by asserting that the 'Culprits made race an issue' (Wockner 14/3/03:2), but these comments fail to register any connection between the emphasis on the ethnicity of a specific group of rapists and the purported ethnicity of their victims, and the claims that these incidents are typical of a particular ethnic background or faith, as several examples above suggest. Since the rapes, new incidents of sexual assault, and especially gang rape, have become key news items, and are often framed by reference to the 'ethnic gang rapes'. One article stressed, somewhat unnecessarily, that: 'Police officially say it is too early to establish any link between the attack and a spate of rapes by Lebanese youths who prowled the western suburbs in 2000' (*Daily Telegraph* 7/5/03:5), thereby implying that it could be related, and thereby reinforcing the idea that rape is typically perpetrated by Arabic-speaking youths.

Despite his earlier caution, the judge in the gang rape trials sentenced the ringleader of these rapes to 55 years, one of the heaviest sentences ever handed down in NSW (Wockner 16/8/02:4). It is hard not to see this sentence as being partly the result of a context of intersecting and escalating panics — about increasing crime and soft sentencing, cultural diversity and immigration, moral decay, the failure of political authority, the loss of social order and cohesion, and so on. We will return to these below, but it's important to stress here that moral panics such as the ones we are describing here are complex, layered social phenomena whose explanation is not immediately apparent. Over the last few years, the 'panic' is not simply about 'Arabs' or Muslims per se, but about a whole raft of issues and concerns which largely emanate from within Australian society but which are projected onto 'external' or marginal groups. This was also the case in the anxieties expressed towards refugees and terrorists during the months following the 'Gangland' and 'race rapes' panics.

The 'boat people'

Throughout 2000 and up to August 2001, the media presented stories of a seemingly endless and unstoppable flow of refugees and asylum seekers invariably described as 'Middle-Eastern' arriving on Australian territory off the coast of Western Australia. In fact, the numbers were well within Australia's planned immigration provision for refugee intake of 12,000 per annum; the moral outrage was supposedly directed at their purported 'queue jumping' and at the predatory industry of 'people smuggling'. Thus:

> December 16, 2000: Boat carrying 117 people, including 32 children, found off the Ashmore Islands. Second boat had 115 people. Refugees mainly Iranians, Syrians and Palestinians.
>
> January 16, 2001: 151 people of Middle Eastern origin aboard Indonesian inter-island ferry near the Ashmore Islands.
>
> June 6, 2001: 235 Iraqi men, women and children land in the Ashmore Islands, 800 km west of Darwin.
>
> June 14, 2001: Boat lands at Christmas Island with 200 asylum seekers from Iraq and Afghanistan (*Daily Telegraph* 17/8/01:8).

Journalist Nadya Stani pointed out as early as 2000 that in reporting on the 'boat people' the media were depending on and accepting information supplied by government ministers and officials, and that this was engendering a panic about refugees (Stani 27/1/00). Stani demonstrates how the media fixed on the means by which the asylum seekers came to Australian territory instead of reporting what they were fleeing from. Her analysis shows that stories invariably originated from 'the information given to the media by the Department of Immigration and Multicultural Affairs, and its Minister, Philip Ruddock, in numerous press releases and interviews':

> The stories concentrated on people smugglers, mafia-type operations, queue jumping, assaults on our shores, the national emergency, and the middle-class status of the refugees ... It was also the language of fear, and, say refugee advocates, it undermined the possibility of any public sympathy (Stani 27/1/00).

23

Stani enumerates that, out of 16 main articles and editorials published over October to December 1999 in the broadsheet *Sydney Morning Herald*, a mere four presented the situation of the asylum seekers with any sympathy. The remainder were couched in the language of 'illegal immigrants', 'human cargo', 'people smugglers', 'queue jumpers', and 'invasion' (Stani 27/1/00). This pattern was even more pronounced in the tabloids and on talkback radio. The following year, Christine Jackman in the *Daily Telegraph*, seriously attempting to be even-handed, attempted to 'kickstart the debate' thus: 'the so-called humanitarians screeching "racist" at anyone who questioned the right of the 438 on the Tampa to automatic entry, should explain what is so humanitarian about indulging people-smuggling'. She went on to use the term 'people-smuggler' twice more in the piece, as well as 'human cargo' (Jackman 4/9/01:17).

On 26 August 2001, the KM Palapa, a somewhat dilapidated ferry carrying over 430 asylum seekers, mainly from Afghanistan, began to sink in the Indian Ocean. Those on board were rescued by the MV Tampa, a Norwegian freighter, about 75 nautical miles from Australia's Christmas Island and almost four times that far from the Indonesian port of Merak (Marr & Wilkinson 20–21/10/01; Burnside 23/1/02; Senate Select Committee on a Certain Maritime Incident 2002). The Captain, Arne Rinnan, decided to head for Christmas Island, as many of the asylum seekers were ill and in poor condition; he radioed Australia for medical assistance, but none was provided. Having entered Australian territorial waters, Captain Rinnan was abruptly threatened by an officer of the Department of Immigration and Multicultural Affairs with the punishment meted out to people smugglers under the *Migration Act* — including the possibility of huge fines and confiscation of the vessel — if he did not turn around and head towards Indonesia (Marr & Wilkinson 20–21/10/01; Burnside 23/1/02). With a federal election fast approaching, the government had apparently resolved to stop these asylum seekers from reaching Australian land. As

Julian Burnside QC puts it, 'This odd decision has never been explained, except with the rhetoric of "sending a clear message to people smugglers and queue jumpers that Australia is not a soft touch"'. Burnside, who argued the case for the asylum seekers' challenge to the Government's actions in the Federal Court, infers that the Prime Minister was calculating that:

> a show of toughness against helpless refugees would be electorally popular amongst the large number of Australians who had responded positively to aspects of Pauline Hanson's unattractive [anti-immigration] platform (Burnside 23/1/02).

The ship was stopped four miles from Christmas Island. It was boarded and taken over by Australian SAS forces, and communications were strictly limited by the Australian military. Rinnan and others later characterised this as an act of piracy. Eventually after more than a week of stand-off, the asylum seekers were transferred to an Australian naval vessel, for eventual transportation to the impoverished Pacific island of Nauru, with which a multi-million dollar deal had been done that they be detained and processed there, allowing the Prime Minister to keep his promise that the asylum seekers aboard the Tampa would not set foot on Australian soil. This populist venture immediately registered in the opinion polls, and election campaign articles began to talk about Howard's 'Tampa-led recovery' and his political exploitation of the plight of the boat people (Manne 6/10/01:16).

Two key stories — one short-lived, the other sustained and leading to an inquiry — buttressed the growing support for this 'get tough' stance. The first linked the asylum-seekers to the deepening concern regarding terrorist activity, arising at the same time as the refugee crisis: the *Daily Telegraph* in its editorial column claimed that, 'While on board, SAS members were able to place under surveillance a suspected agent of the Osama bin Laden terrorist network' (*Daily Telegraph* 13/10/01:24). As there was never a subsequent report about the suspected Al Qaeda terrorist being arrested or tried, we can only assume that the suspicions or the report were unfounded. Nevertheless, beliefs that terrorist cells are infiltrating Australia have escalated over the last two years, and these have been linked in the minds of Australians with the threat of increasing boatloads of refugees.

The other story was the now infamous 'children overboard affair'. On October 6, another unseaworthy vessel, a fishing trawler laden with 223 Middle Eastern asylum seekers, was intercepted by the Australian naval frigate, HMAS Adelaide, in Australian waters off the west coast. Shots were fired across its bows and it was boarded. Over the following day, navy personnel tried in vain to prevent the vessel from sinking, so that it could be towed out of Australian waters. As the boat finally did sink, asylum seekers, including children, had to be rescued from the water. A video was taken by navy personnel. That very day, a Canberra bureaucrat told the People Smuggling Task Force that asylum seekers had thrown their children overboard in an attempt to prevent the Adelaide turning their vessel back (Wilkinson 16–17/2/02:23; Ramsay 16–17/2/02:35). The assertion was repeated publicly many times by the Defence Minister, the Prime Minister, and those campaigning for them, and it was echoed in tabloids and talkback and taverns and tearooms across the continent. A Senate enquiry has since concluded that it was false. It has, moreover, been demonstrated that images from the video depicting children in the water, shown on national television by the Defence Minister during the election campaign, were cut down so as to exclude the view of the boat sinking in the background, and were misrepresented as being of the previous day when the incident of tossing the kids into the sea was supposed to have taken place. It has also been amply proven that the Prime Minister's office and that of the Defence Minister were warned soon afterwards by navy personnel conveying firsthand knowledge, of the falsehood of the story they were presenting, which they nevertheless continued to defend as true until well after the election (Senate Select Committee on a Certain Maritime Incident 2002).

As with the link to terrorism, the imputation that the asylum seekers were bad parents only served to strengthen the popular opinion that refugees would not be good and decent Australians. Prime Minister Howard repeated, 'I don't want, in Australia, people who would throw their own children into the sea' (*Four Corners* 15/4/02). He told Alan Jones's commercial radio audience on Sydney's highest-rating talkback program on 8 October, 'I don't want in this country people who are prepared, if those reports are true, to throw their own children overboard' (Wilkinson 16–17/2/02:28). This intensely moral view of the refugee situation became interwoven with an appeal to national sovereignty and self-determination. One of the oft-repeated and obviously successful slogans of the Liberals' election campaign became, '*We* will decide who can come to this country'. Column-writers such as Piers Akerman repeated the Government's line:

> As for those who threw their children into the sea on Sunday and the malcontents who trashed the Manoora — it must be made absolutely clear that not only is such behaviour totally unacceptable but will in fact mitigate (sic) against any future consideration for admission into Australia (Akerman 9/10/01:16).

The Senate reports show that the Government misled the public on the various aspects of the 'maritime incidents' during 2001. Commentator Hugh Mackay observed that, 'the "children overboard" incident ... show[s] us just how vulnerable Australians have become to political spin'. He argues that 'we *wanted* to believe the kids had been thrown overboard, because we had already been worked over by a slick propaganda machine that had created a "refugee crisis" out of a couple of hundred people rescued by the Tampa' (Mackay 16–17/2/02:31). Manipulating this vulnerability, the Government 'encouraged Australians to see all those using the services of people smugglers to be as undesirable as the criminals exploiting their desperate endeavours to get to Australia' (Kitney 24/10/02:4). In equating the smugglers with the refugees, the Government affirmed the pervasive idea that people from the Middle

East, understood broadly, were immoral, dangerous and violent criminals, a view that paralleled the increasing alarm at terrorist activity.

'Bin Laden groups in our suburbs'

A number of terrorist actions over recent years — most notably the airborne attacks in the US in September 2001 and the Bali bombings in October 2002, but including a number of other incidents — have cemented an ideological connection between Islamic fundamentalism, extremist organisations and the incidents we have already described.

On 11 September 2001, two hijacked aeroplanes were flown into the twin towers of the World Trade Centre in New York, a third hit the Pentagon in Washington, and a fourth plane, surmised to be intended for the White House, crashed outside Pittsburgh. Initial reports had the death toll at 10,000, and the event was immediately pronounced 'world terror' with Osama bin Laden, a Saudi billionaire and leader of the militant organisation Al Qaeda, quickly identified as the main suspect (*Daily Telegraph* 12/9/01:1,2,7). The details of the attacks, the aftermath in New York, the investigation and subsequent invasion of Afghanistan, have now been frequently told. Our primary concern here is not this story but rather the way these events amplified an already pervasive fear of the Arab Other through the concern with Islamic fundamentalism. US President George Bush Jnr stated that, 'The enemy of America is not our many Muslim friends. It is not our many Arab friends', yet his rhetoric quickly followed an 'us versus them' structure: 'Either you are with us, or you are with the terrorists'; 'freedom and fear are at war' (Johnston 21/9/01:1). This polarity left little room for the complexities of cultural, social and national difference. As the 'war on terror' widened, it became clear to at least some commentators that the objective was not simply to target suspected terrorists, but all 'enemies of the US' (Fisk 29–30/9/01:35).

This identification of terrorism with Islam was echoed in Australia. The us/them binary meant that, while this was ostensibly an overseas event, the threat was experienced by many Australians as a local one. Just as during the Gulf War, opinion-leaders in the media raised the spectre of the 'divided loyalties' of Australia's immigrant population, and called upon Arab and Muslim Australians to demonstrate their loyalty to this country: 'Australian Muslims will have to decide whether they are Australians first ...'. (Akerman 16/12/01:109). Fictitious stories circulated on talkback radio that, after the September 11 attacks, there were celebrations on the streets of Lakemba, and a number of threats and attacks on Muslims and mosques followed. The vehemence was indiscriminate: racial slurs were scrawled on a Russian Orthodox church in Lidcombe in Sydney's west; graffiti on a Brisbane wall announced, 'We will kill all Arabs ... Scum will die' and a school bus full of Muslim children in Queensland was pelted with bottles (Burke 15–16/9/01:4). Among a number of more violent attacks, a mosque in Brisbane was torched — but the ethnicity of the arsonists was not mentioned in the media reports (Roberts & Glendinning 24/9/01:9).

Very quickly, moreover, stories began circulating that there were terrorist cells in Australia; a story which was linked in the public mind with the stream of asylum seekers. On 12 October, 2001, the *Telegraph* front-page headline screamed, 'TERROR AUSTRALIS: Bin Laden groups in our suburbs' and the article detailed raids on homes of Arab and Muslim immigrants in Western Sydney by the Australian Federal Police and the Australian Security Intelligence Organisation (ASIO). It reported that 'More than a dozen men from Egypt, Jordan and Tunisia currently applying for refugee status, have been identified as having connections or membership with radical Al-gama Islamiya, Al-Maqdesi, Al-Dawa and Al-Nahda groups' (Miranda 12/10/01b:1,4). The editorial of that day headlined 'Entry is a privilege not a right', and warned of 'up to a hundred operatives in Sydney' suspected of raising funds for 'bogus charities that have been found to have links to terrorist networks'. It urged 'firm and immediate action', and cautioned that 'the existence of these groups should sound a warning over the standards required to gain entry to Australia (*Daily Telegraph* 12/10/01:20). There has still not been a report of any charges, let alone a trial, for any terrorist activity, but new stories of terrorist activity in Australia have burgeoned since the bombing in Bali and the subsequent trials in Indonesia.

The naturalisation of the links between terrorism and Islam were cemented by the endorsement of Huntington's 'clash of civilisations' thesis by politicians and journalists (see, for example, Crittenden 19–20/7/03:4–5). Huntington's argument was that 'culture and cultural identities, which at the broadest level are civilisation identities, are shaping the patterns of cohesion, disintegration and conflict in the post-Cold War world' (1997:20). Culture and civilisation are understood primarily in terms of ethnicity and religion, and become central to Huntington's version of the 'decline of the west' and the rise of Asia and Islam. Although he initially rejects a simple us/them opposition, he nevertheless uses this opposition to portray Islam (and Asia) as a relatively coherent entity that has become a major source of conflict, violence and destabilisation, while the reassertion of western culture and its democratic values is seen as the solution to global conflict (1997:33,36,28). These claims, at an international level, echo and confirm the concerns about conflict between cultures at national and local levels in Australia; a link which is seemingly reinforced by the terrorist attacks on the island of Bali in Indonesia.

On October 12, 2002, two bombs were detonated in or near the Sari nightclub and Paddy's Irish Pub, in Kuta, in Bali. The venues were frequented by many western, and especially Australian, tourists, and speculation immediately arose as to whether the attack was the work of Islamic fundamentalists with links to Al Qaeda. In November several suspects were identified and some arrested; Indonesian and Malaysian Muslims who belonged to the radical Islamic group Jemaah Islamiah. Some of these have since been tried and found guilty.

What was terrifying about Bali for Australians was that Bali was seen to be, as John Howard said, 'on our doorstep': the bomb blast 'stamping terrorism's bloody fingerprint on Australia's door'. A key theme became 'Terrorism Strikes Home' (Moore & Riley 14/10/02:1), confirming much more than the asylum seeker crisis and the attacks in America that the threat was immediate and 'local', and that Australians were a target. Bali, in fact, becomes our 'watering hole', and the blasts are seen to 'wreck [the] symbolic centre of Australian holiday culture' (Holland 15/10/02:6–7). The terrorists' presence in Australia became an ongoing concern, with reports that Abu Bakar Bashir, leader of Jemaah Islamiah, had been to Australia on several occasions and had written for the local Islamic Youth Movement magazine (Saunders 16/10/02:7). There really did seem to be terrorists 'in our suburbs'.

Another round of high-profile 'visits' by ASIO, Australia's security organisation, accompanied by heavily armed Australian Federal Police, targeted the homes of Muslim, this time mainly Indonesian, communities in Australia's capital cities, including Sydney, Melbourne and Perth (Karvelas & Chulov 30/10/02:1,8). As with the previous year's raids on Arab-Australian Muslims after 11 September, there were no arrests for any terrorist offences, though a few were charged with visa breaches. Those raided were labelled as suspected of having links with Jemaah Islamiah, and the raids were justified afterwards by the Prime Minister who warned that 'sleeper' terrorist cells *could* exist in Australia (English 2/11/02:4).

It is not surprising then that the Muslim community became a target of blame. *Daily Telegraph* columnist Piers Akerman (15/10/02:20) complained that, just a few days after the Bali blasts, Muslim community radio in Sydney aired a lecture calling for 'one vast international Muslim nation', with no mention of the Bali attack, 'no mention of love, compassion or forgiveness'. 'The Muslim community', he demanded, 'has a duty to stop this relentless propaganda'. The letters to the editor echoed this extrapolation from a small number of extremists to Islam per se: Nigel Freitas of Roseville argued that these events showed that Islam was not 'a religion of peace' (15/10/02:22); and John Mayberry of Glenbrook claimed that passages from the Koran 'incite believers to violent acts against non-believers', as 'their religious duty': 'the problem of world terrorism today lies firmly rooted in Islam' (15/10/02:23). Many (non-Muslim) Australians responded to this call to arms: within days forty local attacks on Muslims were recorded (Lipari 28/10/02:6). Letters echoed the binarism of us and them: John Dawson of McKinnon claimed that the aim of Islamic terrorists was to destroy 'our values', 'the Western values of life, liberty, prosperity, and the pursuit of happiness', and that Westerners had been 'butchered on every continent' to fulfil this aim (15/10/02:22).

To achieve the metonymic leap, where specific political acts taking place in particular national contexts come to stand for a whole religion or culture and its pathological tendency for evil, terrorism has to be seen *simply* as a crime, and *essentially* as a gross *moral* error. In constantly framing the terrorist attacks as a 'crime', as Howard did (Hewett 19–20/10/02:3), the specific political and economic dimensions of the attacks in America, in Indonesia and elsewhere are refused. This capitalised on the way, since Iraq's invasion of Kuwait in 1990 and the international banking scandal involving businessmen of Muslim background, Islam had been placed in a context of 'criminal culture' (Ahmed 1992:2). Similarly, in foregrounding the immoral nature of terrorist acts, and again ignoring the political contexts, they are seen primarily in terms of good and evil. Akerman sees the various ('left wing') interpretations of the origins of Islamic extremism as 'Sympathy for the devil in disguise', rejecting any attempt to effectively *explain* the terrorist actions. He instead reduces it to one factor: 'The extremists attack the West because it offers something Islam cannot — freedom of thought' (17/10/02:34). In other words, the totalitarian tendency of the Islamic faith is the underlying fault. This error — of faith and morality — can thus be seen to be shared by an entire community, and manifest in actions other than rape and terrorism.

Rapists, terrorists and queue-jumpers: assembling the Arab

As we have seen, media commentators and politicians talk about the disparate events of the last few years as though there is a natural link in that they share what is perceived as a common ancestry. Many of the terms used to describe this background — Middle Eastern, Muslim and Arab — are deeply problematic terms. The 'Middle East', for example, is not a singular entity, and is shaped more by the geopolitics of Western colonialism than the political, ethnic and religious realities of the region it supposedly designates. It includes people of Arabic-speaking background and those not of this background; it includes Muslims and Christians; and it includes countries whose cultures and political systems are quite diverse and distinct (while also including some countries whose status as Middle Eastern is arguable — such as Afghanistan — and seems to exclude one country — Israel — which *is* located in the Middle East). It also includes great internal differences of class and of the urban/rural divide. When 'Middle Eastern' is used to describe residents of Australia, it is even more questionable: it includes those born overseas and those born in Australia (including some whose parents were born in Australia). With the apparent global reach of Islamic fundamentalism, this Other is now seen to include Muslims of Indonesian or other South-East Asian citizenship and their involvement in what Huntington sees as an 'Islamic civilisation'. Nevertheless, some essential Arab-ness or Middle Eastern-ness or Islamic-ness *is seen to be* central to this group of people, to weave them into a single entity. This link is repeated again and again in media items and public statements.

The point of this chapter is not to apologise for crimes committed by Arabic-speaking Australians or Muslim terrorists, but to show how, via chains of association, Arab-ness and Islam and Middle-Eastern-ness are seen to be the same thing, and are seen to be essentially and pathologically evil, inhuman, violent and criminal. As a result of the signification spiral, in which discrete events are ideologically associated and linked to wider discourses of national experience, whole communities are made to share the burden of blame and carry responsibility for social cohesion, or its absence (Hall et al. 1978). This is a key issue in the formation of a folk devil: a moral panic occurs when the 'problem' is seen as too horrible and too threatening to be merely 'cultural boundary setting' — that is, it is not just a question of defining a symbolic Other. For the horror to be this great, we need 'true victims' with real suffering, as well as true perpetrators. This way the panic can *essentialise* the.offender, whose actions are not the product of fashion or situation but express the essence of the person they are (Cohen, cited in Scraton 2002). The assembling of a homogenised Other is intrinsic to this process of essentialisation, and useful in elaborating the construction of the folk devil. When Bilal Skaf, who 'terrorised' young women, reportedly sent an envelope containing white powder to a prison manager, echoing the anthrax scares in the US and elsewhere, this simply confirmed a perceived link between Lebanese rapists and Muslim terrorists (Lawrence 21/3/03:27). Furthermore, when 'Middle Eastern males' 'created havoc' at an anti-war rally in Sydney in March, 2003, the protest was described as being 'HIJACKED BY HATRED', echoing the hijacking of planes on September 11, 2001. This confirmed the idea that violence was endemic in Arab or Muslim culture — this item provided a visual illustration of the clash of civilisations, as white police (protecting social order) were pictured in 'clashes' with 'Middle Eastern males' (violent, inciting trouble) (Clifton & Lawrence 27/3/03:1–2).

The concept of the 'Other' has become a key term in social and cultural analysis to explain the ways dominant groups characterise subordinate groups as problematically different. The most significant and well-known expression of this argument in relation to the Middle East is in the work of Edward Said (1978). Said analyses what he calls 'Orientalism': the discourses and practices emerging from the colonial occupation of the Arab world by Western powers. He argues that the coloniser generates distinct forms of knowledge about the colonised — academic, imaginative and bureaucratic knowledge — which construct an imagined, coherent entity named the Oriental with a distinct 'character', and which posit a fundamental opposition between the Occident and the Orient, the East and the West. These knowledges aided in the administration of the Orient and the subjugation of the colonised (1978:2–3). This Other is an object onto which the West projects its fears, anxieties and desires, but its construction is naturalised as a scientific truth that hides its racialised assumptions.

Said draws on several centuries of Western representations to show that the imagined Oriental is marked by recurring traits which are conflated into an 'unchallenged coherence' which is then seen as objectively true. The Oriental is seen as degenerate, primitive or backward, uncivilised, unreliable and sexually rapacious, with an 'aberrant mentality' and a tendency to despotism. Orientals are rarely seen as people, but as problems to be solved or confined — and there is a particular fear of the Oriental male (1978:205–7). Said's discussion of the early modern period draws primarily on academic and literary texts, but he shows that in the twentieth century these representations are exacerbated in contemporary popular culture. Film images emphasise the Arab Oriental as dishonest and menacing, physically violent and an 'oversexed degenerate' (1978:285–7).

Said does not develop this point in relation to Arabic-speaking groups within Western nations. It is clear, however, that othering occurs in contemporary societies towards minorities, particularly in the light of mass immigrations. The Other functions in two key ways: it constitutes something against which one's own identity can be defined, either explicitly or implicitly; and it constitutes something against which one's social practices, conventions and customs, values and beliefs can be contrasted. This comparison can be either positive or negative, but the historical tendency is to posit an Other that naturalises one's own identity and practices. This complex argument doesn't need to be rehearsed in its entirety here; what is important for us is that this othering tends to produce a fiction of a homogeneous, deviant Other; a fiction which sustains the idea that the Other is always *less* than ourselves — less capable, less moral, less human.

In contemporary Australia, the assumption of an 'Arab Other' can often be found in an array of social discourses and institutions. It conflates quite distinct groups of people with various experiences and origins, and *reduces* them as people to a singular entity, emphasising their difference to *us* as radical, deviant and dangerous. As Ericson, Baranek and Chan (1991:261–2) argue, the news media are rarely interested in explanations, and when they do offer them they are inseparable from political processes of the laying of blame. Explanations that address issues of social power are largely erased.

In this section we want to show how, across the incidents described above, there is an assumption that they are linked because they commonly involve the Arab Other, defined by supposedly shared ethnicity, cultural traits and faith. We want to demonstrate how this Other is construed negatively, as potentially inhuman and evil, and to show that this radical difference posits a link between criminal offences and other practices that are deemed unacceptable or socially threatening.

Miranda Devine, for example, quoted approvingly an opinion pollster, David Chalke, as saying:

> I would suspect that the recent events in outer Sydney, part-
> icularly the gang rapes, the drug problems and the most recent
> bashing of the small boy, will ... deeply offend Australians'
> sense of decency and honesty. In fact, it is our belief that the
> backlash against the Tampa illegal immigrants was founded on
> anger at their breaking the rules (Devine 8/11/01:14).[1]

In one brief comment, the seemingly natural link between gangs, rape, drugs, physical violence and the asylum seekers is established, together with the clear implication the perpetrators, with their Middle Eastern origins, are in opposition to *Australians*. This link is then extended to terrorist activities. In October 2001, as the United States mounted war in Afghanistan, columnist Piers Akerman lauded the Australian military 'preparing to go to sea in the service of their country'. The enemy in each case was equated:

> Some are going to the Middle East, to provide back-up to the civilised world's war against terrorism; others are going to the edges of our territorial waters to dissuade people-smugglers from bringing their cargoes of illegal immigrants to our shores (14/10/01:95).

These juxtapositions are more powerful than any claim, easily disproved, of real links between terrorists and refugees. They are further juxtaposed with other events in an opinion piece by David Penberthy, written three days after the September 11 attacks in the United States. Penberthy claimed that what he wrote was 'extending an olive branch to Australian Muslims', though this was 'contrary to instinct'. It is worth quoting at length because, while it presents itself as an exercise of rational tolerance, it appears to assume that Australian Muslims need to bear responsibility for all of these attacks. It also registers the mood of intolerance and irrationality and the blurring of issues sweeping across Australia:

> Whatever tiny shred of goodwill that still existed in this country towards Muslim Australians probably disappeared at the same time the first hijacked passenger jet smashed into the World Trade Centre.
>
> ...
>
> This galvanising of public opinion is not rational ...
>
> In the minds of most Australians, all of these issues have merged into one.
>
> A series of events has overlapped, the result of which is blanket, unprecedented hostility to anyone who would seek to defend Islam and its adherence.
>
> It explains why, as the Lebanese gang rape scandal started to unfold, there was such acrimony directed towards Sheik Hilaly, over his call for a seat in State Parliament to be found for a Muslim, not to mention his absurd suggestion that because the gang rapists were Australian born, their criminal actions reflected more on their new homeland than on their ancestry ...

It explains why, when the Tampa arrived in Australian waters, carrying 434 people from Muslim Afghanistan, most Australians did not want to hear any stories from those on board. They just wanted them to go away (Penberthy 14/9/01:27).

There it is, in one equation, recognised as irrational and yet endorsed as understandable: terrorism, ethnic crime gangs, Islam, misogynist violent crime, Muslim ethnic-religious leader, Middle-Eastern asylum seekers. This is the same equation made by One Nation in an East Hills election pamphlet during the 2003 NSW state election: it was simply headed, 'Immigration-Multiculturalism-Terrorism-Crime' (One Nation 2003). These aggregations are possible not just because the Arab Other coalesces the diverse groups that have been at the centre of waves of panic over the last decade, but because of the common discursive elements used to identify and equate these groups.

Barbarians, animals and evil incarnate

In assembling this Arab Other, the key ideological feature is the systematic 'dehumanising' of those involved, whether they be criminals, terrorists or refugees. The phrase 'human cargo' was frequently used in describing the asylum-seekers, for example. This was by no means haphazard or accidental: news reports and images of the asylum seekers were tightly controlled via the Australian military. Julian Burnside QC, who argued the case for the asylum seekers' challenge in the Federal Court to the government's actions, later wrote:

> The press were not allowed anywhere near the ship. Despite repeated requests from lawyers and others, no Australian was allowed to speak to any of the refugees. The physical circumstances meant that no images of individual refugees were available. At best, film footage showed distant images of tiny figures under an awning on the deck of the ship. By the same technique, the stories of the refugees were suppressed ... Although the misery of the refugees' situation was obvious enough none of them could be seen as human beings (Burnside 23/1/02).

Burnside's analysis of this, expressed in January 2002, was that by prohibiting media contact with the asylum seekers:

the Government was able to advance its cynical objectives with dishonest rhetoric, wholly unimpeded by facts ... Howard's crucial aim was achieved: the refugees were not seen publicly as individual people for whom Australian citizens could have human sympathy (Burnside 23/1/02).

The accuracy of this judgement may be assessed in the light of the revelation on 17 April 2002 at the Senate Select Committee on a Certain Maritime Incident (2002), by Brian Humphreys, Director General of Communications Strategies in the Government's Public Affairs and Corporate Communication: 'Immigration had concerns about identifying potential asylum seekers and so we got some guidance on ensuring there were no personalising or humanising images'. The refugees were not to be allowed to be seen by the Australia people as human beings, as individuals with life stories. This ideological sleight of hand was extended to all those Arabic Others in the public eye, in stark contrast to 'our' own humanity.

There are several ways in which the opposition between the human 'us' and the inhuman 'them' is elaborated; the first is the depiction of the perpetrators of these various actions as 'uncivilised'. Despite the political use of Huntington's thesis about the clash of civilisations, Arabs and Muslims are rarely given the status of being civilised. Piers Akerman sees this contrast clearly: he refers to 'the civilised world's war against terrorism' (14/10/01:95); John Howard described the Bali bombings as 'an act of barbarity' (Moore & Riley 14/10/02:1). The letters to the editor at the time reflected similar concerns. The same letter-writer from Currumbin Waters who had fretted from 1000 km away about Sydney's 'ethnic gangs' in August now asked, 'What uncivilised barbarism is this? ... placing children's lives at risk' (Ford 11/10/01:27). Similar themes were present during the gang rape trials. One of those convicted for the gang rapes was described by Judge Finnane as 'a menace to civilised society', echoing comments he had made in earlier judgments (Knowles 11/10/02:1).

Similarly, there was a surprising amount of heated debate regarding the trial of a woman in Nigeria for adultery. The sentence — death by stoning — was couched in comparable terms: one letter-writer described it as 'a barbaric punishment for being human' (Smith 4/9/02:26). A significant share of the heat — and little light — was generated in Akerman's *Daily Telegraph* columns (22/8/02:28; 1/9/02; 12/9/02:24). Whether this punishment is acceptable or not is not the point here: rather, it is that the way we see this event, which got unusually extensive coverage in Australia during this period of panic, is framed by the same representations that accrue around local issues. A common Western perception of Islam emphasises its despotic nature, its fanaticism and intolerance: a perception that is echoed in local responses to the building of mosques in Australia for twenty years (Dunn 2001). The Nigerian example cues into this perception. It also cues into the image of Islam as patriarchal, and oppressive of women's rights, in contrast to the perceived sexual egalitarianism of the West. Apart from being a selective evaluation of gender equality in the West, it draws on conventional Orientalist tropes regarding the veiled woman (Mackie 2002). The day before the September 11 attacks, the *Herald* ran an item called 'The face of fear hidden behind a veil of tyranny', claiming that 'Bought and sold, denied basic rights, women in Afghanistan are treated only slightly better than farm animals' (McGeough 10/9/01:10). The timing of this article during the initial coverage of the gang rapes, like the Nigerian example, gives these kinds of claims a further ideological function affirming the oppressive nature of Islam, and the tendency of Muslim men towards sexual violence.

The second way in which the opposition between the human and the inhuman is realised is to depict the perpetrators of various crimes as animals. The front page of the *Daily Telegraph* pronounced one of those convicted for the gang rapes a 'WILD ANIMAL', echoing comments by the trial judge (Knowles 11/10/02:1). The young men convicted in August were described as a 'pack of youths', and the *Telegraph* recounted the judge's words:

they 'treated her like wild animals treat prey they have just killed' (Wockner 16/8/02:4). One of those involved in these 'orgiastic attacks' was similarly described as 'a monster' (Clifton 16/8/02:4). Akerman described Indonesia as a 'snake pit' because of the failure of President Megawati to 'stand up to the young Muslim thugs who are protecting Bashir' (29/10/02:16).

The third element is to depict the perpetrators, not their acts, as inherently evil, confirming a long-standing focus in crime reportage on the 'demonology' of the criminal (Ericson, Baranek & Chan 1991), but in this case giving a racialised hue. In September, 2002, the *Daily Telegraph* printed images of the police sketches of three teenagers wanted for a gang rape of a 'Caucasian' girl at Birrong, in Sydney's south west. Despite looking like fairly ordinary teenagers, but 'of Middle Eastern or Mediterranean appearance', the images were tagged 'faces of evil' (Lawrence 20/9/02:21). Osama bin Laden is routinely described as evil; but the more important point is that both he and the rapists are seen not just to have committed evil acts, but to embody the *essence* of evil. Images of two of the 'suicide terrorists' walking through the airport in New York was headed, 'Evil caught on film' (Beach 21/9/01:5). The front page of the *Telegraph* announced, upon the broadcast of a video claimed to show bin Laden commenting on the Bali bombings, that 'Evil speaks' (*Daily Telegraph* 14/11/02:1). John Howard described October 12 as 'a day on which evil struck' (Stephens 19–20/10/02:1). An Akerman piece on dealing with terrorism is entitled, 'Exorcising the devils that live among us' (29/5/03:23). In a perverse aside, stories circulated on the internet that the 'face of the devil' could be seen in the billowing smoke coming from the twin towers (Williamson 21/9/01:6). More recently, during the war in Iraq, (exaggerated) reports that British troops had found a bunker full of chemical 'weapons of mass destruction' was headed, 'EVIL PROOF' (Wilson 28/3/03:1). On its front page, under a coloured picture of the damage after the Marriott Hotel bomb blast in Jakarta, the *Telegraph* announced that 'EVIL STRIKES AGAIN' (Wockner 6/8/03:1).

The fourth way to depict the inhuman is to emphasise the perpetrators' 'inhumanity'. In its most extreme form, this entails describing people as less than human: in the days immediately after September 11, Muslims (and not just terrorists) were described by radio talkback callers as 'scum' and 'garbage' (cited on *7.30 Report* 13/9/01). More commonly, perpetrators of certain crimes are perceived as lacking fundamental human characteristics: during the rape trials, for example, the youths were described by judge and media as 'callous and mean', treating their victims 'with callous indifference and considerable cruelty', degrading and humiliating them, and never showing contrition or remorse during the trial (Wockner 16/8/02:4). Using this common parlance, many Australians would agree with these descriptions; however, the cumulative effect of such language is to symbolically remove any requirement that we act humanely to those that act inhumanely. As we have seen with the spurious 'children overboard' claims, the depiction of refugees as callous and indifferent to their children was politically motivated and buttressed a callous detention policy. Further, the associations we've mapped here, between the perpetrators and their ancestry, is to locate this inhumanity in Islam or in Arabic-speaking cultures. In a further bizarre twist, a furore erupted in Australia when images of the confessed Bali bomber, Amrozi, laughing with Indonesia's police chief General Bachtiar and fellow police were published in Australia newspapers. Politicians and journalists quickly described the images as ugly and heartless, but the implication was that this applied as much to the Indonesian authorities as to Amrozi. Comments by the Foreign Minister, Alexander Downer, were reported in a highly ambiguous way: 'these people are so bloodthirsty. Their sort of ugly, sneering, amused attitude at the slaughter of innocent people is just horrific' (Miller 15/11/02:9). Letters to the editor regarding this 'obscene picture' were more explicit in their outrage at the behaviour of 'Indonesia', lumping together the terrorist, the police and the nation, Osama bin Laden, Saddam Hussein, Islam, Asia and the Middle East (*Sydney Morning Herald* 15/11/02:14). A *Daily Telegraph* article pointed out that one of those in the picture, Brigadier-General Timbul Silaen, was Indonesian police chief in Dili when militias 'rampaged' through East Timor in 'an orgy of ethnic cleansing' (McPhedran 15/11/02:9). Some journalists speculated that perhaps 'it's a cultural thing, something our soft Western minds can't comprehend': but behind the feigned self-deprecation is the assertion that murderous behaviour is common to Indonesian and/or Muslim culture (Lalor 15/11/02:9).

In contrast, the other side of this equation, the victims of the various crimes — such as the girls who were raped or those killed in the terrorist attacks — are represented in all their humanity. Indeed, they become so well known to us they become like family and friends themselves. Again, this is a very conscious strategy on the part of media organisations in particular — we all know how much value personal interest gives to a story. Their humanity is expressed in all its fullness: over a month after the Bali bombings, newspapers continued to have not just coverage of the ongoing investigations, but an ongoing 'honour roll' of the victims, a kind of family photo album. A continuing section entitled 'As we remember them' in the *Sydney Morning Herald* was devoted to 'portraits' of those lost and the 'cherished moments of joy and love' recalled by their families (Cameron et al. 11/11/02:6 — note that this is Remembrance Day; again, weaving national significance into these events. Also note that these portraits continued well after this date). In these items and in the earlier news stories we are given intimate details of their lives — their work, their histories, their achievements, their characters, their tastes and habits; we become enmeshed in their networks of families, friends and lovers; we experience the whole gamut of emotions fundamental to human-ness — sorrow, pain, love, anger, joy, fear, etc — in relation to their lives and their deaths; we learn about their beliefs, their spirituality, and so on. In short, we *know* these people intimately and fondly; we too experience their loss. Similarly, the coverage of the rape trials emphasised the humanity of the victims — their suffering, their bravery, and so on — and the inhumanity of their attackers.

The point here is not to ignore the brutality of the rapes and the terrorist attacks, nor to detract from the personal and social tragedy experienced by many, but simply to show how a stark opposition is created in which some people have humanity, and some — criminals, terrorists and those who are culturally different — are denied this humanity. Similarly, and perhaps what best shows this ideological distribution, is the oft-repeated claim that the Bali bombings represented the loss of Australia's innocence (*Daily Telegraph* 14/10/02:20; 17/10/02:4–5). It is a rhetorical flourish that is almost meaningless: it is a trope that has been used countless times. As journalist Tony Stephens (19–20/10/02:1) pointed out, it was said of the Hilton bombing in Sydney in 1978; it was said of the various 'massacres' in Melbourne (such as at Hoddle Street in 1987), Strathfield in Sydney in 1991 and Port Arthur in Tasmania in 1996; and of course it was said of Gallipoli in 1915. It might have been said, he added, of the massacres of Indigenous inhabitants over many years (although, of course, it wasn't), but we can't keep losing our innocence. Nevertheless, the idea of innocence gives to its bearer a human-ness that is morally pure.

Those who are denied humanity are seen to be *essentially* Middle Eastern or Arabic or Muslim, and their lack of humanity is shifted to a whole community. The judge's opinion that the rapists had brought this 'slur on their own culture ... they are the ones that created this totally false scenario' (Wockner 16/8/02:4), ignores the already racialised context in which these events and their reportage occur. Ethnicity seems to become a significant factor only at selected moments. When over 100 drunken teenagers from 'the esteemed private school' Waverley College went on a vandalistic rampage through Bondi in September, 2002, their ethnicity was not an issue. Indeed, the initial item in the *Daily Telegraph* was only brief (less than 250 words), made no mention of the school or the suburbs the youths came from, and was buried away on page 18 (Yamine 26/9/02:18). It became front-page news the next day, but the key theme then was that the result of the boys' actions was to 'wreck ... their future' (Grant 27/9/02:3). Similarly, these events were not described as criminal, in the way that 'rampages' by 'ethnic gangs' have been. But what is significant here is not simply that these incidents are racialised or not; but the ways they are racialised and the techniques used to construct the Arab Other as less human, and evil.

Labelling something or someone evil, or barbaric, however reprehensible the act is, reduces what may be complex social, political and economic phenomena to a simple moral framework of right and wrong, and it essentialises that wrongdoing as pathological. It functions, as has been noted in the fear of crime literature, as a condensation symbol, simplifying and making intelligible what might otherwise remain unsettling in the social and moral order (Loader, Girling & Sparks 2000:66). Yet it produces the 'pathological stranger' (Hogg & Brown 1998:50) who inhabits the 'landscapes of fear' which seem to increasingly haunt the media and political representations of our everyday lives (Sparks 1992). The creation of these objects of hostility, as part of a wider frame of ethnic difference, has repercussions for the representations of Arabic-speaking people beyond those convicted of crimes.

Crimes and misdemeanours: criminalising cultural difference

It is one bizarre leap of the imagination to assume a link between the criminal activity of some Australian citizens of Middle Eastern ancestry and the terrorist activities of extreme Islamic fundamentalists in different parts of the world; it is another to link this to the attempts to seek asylum by refugees; and it is yet another to link these actions with the different cultural traditions of Arab and especially Muslim Australians, and yet this link is made *naturally*. In this case, a range of behaviours deemed unacceptable or offensive, become linked with and tainted by criminal activity. Once the criminal behaviour of a minority is pathologised as the tendency of a culture, then other acts of difference become imbued with criminality. In Huntington's claim about Islamic civilisation being a cause of global conflict and violence, for example, civilisation here is defined in terms of culture, ethnicity and religion, forging a spurious link between a fictitious Islamic homogeneity and a cultural pathology of violence and conflict. This sweeping assumption is also played out in other, more localised ways.

The *Daily Telegraph* self-righteously proclaimed that Australia should not feel guilt 'over our revulsion at those who care so little for their own children' (*Daily Telegraph* 13/10/02:24), for they break standard rules of parental love. As we quoted earlier, Devine, linking rape, drugs, violence and the refugees, claims 'the backlash against the Tampa illegal immigrants was founded on anger at their breaking the rules' (Devine 8/11/01). 'Queue-jumping' and 'breaking the rules' were powerful and recurring themes in reportage of the Tampa crisis and ensuing letters to the editors, which linked seeking refuge to terrorism and indecent behaviour. These are clearly linked in an item by Akerman, who, we have seen, had already implied that terrorists were uncivilised. Not only were the refugees illegal immigrants, they were also unable to conduct themselves in a proper fashion, like us: 'the principally Iraqi and Pakistani queue jumpers have shown little civility towards representatives of the country where they hope to settle' (Akerman 4/10/01:22).

This is not surprising given the cultural functions of the queue — especially in English-speaking countries. As ethnomethodologists (Livingston 1987) have pointed out, the queue is a crucial practice of social order; it is a way we get things done. To disrupt the queue is to render apart the basic social fabric — agreed rules and practices. This is why the queue is experienced as a *moral* order; it is a proper and fair way of acting. It is also an everyday practice in which political values of democracy are embedded. It is not hard then to see why 'queue-jumping' outraged so many people: it is experienced as a criminal and immoral act that threatens social and political order. But this is only possible if we see it primarily as an *illegal* or *immoral* action rather than one taken by desperate people fleeing political and economic circumstances that we in Australia would not deem acceptable. The emphasis on the illegality of the asylum-seekers was tantamount to the criminalisation of refugees (Weber 2002; Pickering & Lambert 2002.). We can see the kinds of links being made between what are perceived as uncivil behaviours, crime and cultural difference.

Devine (6/10/02:15), in an article almost a year after criticising refugees for breaking the rules, complained about the 'decline in civility' in Australian society. While no mention is made directly about migrants or gangs, Devine, who writes regularly on these issues and was writing this in the midst of the gang rape trials, repeated the claim by researchers for the conservative Centre for Independent Studies that this decline manifested itself in, among other things, 'road rage', 'queue rage', air rage' and 'increased violence', as well as a 'widespread confusion about social rules', for which parents are largely to blame. In other words, there is a chain of causation from 'bad manners' to criminal activity. In an environment where the incivility has repeatedly been linked to ethnicity, there is an implication that the presence of migrants has done much to disrupt our agreed-upon social mores.

This process of criminalisation extends to incidents in which what is at stake is deviation from the cultural norm. This is not altogether recent: an infamous article in the *Australian* by Des Keegan in the 1980s complained about Muslims slaughtering goats in the living room facing Mecca (Castles et al. 1988:3). However, in the current climate the furore is much greater. On the same day that letters to the editor applauded the record sentence for the ringleader of the gang rapes, letters also condemned the Anti-Discrimination Board approval of a gym for Muslim women only. This was denounced as heinous, undemocratic discrimination, 'prevalent Muslim racism' against 'Australians'. As Di Wilson from Balmain (19/8/02:21) put it:

> Unfortunately the hard work done by Australians to encourage assimilation has been ruined …
>
> Why are *we* the ones who have to change?
>
> If these cultures want to come and live in our society, they are the ones who should adapt to our way of life.

We discuss some of these apparently unrelated incidents in Chapter Five, but it's worth drawing attention to some media and public responses to them here because they illustrate the kinds of themes we've witnessed in relation to acts of terrorism and crime. Shortly after the gym incident, an article about a McDonald's that served halal food met with the same condemnation. S Gordon of Fairfield thought it was 'a disgrace that Australia is compelled to adapt to the culture of its immigrants' (10/9/02:16). A month later, an item about a Muslim man threatened with the sack for stopping to pray at work was the occasion for further claims that adherents of Islam were trying to be 'exceptions to the rule' (Saxby 12/10/02:22). Given the context in which it occurs, such rhetoric affirms the prevalent idea that Muslims in Australia disrupt the unspoken rules of behaviour in national life, and asserts the assimilationism that resurfaced during the 1990s. This rule-breaking, like queue-jumping, is implicitly seen to share with gang rape and terrorism an essentially immoral and criminal pathology endemic to Arabic-speaking cultures, the Middle East and Islam. There are deeply embedded anxieties within these responses and the conflation of crime, terrorism and cultural difference which are yet to be adequately unpacked, but these stories offer telling insights into the current climate of panic in Australia.

Conclusion

The processes of racialisation that we have outlined elsewhere, then, are elaborated and extended over time and reach into every corner of the social formation. With the construction of the Arab Other, the association of criminal and other practices results in the criminalisation of cultural difference, which appears to threaten the social and moral order as much as overtly illegal behaviour. Racism, then, is not a 'clean' or rational phenomenon. Just as unemployment and insecurity can become joined ideologically with non-White immigration in the incoherence of the racist imagination, so Middle Eastern can become conflated with Arab, Arab with Muslim, Muslim with rapist, rapist with gang, gang with terrorist, terrorist with 'boat people', 'boat people' with barbaric, and so on in interminable permutations. So the logics of racism are profoundly difficult to disentangle. Yet this chapter has presented striking parallels between ideological constructs of crime-prone Arab immigrants, violent Muslim terrorists, Middle-Eastern queue-jumping refugees with no respect for civilised rules, and Muslims who are seen as failing to integrate. These events, we have suggested, constitute an ongoing cycle of moral panic around the Arab Other.

The notion of a 'moral panic' has entered common parlance, but in doing this, it has been watered down to cover almost any moment of public outrage, or any form of cultural construction or boundary setting. It's easy to dismiss the recourse to the language of moral panic in scholarly analysis (Burchell 2003), but this would ignore the valuable insights the model offers. We want to retain the conceptual category of moral panic because it is a productive and critical concept, able to draw attention to the recognisable patterns of cultural meaning-making and their relations to social power. Moral panic and the construction of folk devils are both much more complicated social processes than is typically captured by common uses of these terms: they articulate individual events to broader national experience and structures of institutional power, legitimising and extending forms of state control, solidifying moral values and social divisions, and marginalising dissent and deviance (Scraton 2002).

This chapter, in exploring the construction of the Arab Other in contemporary Australia, has raised several important issues in relation to the formation and maintenance of moral panics. What are sometimes described as moments of social concern, are, in fact, layered, complex and ongoing phenomena, suturing a series of events into shared narratives so that they have cumulative power, and so that each discrete event becomes symptomatic of larger social, moral and national concerns. These ongoing phenomena ebb and flow, depending on particular events and their specific contexts, but are woven into wider social discourses — like narratives of law and order, social cohesion, institutional decay — which exist beyond these moments of panic but which are given life through them. The folk devil that is constructed in these ongoing processes, and is central to them, is a similarly complex entity, drawing together diverse groups into a homogeneous Other which is then naturalised through iteration and association. This Other is constructed through an array of ideological resources which affirm each other through the cumulative power of the waves of panic. This Other embodies a range of social anxieties, operating at a number of levels. We'll unpack these later, but we can indicate that present within the events we have just described is a set of interrelated fears — about increasing crime, cultural diversity, social cohesion, moral decay, the failure of political authority and various state institutions, globalisation and economic change, and so on. This Other functions not only as an object of hostility, therefore, but also as a form of ideological explanation of a range of social problems, understood as moral problems originating in the cultural pathology of the folk devil and providing a simple narrative of us and them, good and evil, victim and wrongdoer.

Having examined how the Arab Other is 'assembled' through linking criminality, terrorism, lack of civilisation and lack of humanity and equating this with Middle Easternness and Islam, we want to develop further an understanding of the fusions which forge this Other and the processes which cast it as such a terrifying threat. To this end we explore in the following chapter, the crucial role of military metaphors in these ideological equations.

1   The reference to the bashing of the small boy in this context seems to imply that it was committed by someone of Middle Eastern origin. It was one Paul Voss who was eventually convicted of the crime (Knowles & Casella 5/10/02:4).

2

Acts of war:
engaging the terrorist

'ACT OF WAR' was the headline emblazoned on the front page of the *Daily Telegraph* the day after the terrorist attacks on the World Trade Centre and the Pentagon (12/09/01:1). It continued to feature as a header for some days thereafter. But 'AN ACT OF WAR' was also the headline the *Telegraph* used in November 1998, after shots had been fired at the Lakemba police station from a passing car, two weeks after the fatal stabbing of Edward Lee in Punchbowl (Ogg & Casey 2/11/98:1).

Our intention is not to trivialise the events of September 11 by such a comparison; rather, we want to argue that, through the political and media alignment of the events we described in Chapter One, the previous several years of media reportage of 'Lebanese youth gangs' in NSW get their ideological 'pay-out' after the Tampa crisis and the terrorist attacks. The discursive arsenal used to explain the terrorist attacks bears remarkable similarities to that deployed in explaining 'ethnic gangs' — there is a common language of war — and there are echoes in the representation of the asylum seekers. The 'narrative accrual' of such representations over the previous years came to fruition in the coverage of the recent and ongoing international events — a process that enormously benefited the Liberal-National Party coalition in the 2001 federal election campaign. This accumulation of warring images in the reportage of gangs, rape and refugees crystallises in the terrorist 'attack on America', naturalising the dangerous Otherness of those of Arabic-speaking, Middle Eastern or Muslim background. The Arab Other becomes not simply an uncivilised, animalistic queue-jumper, but an immediate and violent threat whose reach stretches from the Middle East to our own backyard and endangers the innocence of the ordinary Australian citizen. This threat is deployed to justify a reactive 'war on terror' at the international level, but also a regime of aggressive, domestic policing and security.

There is another narrative about the Arab Other, however, which also relies heavily on the metaphor of war. This second narrative recognises to some extent the moral duplicity of both combatants: it registers the culpability of the state as well as that of the Other which, we shall later argue, contributes to a culture of fear. This chapter explores these two narratives and suggests that they both try to recuperate the morally innocent position of 'the ordinary Australian', but in doing so they both sustain and erode white Australian nationalism. In granting agency and causal power to the Other, they create a sense of threat in the suburban heart of the imagined Australian national community, which exacerbates the sense of vulnerability.

War, crime and metaphor

The choice of language and image in dealing with complex social events is crucial because it organises the ways we think about and respond to them. It is important to stress that these choices are not natural or innocent; there is not a self-evident way of characterising such complex social phenomena as terrorism, for example, as a 'war' or a 'crime'. Wars and crimes are quite different things, even if there seems to be a lot of overlap between some crimes and some acts committed during a war; terrorist acts are not quite wars and yet are more (or less) than crimes. Moreover, what counts as each can be different. The US assassination in Yemen in 2002 of an alleged Al Qaeda operative would be an act of terrorism to some, but to the US government it is part of the 'war *on* terror'. Certainly the White House would call it a 'crime' and terrorism if it were perpetrated on the US.

The discussion of the Bali bombings, however, moved seamlessly between the two registers. The bombings were described on the one hand as a 'crime' (*Daily Telegraph* 15/10/

02:20), in which policemen talked about 'suspects', or people who could help 'solve this case' (Heinzmann, Farr & McDougall 15/10/02:2). On the other hand, those killed were 'VICTIMS OF WAR' (*Daily Telegraph* 14/10/02:1); the event was explained as an 'atrocity' (Akerman 15/10/02:20), and loss of life was compared to World War II (Lawrence & McDougall 14/10/02:2). As a consequence, 'Australia mourns its fallen' (Heinzmann, Farr & McDougall 15/10/02:2); this movement between war and crime does particular kinds of things in the way we understand and react to these events.

As Lakoff (1991) argues in his paper 'Metaphor and War', widely circulated during the (first) Gulf War, metaphorical thought is a commonplace tool for understanding complex situations. The metaphor of war is particularly functional in characterising and giving shape to events involving conflict. However, metaphors of war have a decidedly moral and political character, serving to legitimate state action and entrenched interests — and to render illegitimate those of an opponent. Crucial to this, Lakoff adds, is the equation of war with crime, particularly violent crime — and he cites the characterisation of the Iraqi occupation of Kuwait in the early 1990s as 'rape' as an example — because crime is more recognisable in terms of a discourse of morality and justice. This, he argues, displaces the political and economic dimensions of war. Making war a 'crime' not only reduces it to a simple paradigm of the rights and wrongs of adhering to social laws, it makes it containable as an event, something we can respond to given our limited institutional and symbolic resources.

The equation of war and crime works the other way as well. Military metaphors are common in the reporting of violent crime (Young 1996:6–7; Bessant 1995:51–2). As van Dijk shows in his discussion of what he calls the 'riot script' in the reporting of ethnic issues in the English and Dutch press in the 1980s, not only was there an emphasis on the link between ethnicity and crime, but this link drew heavily on of the imagery of war (van Dijk 1991:78).

This included fears of 'race war' and 'invasion' by refugees, and involved images of battles, mobs, attacks, terror, time bombs, guerrillas, and so on (1991:2,55–56,66,93). Images of 'race war' have more recently littered the reportage of disturbances in England (Harris 3/6/01). Here complex economic and political causes are displaced by reference to cultural difference — difference that is construed as (cultural and moral) deviance (1991:21). But its key effect is to enhance the violence of the threat posed, and to extend it to a general, pervasive threat, akin to a warring enemy. Like the chains of association we followed in Chapter One, wars and crimes become phenomena of the same order, but they also ground the suspicions we have that those committing these offences are all of a kind.

'Terror Australis'

Unsurprisingly, then, the metaphor of war is central to the recent representations of 'Lebanese gangs' in Australia — but it is a metaphor that is worked and reworked in various ways. The shooting at the Lakemba police station, as we suggested, was declared to be an 'act of war', with 'Gunshots that broke our peace' (Wynhausen & Safe 8/11/98:13). A 'battle for Bankstown' featured in media and political representations (Harris 26/3/00:91–93) — the events in south-western Sydney have been described as 'urban warfare' (Martin 1998:26–27), a 'turf war over drugs in Bankstown' between 'Lebanese and Vietnamese gangs' (Temple & Trute 1998:5) and 'criminal warfare' (Miranda 8/1/01:4). Most recently, the theft of thirty pistols from a private security firm was described as being linked to 'a new drug war in Sydney's west' (Kamper 4/9/03:5): this item, which came with a large, dramatic photo of thirty pistols, also included discussion of a number of (largely unrelated) shootings, some of which involved men of Arabic-speaking background.

This metaphoric frame was elaborated through a complex array of related images which peppered the commentary; and south-western Sydney was seen to be a region which was 'Under fire' (Bearup 7/11/98:33) and in which there was an 'Ethnic time bomb with a slow-burning fuse' (Williams & Moore 1–2/9/01:14–15). Police Commissioner Ryan wondered where a 'Middle Eastern connection organisation' was drawing its 'recruits' from (Wain-wright 7/8/01:2). Gangs (of varying cultural backgrounds) were said to 'occupy territory', in a place the media called Gangland (McDougall & Miranda 6/8/01:4) — a foreign territory within the nation's borders — which gave a spatial dimension to this criminal activity. Newspapers provided images of 'leaders' facing off — in one case Premier Carr and Sheikh Al Hilaly (Casey & Ogg 3/11/98:5) — a standard juxtaposition in war reportage. The police accordingly responded with a special 'strike force' to deal with street crime (Kennedy 22/10/98:3) and we were given images of organised raids (see Figure 1) which echoed the images of troops in the Gulf, and prefigured the images of troops in Afghanistan and later Iraq. We were often given maps of areas under attack and aerial shots of dangerous places like Telopea Street (the site of Edward Lee's killing) which had a decidedly military feel (Sutton 25/2/01:10), comparable to the images from the wars in Afghanistan (Beach 11/10/01:3) and Iraq (Brenchley 24/9/02:16–19), and the investigations in Indonesia (Ratnesar 23/9/02:30–31).

Even when the issue wasn't about violent conflict, this language still framed discussion: articles described how young people were caught in 'cultural crossfire' (Stevenson 7/11/98:32–3); they complained that the issue of ethnic relations was a 'cultural minefield' (Warren 12/9/01:33); and they dubbed the debate over the sentencing of those guilty of so-called ethnic gang rape a 'judicial minefield' (*Daily Telegraph* 24/8/01:10).

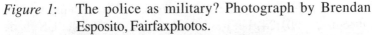

Figure 1:   The police as military? Photograph by Brendan Esposito, Fairfaxphotos.

The language of war to describe conflicts in Sydney — criminal or otherwise — is not new, of course, and it has featured in the debates on crime overseas as well (Stenson 2000). What is significant is its increasing pervasiveness and the growing use of themes of terrorism. It is not just war which is the metaphorical frame, but that particularly heinous form of military action which terrorism represents, and which brings with it a seemingly clearer moral dimension. A *Daily Telegraph* editorial equated the events of late 1998 with 'acts of terrorism' (2/11/98:10) — but it wasn't only the tabloid press that saw this — journalists from the *Daily Telegraph* and the *Australian* decided that we now lived in 'terror Australis' (Miranda 12/10/01b:1; Crawford 2/11/98:1) and the ABC's Michael Brissenden observed that 'Australia is no longer immune from acts of urban terror' (cited in Poynting, Noble & Tabar 2001:78).

One politician even evoked the idea of the 'enemy within' (Piccoli 23/8/01:24) before the terrorist attacks in the US made this a concern of Western politicians and media organisations, and its ethnic resonances echoed the ensuing anxieties around the use of mail containing anthrax spores. Since then, talk of the 'traitors within' (Goodsir 14/7/03:1) and the 'conspiracy of silence' which has turned us into a 'soft target for turncoats' and the 'traitors in our midst' (Reed 14/4/03:15) have become a staple of the news media. In the panic around Gangland, a month before September 11, many of these gangs (including 'Asian gangs') were described in terms reminiscent of terrorist cells: they were 'secret societies', 'obscure' and 'secretive', identifiable by their peculiar tattoos and secret hand signals (McDougall & Miranda 6/8/01:4). Secret hand signals recur as a figure of violent and criminal behaviour — much was made of the hand signals of the 'Punchbowl boys' (Casey & Ogg 3/11/98:1) — and this is similar to the claims that bin Laden had been 'using secret hand signals' in videos to order new attacks (Johnston 5/11/01:9). Thankfully, we were given detailed briefings and maps of the various groups (McDougall & Miranda 6/8/01:4); much as we have been given similar information about Al Qaeda (*Time* 2001:30–31).

Similarly, during the panic around 'race gang rape', the *Sun-Herald* described these incidents as 'terror in the suburbs' (Kidman 29/7/01:4): the youths were described as having 'terrorised women' (Wockner 16/8/02:4). The young female victim's evidence became 'her only weapon' (Wockner 31/5/02:6). The judge emphasised the almost military-style operation of the attacks: the 'considerable degree of planning and co-ordination' involved in these attacks, which differentiated them from other cases of gang rape (Wockner 16/8/02:6). He also likened the crime to, in the *Telegraph*'s words, 'the unforgiveable attacks against women at a time of social breakdown caused by war' (*Daily Telegraph* 16/8/02:22).

The link between local gangs and overseas terrorists is extended with the claims, mentioned in the previous chapter, that boatloads of asylum seekers also contained terrorists. Yet the links were more complex than the questionable, literal claims. The reportage of the refugees was couched in the same kind of language we have witnessed in the recounts of gang activity. The *Telegraph* pointedly headed the section dealing with letters on the refugee crisis 'Terrorism on the seas' (*Daily Telegraph* 11/10/02:27). In August 2001 there was a meeting between New South Wales Premier Bob Carr and the federal Minister for Immigration Philip Ruddock after Carr had demanded the tightening of immigration policies to reduce 'ethnic crime' in Sydney (O'Malley, Jacobsen & Kennedy 29/7/01:3; Wainwright 7/8/01:2). Carr expressed concern that 'people with military experience' were allowed to enter Australia, and called for a federal-state plan designed to make it harder for 'criminals' to get into Australia and easier 'to kick them out' (O'Malley, Jacobsen & Kennedy 17/8/01:3; Morris 17/8/01:8). Boxed in by the *Herald* article on this was another piece, headed, 'Authorities brace for more arrivals as ailing asylum seekers end horror voyage' (*Sydney Morning Herald* 17/8/2001:3). The *Telegraph* story on the same day was more strident, and on the other side of the page from the military migrants story and another one about a new police anti-gang squad (Miranda 17/8/01:8). Its headlines read, 'Leaky boat lands 348: Human cargo arrives with more on way' and 'The illegal armada keeps coming' (*Daily Telegraph* 17/8/01:8). The literal sense of 'armada' could not but reinforce the notion of immigrants armed with weapons — earlier in their homelands and later in Australian streets — especially in the context of continual reporting about the crime-ridden suburbs being a 'war zone' (Clennell 9/11/98:4).

This web of connection between gangs, immigration and refugees was repeated frequently. Mark Day complained: 'We are importing the problem', whether it be in the form of 'immigration officials ... welcoming members of the Southern Lebanon Army ... with no qualifications other than being trained to use machine guns', or 'Pacific Islanders, who know nothing other than how to wield a machete' (Day 8/8/01:27). One *Telegraph* correspondent from close to Pauline Hanson's heartland in Queensland wrote, 'It is a fact that gangs of Asians, Pacific Islanders and Arabs are terrorising Sydney' (*Daily Telegraph* 9/8/01:30). In this account, not only was 'war' being imported, but also 'terror'. All this was before 11 September.

Australian politicians, of both major parties as well as One Nation, linked asylum seekers with terrorism and crime during and after the 2001 election campaign. On 14 September that year, Defence Minister Peter Reith warned that Indonesia could serve as a 'launching pad' for terrorism against Australia and other countries: 'the clamp down on border protection against boat people went "hand in hand" with efforts to combat terrorism' (Allard 14/9/01:6; *PM* 14/9/01; Farr 14/9/01:8). Immigration Minister Ruddock warned on 17 September that boat people entering Australia were a potential security risk, and that some of them had criminal records (AAP 19/9/01). The Prime Minister said much the same in a television interview on *60 Minutes* the previous evening. Attorney General Daryl Williams called for closer surveillance of immigrants, and Queensland Liberal MP Peter Slipper asserted 'an undeniable linkage between illegals and terrorists'; it was undeniable because 'many refugees came from Afghanistan' (Phillips 20/9/01).

Unsurprisingly, the media, after September 11, warned of 'Bin Laden groups in Sydney suburbs' (Miranda 12/10/01a:5), linking the Lakemba-based Islamic Youth Movement and individuals who had received 'military training'; and thereby linking — first implicitly and then explicitly — 'Lebanese gangs' in south-western Sydney with Islamic fundamentalism and terrorism, in much the same way that refugee boats were claimed to have contained terrorists. This connection followed effortlessly from the parallels between representations of Lebanese gangs and the terrorist attacks on New York; parallels based on the accrual of a shared imagery. Both groups engaged in 'acts of war'; both events required military responses and tactics (aerial photos and so on); both groups displayed obvious signs of 'terrorist behaviour' — violence, secret signals, clandestine organisation, extremist association, and so on. Both exhibit, indeed, a common origin in a 'culture of violence'.

When, after the Bali bombings, claims that Muslim terrorists were present in Australia were asserted again by politicians and media, this time the claims seemed real and uncontroversial. The year before they had seemed bizarre, and even hysterical, but given that Bali was 'on our doorstep' the threat had become immediate and local. Yet this claim about terrorists in the suburbs, especially given the so far fruitless ASIO raids on suspects, is possibly more believable only because of the years of casting petty criminals, rowdy boys, asylum seekers and migrants as terrorists. The weekly reminders that Australia was now a 'prime target' for overseas terrorists (Baker 23–24/11/02:1) and under 'DIRECT THREAT' (Dickins & Farr 20/11/02:1), were complemented by claims that 'sleeper cells' existed in Australia, that Jemaah Islamiah terrorists were being trained in the Blue Mountains, just outside Sydney (Barrass 30/11/02:6), and that 'deadly instruments of terror' — like a 'suburban rocket launcher' — were found at Lake Macquarie, near Newcastle (Cock & Williams 30/11/02:5). More recent articles have continued to claim the existence of terrorist networks in Australia (Goodsir 14/7/03:1; Goodsir 4/9/03:1). We are not suggesting that there is no possibility of a terrorist attack in Australia; just that the hysterical nature of the claims about the threat accentuates the fear of the Arab Other.

We shall return to the nature of this fear later, in Chapter Seven; the point here is that the Bali reportage sustains this web of connection between crime and terror. These parallels are not 'natural'; nor indeed are they innocent, but work to naturalise ideological links and produce substantial effects. A number of instances of racial vilification in recent years were reported to have connected the terms 'Arab' or 'Muslim' with 'terrorist', and we will return to these below. This pattern was observed during the 1991 Gulf War, long before the 2001 September 11 attacks (HREOC 1991). These representations have a long history that is crystallised at a particular moment, not simply as representations, but as rationales for racist attacks. They become so because the military metaphors turn a deviant Arab Other into a pathologically violent and direct threat.

The Other is armed

Metaphor works through association, reinscribing complex phenomena in terms of the familiar, and through processes of opposition, reduction and conflation, turning people and events into essentialised, contrastable categories. War metaphors, for example, involve an apparently morally clear battle between an 'us' and a 'them'. Lakoff (1991) notes the pervasive use of a 'fairytale' cast of villain, victim and hero — with an accompanying simplistic moral structure — in explaining and hence justifying military action and demonising the enemy. But these metaphoric framings also invest in the villain, the Other, an agency with the capacity for disorder and violent destruction. In representations of Lebanese gangs and the array of incidents seemingly involving the Arab Other, the enemy was not always so clearly defined, but it was understood that this enemy was pitted against government, the police, and right-thinking Australia, and was deemed a real and present danger, much like international terrorism.

The opposition between good and bad, however, is primarily construed as a cultural division. Central to these representations is the creation of the problem as an 'ethnic problem'. This involves mobilising the racialised Other we have detailed: a 'them' against whose 'difference' a dominant national, ethnic 'us' is defined. In these images a racialised Other is created to bear the brunt of blame — the circumstances are deemed to be an 'ethnic situation', the problem identified as an element within the Arabic-speaking communities. This thematises (van Dijk 1991:116–7) a link between ethnicity, crime and violence, producing the overwhelming image of ethnic difference as a social threat and the source of conflict and deviance. This racialised 'them' is set in conflict with an unproblematised 'us': the *Daily Telegraph* is clear on the point that '*Sydney* battles gang crime' (23/8/01:1, our emphasis). The recurring claim that members of Arabic-speaking communities have put up a 'wall of silence' best reflects this divide — 'they' are not talking to 'us' (Poynting et al. 2001). The crucial element here is that this Other is always seen to be the one who initiates disorder and contravenes social rules. In the media coverage of the halal hamburgers, the women-only gym and the praying worker (mentioned in Chapter One and detailed in Chapter Five), the letters to the editor were clear about who had unsettled the peace. Moreover, as with the gang rapists, it was stressed repeatedly that 'they' were the ones who were racist in insisting on maintaining their ways at the expense of 'ours'. The Arab Other is always seen to be the aggressive transgressor, someone who brought conflict here.

As we have already seen with the refugees, a common theme in reporting gangs was the way war had been imported, from places like Beirut, along with the cultural baggage of migration. These 'wars', we were reminded, were 'A grim echo of Beirut' (Charlton 3/11/98:11). Significantly, Beirut has become a figure of urban and social decay, particularly when it is used to describe a place such as Bondi that has been the centre of concerns about the disruptive presence of Arabic-background youth (Skelsey 2/3/01:13). Comparisons were also drawn between south-western Sydney and Israel and Kashmir in one *Daily Telegraph* editorial (2/11/98:10).

Much has been made of the military background of those involved in criminal activity and the so-called gangs (McDougall & Miranda 6/8/01:5). The Premier referred to the weapons training these 'gangsters' have received in military organisations (Wainwright 7/8/01:2) and murdered gang boss Danny Karam's military experience was noted, though without emphasis on the fact that it was with Lebanese *Christian* militia (Sutton 25/2/01:10–11). This was often linked to the 'culturally institutionalised' violence of Middle Eastern countries: anthropologist Richard Basham from Sydney University was quoted as saying 'it's part of their culture', while police were reported as suggesting that gang activity was 'part of their cultural upbringing' (McDougall & Miranda 6/8/01:5). Sutton

(25/2/01:10–11) explicitly traced the 'Telopea Street Boys' associated with the Edward Lee manslaughter to a Sunni Muslim village in the Al Dunnieh region of Lebanon, while retiring Federal Police Commissioner Palmer claimed that knives and guns were more commonly a feature of 'Lebanese culture' (Mercer 12/3/01:1). No distinction is made here between those of Christian and Muslim faith, between those from Lebanon and those from elsewhere in the Middle East, and between those born overseas and those born in Australia. As in the article expressing a concern about bin Laden groups in Sydney, a *Daily Telegraph* editorial — 'Entry is a privilege not a right' — links international terrorism, local Arabic-speaking communities and problems with lax migrant and refugee entry rules (yet denies this is an issue of racism) (12/10/01:20).

As we have already argued in Chapter One, the imagining of this Other ignores complex distinctions between religions, places of birth and country of ancestry, making internal differences inconsequential. There is a semantic chain of equivalence that links, unproblematically, Australians of Lebanese background, the Middle East, Afghanistan, the Taliban, Arabic-speaking groups and Islam, as though these are all of the same order. A homogenising classification is a characteristic feature of racialised knowledge and the way it constructs its Other (Goldberg 1993:150). Further, this homogenised Other is explained culturally — these categories are 'ethnicised' and a similarity found in this imputed cultural homogeneity. A semantic chain is also established culturally between (exotic) masculine bravado, civil disobedience, organised crime, violent crime and terrorism, and linked to lack of civilisation, misogyny, deviant masculinity, cruelty, irrationality. Analysis of fear of crime has shown many times over the ways criminal activity is explained in terms of individual pathology (Barak 1994:20–1); here we are seeing a more cultural explanation of criminal, violent, and terrorist activity, shorn of any sustained attempt to contextualise such activity, and building on the existing racialisation of youth crime (Collins et al. 2000; White 1996).

An oft-repeated claim was that the activities in the spotlight — drug dealing, crime, gangs, violence, interethnic conflict, uncivil youth — were new and intrinsically 'foreign', imported into Australia through decades of immigration, especially from countries and regions where conflict and war were familiar and ingrained aspects of cultural life. Much of what we had witnessed since late 1998, it was perceived, had to do with 'Arab culture'. In Premier Carr's complaint that 'we import gangsters' (Wainwright 7/8/01:2), the emphasis is on the threat that derives from elsewhere, laying the blame for 'Lebanese gangs' squarely at the feet of the Arabic-speaking community leaders (Jackson, Harris & Nason 3/11/98:5). This amounted to the criminalisation of (especially young) people of Arabic-speaking background. They have become the pre-eminent 'dangerous Other', the 'unpredictable stranger' in Australian cultural life (Lupton 1999a:14) onto which we project our deepest fears about social and moral disorder.

In producing knowledge about this Other, the process of racialisation identifies, if only implicitly, a set of characteristics or behaviours, even a pathology, used to explain social and cultural difference, and to naturalise social exclusions (Goldberg 1993:151). This involves the projection of anxieties about social problems onto the Other, which becomes seen as the cause of those problems, the source of conflict and disorder. The Other is not only a source of conflict, but embodies a lack of moral order. Societies create cultural boundaries and oppositions as a way of maintaining order: they differentiate between those who belong and those who, owing to cultural differences, are seen as out of place (Douglas 1966). In order to legitimate these divisions, those who are seen as Other are constructed as moral threats. The metaphor of war, and the theme of terror, locate moral right on one particular side of the divide, legitimising the actions taken by the NSW government and its police service. Racialisation, licensed by the metaphor of war, proceeds through a double movement: social problems are defined as ethnic ones, and ethnic 'villains' are inscribed as morally culpable on the basis of their ethnicity, allowing the 'non-ethnic' heroes to remain morally pure. It is not just the characterisation of the Other as deviant at issue here, but the imputing of violent agency to the Other: the 'puritanism of good feeling', as Flahault (2003:75,108) puts it, rests on the energy of the villain's agency. This sustains the veneer of the moral innocence of Australian society, but at some cost, we shall argue.

The ideological conflation of 'Lebanese gangs' (even though this was concentrated on NSW) and Arab terrorism produced a windfall for the conservative parties in the 2001 federal election. Together with the refugee crisis, these events intensified the racialised discourse that pervaded the campaign, even when it was not explicit. After both the Tampa crisis and September 11, electoral support for the Coalition rose by about 5% on each occasion (Manne 12/11/01:10). In Sydney, the centre of the ethnic gang panic, the swing to the Liberals was greater than in any other capital city — in some parts of Sydney it was over 8% (Clark et al. 17–18/11/ 01:27). Prime Minister Howard made much of this situation — evoking our uncertain times and the need for firm action. This discourse racialised issues around global inequalities, humanitarian policy, cultural difference and so on, but *articulated* them as issues of right and wrong, villain and victim. The increasing incidence of harassment and vilification, here as in the US, both official and unofficial (Riley 10–11/11/01:18; Jopson 20–21/10/01:18), bears testimony to this implicit 'understanding' of the links between cultural difference, crime, terrorism and moral and social order.

In 'arming' the Arab Other, fashioning a folk devil who is aggressive and violent as well as deviant, Australian politicians and media imbue this figure with an agency that props up the belief in the moral purity of the nation and 'demands' an assertive response. Howard's election campaign appealed because it reasserted a degree of agency in 'defending' the nation; just like state-based 'get tough' policing policies — but in both cases they exhibit a certain hysterical machismo endemic to Australian politics. Overall, these responses serve to feed a deep-seated anxiety about Australian social and political life. In an insightful cartoon and poem entitled 'The Warlords of Suburbia', Michael Leunig captures something of this: an embittered male watches international events on his TV, and domestic events inside and outside his own home, and vents his own frustration and sense of impotence by wishing misfortune upon the world. A classic representation of the passive/aggressive element in Australian suburban life, Leunig's work captures our eagerness for the suffering of others and the hypocrisy our double standards, while only barely masking deep anxieties and disillusionment (24–25/11/01:2).

The Gulf War, or the space in between

This first narrative — innocent 'us' versus aggressive 'them' — only works up to a point. The coverage of the events around gangs — like the events around the refugee and terrorist crises — was, however, always more complex than this portrayal suggests. A second narrative has emerged in the representation of youth gangs which, while it still operates around the metaphor of war and its attendant reductions and associations, uses it differently from the manner suggested in Lakoff's analysis. During the ethnic gangs panic, the distinction between 'us' and 'them' became a little murky. Van Dijk (1991:143) suggests that the us/them schema always involves complex sub-categories. But something more complicated is happening in these representations. On the one hand, there is a sense in which 'we' are caught in a battle between warring elements, innocent victims of a bloody battle. Here 'we' are the civilians in the 'war'. As Charles Miranda suggests, 'gangs battle for control of *our* streets' (8/1/01:4, our emphasis). This innocence and removal from wrongdoing is a common theme in these stories, but there is something else here.

In the earlier narrative, the police were initially cast as the defender of good. As well as being seen as avengers, responding to aggression with a special 'strike force' to deal with street crime

(Kennedy 22/10/98:3), police were also described as the *target* of 'Terror Australis' (Crawford 2/11/98:1). Ogg and Casey (2/11/98b:1) likewise describe how police had to 'dig in against gang attacks' (which aligns the police with the revered World War One 'diggers'). Both victim and defender are morally justified positions because they are not seen to initiate unjust aggression. Yet the image of the police-as-victim also opens up the problem of a sense of incapacity to act and resolve the problem, and eventually leads to a sense of police as part of the problem (Warren 16/8/01:23). Narratives that rely on the fairytale genre and metaphors of war work on a particular distribution of blame and of agency (or cause and effect). To shift blame onto the wrongdoer, they must grant agency to them, leaving the hero as reactive. If the required restoration of order does not ensue, as is the case with both the NSW 'crime wave' and the 'war on terror', then this leaves the hero open to charges of impotence. Further, the metaphor of war only works if the hero can sustain the burden of moral purity. Over the last few years, impotence and moral laxity have become marked features of the actors — the police and the State — deemed to be the heroes.

Inept policing has become a common theme. We see not only gang warfare, but wars within the ranks — one article talks about police wars, wars of ideas regarding how to deal with drugs and crime (involving both police and politicians), as well as the turf wars between gangs (Lagan 2001). A cartoon lampoons the 'gang wars at the coppers' club' (Moir 8/3/01:13). War has erupted all over the place. Rather than positively representing the police and politicians, much media reportage has become much more ambivalent — even critical — of their actions and pronouncements: a marked difference from 1998 when some news articles restated police media releases with little alteration. This does not just revolve around incidents in the Bankstown area or those involving the Arabic-speaking communities alone, but includes a number of events and issues. Alongside this perception of ineffectuality is the long-standing recognition of police corruption. Over the course of many years, police have increasingly come 'under fire' for corruption, drug-taking and violent behaviour as well as bureaucratic in-fighting, poor policing policy and strategy, echoing the image of a corrupt force pictured by the Wood Royal Commission (Horan 26/12/99:19; Miranda 24/10/00:7; Chan 1997). The failure to resolve factionalism in the NSW Police Service, of course, was one of the factors in the 2002 sacking of Commissioner Peter Ryan by the NSW Labor government, which had employed him from England to become Australia's highest-paid public servant to reform the hitherto notoriously corrupt NSW police and to bring (supposedly rampant) crime under control. Extravagant promises about the latter, while successful image-builders in the talkbacks and tabloids, proved to be Mr Ryan's downfall when he was unable to deliver on them and the media turned against him, outraged when his publicity machine misrepresented failures as successes (Mercer 16–17/2/02:25).

Here we do not merely see the mitigation of police acts in representations of ethnic situations, as van Dijk claims (1991:198), but an ambivalent relationship with the police; sometimes supportive, sometimes critical. Often there is a recognition that aggressive (as well as corrupt and inept) policing is part of the problem of conflict, not the force defending us. The coverage of the police response was meant to reassure us that the police were on top of crime, but the images of mass police action — often military-style — produce the anxiety they are meant to dispel. The columns of police marching into Telopea Street with helicopter cover in August, 2000, were intended as a conclusive show of strength — 'Police raid tames a street of silent fear' — but it represented for some the image of a military state (Lawrence 3/8/00:3). This image was circulated on the Internet with the ironic caption 'community policing?'

The representation of NSW politicians and the state Labor government has been similarly ambivalent. In an item on Bob Carr's mid-term report card which focused on his new drug laws, for example, the overwhelming emphasis in news coverage was a disillusion with political grandstanding which papers over ineptitude and ineffectual policy (Jacobsen 26/3/01:6). These drug laws were dubbed 'Nazi-style' (Lagan et al. 29/3/01:4). On top of these claims, in response to the gang rapes there was the recurrent accusation that Australia's courts were failing to reflect community concerns and were 'soft' on criminals (Devine 30/08/01:12): another public institution failing to protect the citizenry. A One Nation (2003) campaign leaflet for East Hills in the NSW election similarly lumped together criticisms of multiculturalism and its role in escalating crime and terrorism with criticisms of judges, policing, and other public institutions.

Similar themes of the incompetence and corruption of those institutions designed to protect Australian citizens has emerged in the asylum-seekers crisis and the investigation into the terrorist attacks, especially in relation to Bali. As we saw in Chapter One, the Senate Select Committee on a Certain Maritime Incident (2002) found politically motivated acts of misrepresentation over the 'children overboard affair' occurring at many levels, from the Prime Minister's office through the Defence Ministry and elements of the armed services. Similarly, very soon after the Bali bombings, questions were being raised about the competence of the investigation, Australia's intelligence services and the political management of public concerns. While an inquiry eventually cleared Australian authorities of any failure to notify the Australian public about terrorist dangers (Morris & Stewart 11/12/02:10), a common response was that there were still 'questions unanswered' about Australia's intelligence and security capabilities (*Sydney Morning Herald* 14–15/12/02:32). More recently, evidence that the Australian government, like the UK government, exaggerated the threat of Iraq and its 'weapons of mass destruction', and ignored advice that war would increase the likelihood of terrorist attacks on Australia, have undermined the strong and popular position taken by the government (Allard & Fray 13–14/9/03:1).

Ambivalence towards political life was seen in other ways. Australian politicians were, like the police, seen as unprofitably divided: Prime Minister Howard and Opposition Leader Simon Crean were seen to be 'at war over terrorism' (Banham 14–15/12/02:1). The ASIO raids of the homes of people with suspected Jemaah Islamiah links were, while generally endorsed by the Australian public, also the basis of concern over 'heavy handed' responses (*Sydney Morning Herald* 1/11/02:10). On the other hand, viewers of Channel Nine's *Today* (18/11/02) responded by email to a question about whether Australian authorities were 'doing enough' to prepare for a terrorist attack were scathing, describing Australia as a 'soft target'. As one viewer argued, 'our intelligence agencies are so far behind the times we wouldn't stand a chance'. Janet Albrechtsen (4/12/02:15) managed to link terrorism and refugees again while shifting the blame for the threat of attack onto the High Court who, she argued, were 'inviting terrorists' to Australia. This theme had appeared in a Warren cartoon in the *Daily Telegraph* after September 11, showing a bewigged judge sitting in his lounge room with four bearded, turban-wearing Taliban-like figures drinking cups of tea while saying to his wife, bearing the tea tray, 'I'm sorry dear — I told them it was okay to stay' (Warren 12/9/01:33).

The initial war narrative cannot contain the populism in Australian political life, a deep and abiding ambivalence towards political institutions and associated authorities. While Australians generally supported a 'tough' stand on terrorism, they also saw the Federal Government's anti-terrorism as 'political grandstanding', as the *Telegraph's* tele-poll showed (4/2/03:16). At stake here is not just the negative portrayal of police and politicians, just as the images and headlines discussed were not *just* about those of Arabic-speaking background — but a distancing from the very institutions that are supposed to guarantee the rights and freedoms that define Australian society. While in the earlier narrative the attempt to find the moral high ground included those institutions, now the need to find a morally innocent position works by excluding those institutions. In setting up an opposition between interests that are equally 'to blame' (see 'Lebanese leaders attack Carr', *Daily Telegraph* 6/11/98:4), the media representations provide us with a position from which to reject all sides, to find a space 'in between', so to speak. The metaphor of war here is not of one in which we are fighting, nor a war where one side is any longer 'our side' — it is a futile, endless war which we view from a distance, or as victims. This is how we have come to view conflicts in Northern Ireland and the Balkans, yet what is significant here is the way this is mapped onto domestic politics. This second narrative, which emerged over the last four years, registers a deep if inarticulate ambivalence about the very foundations of the Australian polity, even as it hangs on grimly to the moral purity that is often seen to be attached to Australian society.

A particular kind of image began to appear in the last few years that captured this sense of antagonistic parties and a neutral space between them. In this image — see Figure 2 (Kennedy & O'Malley 25/11/00:9) — we have a scene from Kathleen St, Lakemba in western Sydney, after a shooting that took place there. Six police officers, striding down the street passing suburban homes, are walking away from us, and are positioned on the far left side of the image. A Muslim woman, in traditional garb, and carrying her shopping, is positioned on the far right side. It is supposed to reassure us that police are on the job, but it resonates rather with a profound sense of the gulf between the police and Arabic-speaking communities — a gulf expressed not only in the physical distance between a group of police and a Muslim woman at either edge of the photograph, but also in the fact that backs are turned against each other — a sign of both disrespect and an incapacity to engage. In this image we are being placed *between* them and away from them: not asked to side with either, but against both.

There are two things noteworthy here: first, we are removed from being protagonists in the conflict, but are caught in it. Second, what is in the middle — well, not exactly the white picket fence from John Howard's 1988 'Future Directions' campaign, but it is a front yard and a gate of an ordinary suburban house — a symbol of ordinary Australianness. The battle that is being fought, then, is over the heart of Australian life, and 'ordinary Australians' are caught in the middle. This is conveyed in other ways. The headline, 'Mum gunned down' (Westwood 24/11/00:3), focuses not on the ethnicity per se of the person killed, but the fact that she was a 'mum', an ordinary person from an ordinary family (whether she was or not is irrelevant). Elsewhere we have other images of innocent and ordinary Australians — like children (Clennell 9/11/98:4) — being caught in the crossfire, not able to believe that this is happening in their own back — or front — yards. In these images, ethnicity is largely erased from the victim of the crime. This narrative, reworking the representation of distant wars, allows us to recognise and explain local conflict and yet remove ourselves from it, to see ourselves as victims, even as the ethnicity of the real victims is largely erased.

Figure 2:   The space between. Photo by Jessica Hromas, Fairfaxphotos.

It is no wonder that the suburban setting of these criminal acts and of the ongoing conflict between police and communities is constantly stressed — perhaps if they happened at a longstanding drug and prostitution hub of the city like Kings Cross we would be less shocked. But the 'sleepy suburbia' of ordinary Australia was under attack (Wynhausen & Safe 7–8/11/98:13), just as after the World Trade Centre attacks the media worried about 'Bin Laden groups in Sydney suburbs'. Another image captures the same sense: two foreigners in exotic clothes and two police officers, backs turned. We do not identify with either of them, but with, in the middle of this suburban street, an ordinary looking fellow (Humphries & Marsh 3/11/98:1). On closer inspection, this ordinary fellow could be of 'Middle Eastern appearance' too, but his western clothes — in contrast to the distinctive apparel of those on the right of the picture — emphasises his assimilation to Australianness as well as his difference from uniformed authority. This article states explicitly that this attack 'was un-Australian'.

Ordinariness is, of course, a key figure in any populism. An enormous investment is made in the idea to embody the goodness and decency of the populace. A *Telegraph* editorial (28/10/02:14) stressed this ordinariness in arguing that 'ordinary people' were increasingly the targets of global terrorists — 'in their sights' — resulting in the loss of 'innocent lives'. Ordinary and innocent are virtually interchangeable here, and contrasted to war and terror; and if these latter two are associated with the Arab Other, then innocence and ordinariness are also aligned in particular ways.

War is not just a metaphor, then, but is central in constituting a complex frame wherein a range of social problems, which include inept policing and political grandstanding as well as the specific concerns around 'ethnic crime', are structured by a moral discourse which perceives issues in terms of simple right and wrong. It also works to construct these problems in terms of an aggressive 'threat' to moral innocence: a world populated by villains who threaten victims. This frame works, not by telling us what to think in any singular sense, but by drawing a border around what we see, and directing us to what is to be seen: it includes some things and excludes others, and sets the parameters by which the object is perceived and interpreted (McLachlan & Reid 1994). Yet it also helps us forget where we are looking *from*. By focusing in this chapter on the metaphoric frame we can move away from the content of the images and headlines to the ways we see this content and the position from which we see it.

Note that those shots fired at Lakemba police station were 'Gunshots that broke our peace' (Wynhausen & Safe 7–8/11/98:13) — *our* peaceful existence was disrupted from outside. A *Herald* letter-writer warned that 'It is Mr and Mrs Average who will wreak revenge' for these crimes; but this 'middle Australia' is clearly identified as an 'Australian-born underclass' (Murphy 10/3/01:35). This theme of the un-Australian nature of the attack, and by implication, of the perceived culture and traditions of the perpetrators, is not new, of course. At one level it confirms the us/them schema we have already discussed. But the 'us' sometimes may contain moral duplicity. Recognising how the frame of war hides the position from which we view these incidents, we can see that the problem will always be seen to be someone else, coming from somewhere else — whether it be Arabic-speaking people, police, politicians, or whatever — and 'we' are removed from it.

But who is this unseen ordinary Australian that is at risk? Who is the 'we' that is understood in this discourse? The 'Let's look out for Australia' anti-terrorist campaign (Commonwealth Government 2003) emphasised the need to protect 'our way of life' — despite the fact that in contemporary Australia such a concept is almost meaningless — and it did so by contrasting this with suspicious activity that is 'out of the ordinary', a 'lifestyle that doesn't add up', and even people with 'false or multiple identities': remembering that we have been reminded that many refugees had false identities, and multiculturalism is predicated on a recognition of multiple identities. This position of ordinariness then is not available for all to take up. If one side of the polarisation is the exotic, third-world-looking migrant — as Hage puts it (1998) — then this hidden position 'in between' is necessarily 'white'. This may have class inflections too — this was clearly seen when the debate, and the anxiety, was upped a notch or two when it was suggested that criminals from 'other areas' were invading Sydney's north shore (Gilmore 6/11/00:5) — the heart of the white, Anglo middle-class Australia. The editorial of that issue of the *Daily Telegraph* (6/11/00:20), entitled 'Community fighting for our children' — note the 'our' again — spells this out: 'In communities which, by and large, typify our ideal of a safe, suburban environment, such a scenario seems all the more disturbing'. National belongings always have these inflexions of race and class and gender, and this is no exception. Perhaps the more important aspect here is that safety, civility, decency and order are always on *our* side, and this side is white — an implication also evident in the terrorist coverage.

Conclusion: for a war on ordinariness

We have seen two narratives used in the representation of Lebanese gangs, as well as Muslim terrorists, both of which revolve around the metaphor of war, both of which involve processes of racialisation and both of which seek to preserve a morally innocent position of ordinary Australianness. The frame of war not only embroiders the representation of crime and ethnicity, it is an emotionally charged force which shapes the ways we understand social relations as moral relations. As Bauman (1993:183) has argued, responsibility is fundamental to the structure of subjectivity. These two narratives provide ways of dealing with responsibility and morality. One puts us into battle against a racialised Other in a classic war of good versus evil which resonates with contemporary representations of terrorism; it casts the Other as aggressor and as evil and posits us on the side of good as both victim and avenger; the second acknowledges that the two warring sides are not quite so easily separable but finds not only a safe haven between them, but a space where we can recuperate moral good. Either way, it is always someone else's fault, and either way the moral positions are highly racialised. The value of the second narrative is that it allows us to abrogate responsibility when our institutions are at fault. These two narratives, then, also provide a kind of ideological space — a repertoire of positions and representations which politicians, media commentators and audiences draw upon in attempting to make sense of social relations and in particular the concerns and tensions related to cultural diversity, crime and social policy. The different narratives can be mobilised according to the situation and speaker, giving the dominant cultûre a kind of hegemonic flexibility. At their heart both narratives attempt to retain a morally 'pure' position which is attributable to some core ordinary Australianness that retains the possibility of a pure national community, relegating to an ethnic Other the tendency towards criminality.

Nation-states and elements within their social formations have always promoted strategies of 'purification', aiming to create senses of national and local space from which impurities — of race and ethnicity, for example, or criminality and deviance — can be excluded, such as in restrictive immigration laws or in white, middle-class gated communities (Morley 2000:141–144). However, purification can also refer to the specifically moral nature of national identification, creating a sense in which the ordinary citizen is freed of the impurity of ethnic conflict, crime or institutional corruption. The identification of Gangland is one way in which moral impurities can be located and externalised; the identification of a pathologically violent Other that imports crime and terror similarly sustains this purity.

Ironically, however, these strategies also serve to problematise the very foundations of national identification. On the one hand the shift in narratives demonstrates that impurity is increasingly hard to conceive as external; it is becoming increasingly internal to

Australian society, not because multiculturalism allows us to 'import' conflict, crime and disorder, but because Australian institutions themselves are increasingly seen as corrupt and disordered. On the other, the association of innocence and victimhood produces a 'weak' nationalism. In investing in the criminal Other the capacity for aggression and disorder, these representations invest in 'us' the capacity to be harmed, a passivity which guarantees the moral status of victimhood but which robs 'us' of agency. This is like the tendencies of crime surveys generally, which construct simple categories, founded in opposition between victims and offender, but which exacerbate the sense of risk and of the likelihood of victimisation (Stanko 2000:13). We will return to the consequences of this for an emerging 'paranoid nationalism' (Hage 2002), a culture of anxiety around our national attachments; suffice it to say here that the theme of fragmentation (Seccombe 17/2/01:25,30–31) has been common to those ongoing debates about Australian national identity and multiculturalism for many years.

The identification of a pure Australian ordinariness underlies the strong association of crime and ethnicity, and, as we have seen, it licenses the 'criminalisation' of cultural difference. We need, therefore, to problematise the ordinariness we often take for granted in national life. We need to question the apparent innocence at the heart of Australian identity and reveal the 'warlord of suburbia' that lies within, and to deconstruct the essentialised understandings of ethnicity underpinning our everyday assumptions about cultural difference and national community.

3

The lost boys:
caught between cultures or resisting racism?

War is not the only metaphor in terms of which the 'Arab Other' is conceived. In this chapter we examine the image of being lost, caught or trapped between two cultures, that sets the horizons of intelligibility for much influential discussion and practice in relation to young second-generation Arabic-speaking background immigrants in Australia. Of particular interest and focus here are the young working-class men who are encountered by the State as a problem to be resolved or dealt with: not least during the widening gyres of moral panic. In both versions of the metaphor of war analysed in Chapter Two, the Arab Other tended to be presented as the enemy of those hegemonic 'us' who were constructing this message and of those of 'us' with whom this message was intended to communicate. 'We' are sometimes the innocent victims of an enemy within, a cultural or actual fifth column from which we must be protected by the police and, if necessary, security forces and other repressive arms of the State. 'We' are sometimes the innocent, put-upon hosts of ungrateful, bad-mannered and downright immoral guests within our home, who cannot or will not learn to do as the Romans when they are in Rome.

In the first version of the war metaphor, the police and security forces are on 'our' side, and the enemy is to be defeated, put, down, repressed. This corresponds in part to the 'zero tolerance' approach towards second-generation young men in public spaces, which has been analysed in Poynting (1999) and Collins et al (2000) and is not the major focus of our attention here. The second version of the war metaphor, as we have seen, leaves the 'us' in the space in between the Other and the heavy-handed or bumbling police.

This second version of the metaphor of war places the immigrant in an either/or position: either become 'one of us', or remain (at best) on the outside as the Other or even (at worst as in the 1991 Gulf War, the 'War on Terror' from 2001, or the ensuing second Gulf War) on the side of the enemy, a traitor.

Young, second-generation immigrants are positioned especially invidiously and unrealistically within this framework, as we shall see in this chapter. In addition to the ethnic profiling and 'zero tolerance' approach, the State has a gentler way of dealing with them within its repertoire, more apparently consensual and less coercive. Well-meaning liberals, worried ethnic leaders and community workers — and even in some contexts concerned parents and the marginalised adolescents themselves — can come to see this second generation as lost between cultures, and thus contrive or support measures to find, rescue or save them.

This popular notion that second-generation immigrant youth of Lebanese background are 'caught between two cultures' is widespread both in the dominant culture and among Lebanese-Australian communities. Indeed, this belief is held in both academic and common-sense forms, of second-generation immigrant young people generally. It is often put forward to explain a range of social problems involving these young people: from education to youth culture and the criminal justice system. In the context of the criminalisation of young people — especially young men — of Arab and Muslim background which is the focus of this book, the 'Lost between Cultures' thesis offers an ideological 'explanation' of the taken-for-granted criminality.

This chapter demonstrates, firstly, that the thesis does not stand up to empirical test. We show that the premise of two neatly bounded cultures with second-generation immigrant youth trapped in between does not accurately represent the lived reality of the young people concerned. Secondly, this calls into question the range of redemptive measures that are prescribed by well-meaning and right-thinking experts: from reactionary to progressive. These comprise contradictory and complexly interrelating strategies of assimilation, conservative cultural maintenance, and liberal cultural pluralism. We argue that these prescriptions are generally futile, for they depend on a deepseated ethnocentrism in education and criminal justice systems which are part of the problem. We conclude, rather, that recognition and provision of social space to develop cultural hybridities could be part of the way forward. We also emphasise that it is necessary to deal with the realities of class inequality, including unequal means and power in the production and valorisation of hybridity.

There is a difference between being lost and being told to 'get lost'. This chapter advances the argument that these distinct approaches comprise two complementary hegemonic strategies deployed by the State in the social control of young, male, working-class, second-generation, Arabic-speaking background immigrants.

Some definitions

Let us begin by defining some key terms which we will use in the analysis presented in this chapter. We are using the concept of 'hegemony' as developed in the 1920s and 30s by the Italian social theorist and revolutionary, Antonio Gramsci (1971). Hegemony is a form of class domination through a political-cultural alliance of ruling-class fractions, in which the ruling class secures a decisive measure of consent by the subaltern classes to their own domination. It involves intellectual and moral leadership by the ruling class, through its domination of institutions such as schooling or the press, and the influence of the intellectuals organic to the ruling class, such that the everyday ways of seeing and acting in the world, of the masses of ordinary people, become aligned with, or present no viable challenge to, the interests of the ruling class. This consent, however, is never uncontested and must be continually won by the ruling class if it is to maintain its rule; moreover, it is always backed up by coercion — the repressive arm of the state — in the army, the police, the courts, the gaols. Coercion and consent are always linked: the press and the schools have a coercive function as well as an informative and educative one; and the courts and even the police also have a pedagogic function. The concept of the State, in this theory, takes on an expanded meaning, and incorporates privately-owned media, say, as much as publicly owned schools. It is 'the entire complex of practical and theoretical activities with which the ruling class not only justifies and maintains its dominance, but manages to win the active consent over those whom it rules' (Gramsci 1971:258).

A crisis of hegemony

We conjecture that the moment of Hansonism represents a crisis of hegemony in Australia: an instability, pending realignment of the dominant class fractions which, in their hegemony, represent the people to themselves. Cope and Kalantzis (2000) call it a 'watershed'. They compare it in significance to the Federation settlement, in which crisis was resolved by a white and male-dominated working-class movement accepting State limiting of class struggle through arbitration, in return for considerable concessions, including immigration restrictions: the 'White Australia Policy'.

So-called 'globalisation' — the increasing and accelerating interchange of capital, commodities, information, population — has brought economic and cultural insecurities to particular sections of the populus in recent decades. It has, for example, advantaged those sections of capital which are most mobile and most easily bridge or jump national boundaries. Workers employed by these capitals have enjoyed better conditions and prospects in recent years: jobs for those producing commodities in the information sector, or certain service industries, for example, for the world tourist market have increased, while employment in manufacturing industry has dramatically declined. In the context of this unsettling change, many have been susceptible to the ideology that the attendant insecurities are caused by immigration, by migrants, by foreigners. This has occurred over much the same period in France, Germany, Austria,

Spain, the Netherlands and other countries, as in Australia. In such a context, 'ethnic crime' can be identified as a source of fears and insecurities whose causes are more deep-seated and less understood[1].

White Australian xenophobia marked the previous turn-of-century in the wake of the 1890s depression, and the Federation settlement of that time. One cartoon from the late nineteenth-century *Bulletin* depicted a Chinese octopus with its tentacles inscribed with gambling, vice, drugs, disease, corruption (see Figure 3, reproduced in Coleman & Tanner 1978:188). This cartoon is uncannily echoed a century later by a Warren cartoon in the *Daily Telegraph* (28/10/02, see Figure 4), showing an octopus with the head of Osama bin Laden entangling much of the globe in its tentacles. Most of the evils of immigration which troubled the *Bulletin* at the birth of the White Australia policy have concerned the contemporary One Nation Party as the policy was born again. So the fear of 'ethnic crime' is not new, but cyclical moral panics about it can be manifestations of more deep-rooted anxieties arising from real, structural insecurities. Nor is the fear of youth 'gangs' a recent phenomenon: also in the late nineteenth century, there was a moral panic about working-class youths loitering in public spaces, their supposed criminal propensities, and the offence and alarm they caused to passing respectable citizens. These were the original 'larrikins' (Finch 1993; Morgan 1997).

In the context of economic recession and crisis-level youth unemployment of the mid-1980s, the 'Blainey debate' about 'Asian immigration' instigated by right-wing historian Geoffrey Blainey in 1984 and endorsed by then Opposition Leader John Howard in 1988, slated immigration, especially of South-East Asians, for increasing unemployment and potential social unrest. There was much talkback radio chatter and tabloid troubling about 'ethnic ghettoes' like Cabramatta in south-west Sydney being centres of crime as well as strange sounds, smells and shop signs. When in 1994, Cabramatta state MP, John Newman, was shot outside his home, there ensued a media panic about 'Asian gangs' (Walsh 20/9/94:26). This led to a campaign of police harassment of young, South-East Asian background people in the Cabramatta area, where humiliating public strip-searches and other civil rights violations became common (Maher et al. 1997). At the same time, there was a proliferation of seemingly sympathetic media stories about young orphans and refugees from broken homes and a war-torn background being 'lost between two cultures': a liberal gloss on the social marginalisation, largely of racism, which is a strong causal factor in crime.

So the two modes of State dealing with young, working-class, non-English speaking background (NESB) youth — coercion and moral rescue — were already well rehearsed by 1998.

Figure 3: Anti-Chinese cartoon in the *Bulletin* 1886.

Figure 4: 'Warren's View' cartoon, *Daily Telegraph,* 28/10/ 02. Cartoon reproduced courtesy of Warren Brown and the *Daily Telegraph*

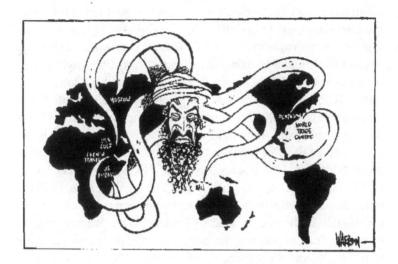

The hard line

From 1994, a whole battery of coercive legislation was passed in NSW to deal with groups of young people in public places. These were conceived as part of a populist strategy of focusing on law and order issues in the state election campaign, resulting in an 'auction' between Labor and the conservative Coalition as to who could be tougher and more punitive. In an ideological manoeuvre which we shall analyse in Chapter Five as 'Dog-whistling', it was never stated explicitly by the bidders in the auction that the targets of the 'get tough' approach were especially Indigenous youth and youth of non-English speaking immigrant background. Yet the message got through to those disaffected voters for whom it was intended. In 1994, the *Children (Parental Responsibility) Act* was passed, though opposed by the NSW Police Association, the Federation of Parents and Citizens Associations, the Bar Association, the Law Society and the Council for Civil Liberties (Legal Information Access Centre 1997). This law was extended under the Carr Government in 1997, with the *Children (Protection and Parental Responsibility) Act* 1997. This allowed police to pick up young people under 16 from public places at any time, night or day, if they are not under the supervision of a responsible adult and the police believe they are 'at risk'. Police may use 'reasonable force' to do so (Irwin 2000). In the same year, the *Crimes Act (Street Safety) Amendment Act* was announced, allowing police to break up groups of three or more in the street if they have 'reasonable grounds to believe the group's behaviour is likely to obstruct, harass or intimidate' (Humphries 29/3/97:1). The legal measure of likely intimidation is if a person of 'reasonable firmness' would feel intimidated in the circumstances (Sanders 2000). We have argued elsewhere that, in practice, the embodiment of this person is likely to be Anglo, and more often elderly (Collins, Noble, Poynting & Tabar 2000). Despite opposition by some Labor members of the Legislative Council (NSW Upper House) and the Council for Civil Liberties, who said that the law would militate against the young, Indigenous people, and immigrants, the *Crimes Legislation Amendment (Police and Public Safety) Act* was passed by the NSW Parliament in 1998. Also in 1998, the *Police Powers (Vehicles) Act*, gave NSW police the power to stop and search vehicles if they believed they may have been used in the commission of a serious offence, and to demand identification of the occupants (Legal Information Access Centre 1997; English 1998). As if these laws weren't enough — and the Illawarra Legal Centre (Harvey 2000:2) has argued that they are more than enough — various local councils in areas of high unemployment, such as Bankstown and Wollongong, have passed anti-loitering laws: without any legal definition of what constitutes loitering.

'The lost boys' and the 'soothing show of force'

In November 1998, the Sydney tabloid newspaper, the *Daily Telegraph* had a coloured, front-page banner advertising its lead story with the label, 'The lost boys: caught between cultures in Lakemba' (*Daily Telegraph* 3/11/98:1). The six Lebanese-Australian young men pictured on page one were not lost; they were on their way home from a south-west Sydney suburban state secondary school, yet they were being mischievously misrepresented by the tabloid as gun-toting gangsters (Collins et al. 2000).

The 'caught between cultures' portrayal was reprised during subsequent cycles of moral panic, most notably in the case of the 'ethnic rape gangs' alluded to in Chapter One and traced in detail in Chapter Four. In some ways, it can be seen as an ethnocentric misreading, or an exploitative and even racist misrepresentation. It is more than that, however, and more shared than that — it is even shared to an extent by the communities of the young men concerned, including sometimes in certain contexts the 'lost boys' themselves.

For their part, the second-generation bicultural young people sometimes see themselves as caught between cultures, while mostly they are moving strategically between elements of each culture, depending on context, and sometimes they recognise themselves as doing this. The 'caught between cultures' positioning can be an assimilationist gloss, or a conservative plea for 'traditional' cultural maintenance, or yet an elitist deprecation of 'hybrid' cultural forms. Each of these informs a range of strategies of social control, of which we canvass examples in this chapter. We also examine the cultural resistances to which these strategies are a response, while at the same time interrogating the extent to which these strategies of social control in turn elicit cultural resistances.

We have earlier mentioned how, in a western Sydney suburban street the media dubbed 'Murder Street' (Lawrence 27/11/00:7), Korean immigrant schoolboy, Edward Lee was mortally stabbed on an October Saturday evening in 1998 after he and his companions, on their way to a local teenage girl's party, became involved in a footpath brawl with a group of youths. The moral panic which ensued is traced in detail in *Kebabs, Kids, Cops and Crime* (Collins et al. 2000). By way of updating the story, we should note here that in 2002, a young man of Lebanese Muslim background on trial for Lee's murder and having pleaded 'not guilty', offered to plead guilty to a charge of manslaughter. In the context of the virulent moral panic raging at this time about lawless Muslim youth, and in the wake of public outcries about charge-bargaining and lenient sentences in the 'ethnic gang rape' cases, the judge, Justice Hulme, (in an unexpected and almost unprecedented response) refused to accept the plea of guilty to manslaughter (Connolly 10/ 10/02:2; McNamara 10/10/02:21). With an appeal pending against this extraordinary refusal, and a retrial due to follow the hearing thus aborted, the Director of Public Prosecutions (DPP) then dropped the charge of murder and proffered one of manslaughter when Moustapha Dib was rearraigned before Justice Barr, who accepted the manslaughter plea (*Daily Telegraph* 10/12/02:9; Glendinning & Connolly 19/12/02:1). This eventual outcome does not allay the reasonable conjecture that the first judgment was called forth by the moral panic which had surrounded the Lee killing and the media's moral outrage which could be anticipated in the case of any sentence that could be portrayed as 'soft'. In the event, when the three accomplices of Moustapha Dib pleaded guilty, as the result of charge bargaining, to being accessories after the fact of malicious wounding, carrying a maximum sentence of 5 years instead of the 25-year maximum for accessories after the fact of murder, the front page of the *Herald* bore the headline, 'Light sentences fall on a boy's lonely grave' (Glendinning & Connolly 19/12/02:1). Moustapha Dib himself was sentenced on 12 February 2003 to a maximum of 10 years' imprisonment, with a minimum of five years to be served, which immediately sparked the Labor Attorney-General (in election mode) to write to the DPP calling for an appeal against this minimum and to reassure the public that manslaughter sentencing provisions were being reviewed by a former Supreme Court Justice, and the Liberal Opposition legal affairs spokesman (in like mode) to call upon the Attorney to appeal against the decision (*News Online* 12/2/03; Connolly 13/2/03:7; Miller 13/2/03:17). The *Telegraph* headline lamented, 'Son's killer may go free in three years' (Miller 13/2/03:17).

Of issue in this chapter are two things. The first is that the media presented the killing at the time as an assassination arising from a 'turf war' between competing criminal 'ethnic' gangs. It is clear now that it was nothing of the sort: rather, a violent schoolboy brawl with tragic consequences — one of a series of such in Sydney, Melbourne, Perth and other Australian cities over 1998–2002.

The second is that, following this portrayal and the moral panic of which it formed a part, the State responded in two opposing and complementary manners: a tough repressive law and order crackdown targeted by ethnic profiling, and an apparently well-intentioned ideological campaign presenting 'at risk' ethnic minority youth as lost sheep, in want of pastoral care to find them and set them on the right path. Yet the right path according to assimiliationists was to abandon the wicked, backward ways of their culture of origin, as we shall see. The right path according to conservative ethnic leaders was to forsake the corrupting influences in western culture and return to traditional values. If the boys of this immigrant generation are 'caught in between' anything, it is between the contradictory demands of these two reactionary politics of culture. As we shall see, these boys are not 'lost'; they do not accept the invidious either/or. Nor is their supposed forlornness in any way an adequate explanation for crudely observable patterns in crime rates.

'Murder Street' is in fact a tree-lined suburban sidestreet, where residents can still live on quarter-acre housing blocks, some twenty minutes by train or car from the city centre of Sydney. A couple of minutes away by family sedan is the local shopping strip where there are signs in Arabic, familiar food in the stores, and familiar faces in the street. It is close to Maronite, Orthodox and Melkite churches and the Lakemba mosque, and is the sort of street where many immigrant families have aspired since the 1970s to make a new life in their new land. It was neither the ghetto nor the 'no-go zone' which the media would represent it as over the subsequent years.

We have shown in *Kebabs Kids, Cops and Crime* how from the beginning, the killing of Edward Lee was causally linked by police and media to ethnicity, the perpetrators were described in racial terms, and a moral panic about 'ethnic' gangs was generated in a feedback loop of police, media and politicians in election campaign mode. The first article to appear in a metropolitan broadsheet presented the attack in the context of clashes involving 'Asian' and 'Middle Eastern' gangs. Middle Eastern appearance is mentioned three times, 'a group of Lebanese men' once more, and 'Asian' gangs are mentioned twice. Television news reports the night after the killing were linking it to a 'gang' and circulating the police description of racial phenotypes alluding to Lebanese immigrants.

The State's 'get-tough' response was to follow swiftly: an intensive police campaign of 'zero tolerance' targeting Lebanese immigrant youth in public spaces of the neighbouring suburbs. While young men of Arabic-speaking background were the focus of the clampdown, older people and teenage girls from their communities were not exempt. The campaign of 'stop and search' and 'move on' was exclusively directed at people of 'Middle Eastern appear-ance' (Ogg & Casey 2/11//98:4–5; Poynting 1999; Collins et al. 2000). 'About 130 police, including mounted and dog squad officers, blitzed the Bankstown area in an aggressive and high-profile push to reclaim the streets', reported the *Telegraph* (Rowlands & Ogg 30/10/98:9). The stated objective of this offensive was 'the lookout for stolen property, outstanding warrants, truancies from schools, anti-social and offensive behaviour' (Rowlands & Ogg 30/10/98:9), which contributed little towards investigating the slaying of Edward

Lee. These resources were not directed at solving the crime, rather at clamping down on whole immigrant communities taken to share responsibility (Poynting 1999). The *Sydney Morning Herald* called this a 'soothing show of force' (Bearup 2/11/98:4): the accompanying photograph of an elderly Anglo woman suggested the sort of people who might be soothed by all this.

The moral panic was given further impetus when, on 1 November, after two weeks of this 'zero tolerance' campaign, gunshots were fired from a passing car into Lakemba police station. No one was injured. There was general agreement that the attack on the police station was in retaliation for the aggressive police operation on the streets (Ogg & Casey 2/11/98:1,4–5). There followed an accelerating round of press briefings from police spokespeople, comment on talkback radio, statements by parliamentarians and other public figures, letters to the editor, press editorials (Collins et al. 2000). These were in general of two types: right-wing demands to 'clean up the streets', and a liberal rhetoric about a younger generation of Lebanese immigrants being 'caught between two cultures'. It is the second frame upon which we focus here.

'A growing divide'

Journalists in the *Australian*, in a relatively sympathetic background piece, expounded:

> Up to 45 per cent of [the local community] are Arabic-speakers, mostly Muslims from Lebanon who came to Australia in the 1970s and *whose children often feel themselves to be outsiders who don't really belong to one culture or the other* — a sense reinforced by the way people react to them. Confronted with the sight of a bunch of them in Nike caps and Fila jackets, many other Australians seem to see an olive-skinned apparition of a bunch of homeboys from South-Central Los Angeles (Wynhausen & Safe 7–8/11/98:13, emphasis added).

Its tabloid stablemate, the *Daily Telegraph*, said much the same thing, that the young people being targeted were 'caught between two cultures', 'caught in the middle, belonging neither to the world of their parents nor the world of their peers' (Stevenson 7/11/98:32). The *Sydney Morning Herald* painted the same picture:

> In all likelihood the gang members ... are Australian. Born and educated here. The sons of hardworking Lebanese immigrants who fled the civil war in 1975. Like the Vietnamese kids of Cabramatta, they are caught between their parents' culture and their new culture, not really fitting into either. The gang becomes their culture (Bearup 7/11/98:43).

The television news of the Australian Broadcasting Corporation (ABC) reported:

> The weekend attack has shocked local Lebanese as much as anyone else. Some say they've lost control of their young people and they're causing a growing divide within their local community (2/11/98).

The main informants for these media representations seem to be ethnic community workers and ethnic community leaders, rather than the young people of Lebanese background themselves.

The account of 'loss' is more typically articulated by the first — their parents' — generation of immigrants:

> The biggest problem would be a generation gap, there is a big backlash because of the generation gap and secondly you've got two cultures: like the parents have a culture and the kids have a part of their parents' culture and also taking on the Australian. So we've got new cultures coming up. And the kids are lost, and the problem is an identity crisis. They don't know who they are, are they Lebanese, are they Australian, are they Arabs are they Turkish, are they Asians? (community worker, male, 33 years, himself a parent of three).

Rob White (1990:165–188) has pointed out how the youth worker performs a function of social control for the State. There is an ideology of dysfunction, which legitimates state surveillance and intervention. The corrective intervention can be one of enlightenment or forceful containment. Here, the youth worker's argument implies the need to educate parents (in the ways of 'whiteness' — the dominant culture), or else the children 'end up on the streets', necessitating repression:

> There is a big communication breakdown within the home itself. The father doesn't see his son much because he is always busy and the father doesn't understand his son's culture. He wants him brought up the way he was brought up by his uncles, so there are always cultural differences at home and a com-munication breakdown. They don't talk to each other much, not like the way they should be talking to each other. If my own son has a problem, by right he should approach me and I should be there to support him and help him out. Otherwise he will be looking for somebody else to be comfortable with and this is why they all end up on the streets (community worker, female, 36 years, herself a parent of four).

Spokesperson for the Lebanese Muslim Association, Richard Mitre, when interviewed by conservative media personality Alan Jones (10/11/98), said that Lebanese parents worry about their children losing the best of their tradition. Jones retorted that parents feel that they are not allowed to discipline their children as they see fit. Alan Jones was here echoing pronouncements by the Mufti of Australia, Taj Al Hilaly, who had been quoted in the *Australian* saying that 'The law doesn't give the power for families to control their kids' (Humphries 4/11/98:5), and Sheikh Chami, of the Lebanese Welfare Centre in Lakemba who had complained to the same newspaper that 'the Government doesn't allow parents to discipline' (Jackson 3/11/98:5).

When young people were actually interviewed, they tended to be misheard: the group of young men interviewed by the *Telegraph* spoke of their solidarity against racism and their demands for mutual respect; the reporters heard and recounted an argument about a 'gang' united by 'Lebanese blood' (Casey & Ogg 3/11/98:4). There were commendable exceptions, of course, such as the documentary on Radio National over a year later by Nadya Stani (2001), who interviewed some of the very same youths:

> *First young man's voice*: Walter here. Walter's never hurt an ant in his life; he never hurt anyone in his life but there he's referred as a big gang member.

> *Second young man's voice*: Because my parents have come from overseas, my parents might be Lebanese and that, but I've lost a lot of my heritage, my parents haven't passed it down to me so therefore I've picked up the Australian heritage so therefore — but inside, I might not look it, but I am Australian ...

If we take the trouble to listen to the young man, he is not saying that he *is* 'lost', though others may say it of him. He has inherited *some* Lebanese culture, 'lost' some, and 'picked up *the* Australian heritage' (emphasis added). He asserts that he is Australian, while conceding that his physical appearance may lead some to think otherwise. He indicates awareness of the calls in his ethnic community for cultural maintenance, and some sense that he *has* 'lost a lot of ... heritage'. There is also a notion that there is something already defined as *the* Australian heritage, which he feels that he has 'picked up'. He is constructing his identity then, within the contradictory demands for cultural maintenance and for assimilation to 'the' dominant culture. There is no lack of confidence in his partaking in the 'Australian heritage', only an implied resentment that others may call this into question because of how he looks.

This is not an idiosyncratic individual case, but an example of a strong pattern which we have encountered again and again among this generation in a series of research projects in Western Sydney since 1996 (Poynting, Noble & Tabar 1999; Noble, Poynting & Tabar 1999; Collins, Noble, Poynting & Tabar 2000).

A very similar formulation was articulated by Paul, a seventeen-year-old student interviewed in a western Sydney high school in 1996:

SP: How do you identify yourself in terms of ethnicity?

Paul: I see myself as an Australian from a Lebanese background.

SP: What does that mean to you?

Paul: Well, I respect my parents what they are and they respect me for what I am. And I like being Australian because I was born in Australia, this is my country and I also respect my parents for Lebanon as their country. Them being Australian citizens has never really been a problem.

Paul considers himself to be Australian, which he is by birth and citizenship. His parents, who migrated to Australia some twenty years ago, are Australian citizens, and Lebanon is seen by him (and probably by them) as 'their country'. His father speaks English and his mother can understand English but not speak it. Paul speaks Arabic with his parents and English with his five brothers and two sisters, mixing the two languages sometimes with his siblings and never with his parents, he says. Paul is confident in his bilingualism and what could be called biculturalism. He speaks highly of the multiculturalism now well established in his school, and speaks critically about racism where he finds it in his neighbourhood and his milieu. Paul is constructing his identity, then, in similar circumstances to the young man interviewed by Nadya Stani. He moves fluidly and competently between two cultures depending on context, but this does not mean that the two are neatly bounded or that he is caught between them. His manoeuvres may be impeded by racism or directed by pressures for cultural maintenance.

Paul's father works long hours as a taxi driver; his mother is occupied full-time in domestic work for their family of ten. His sisters are still very young, four of his elder brothers are working in professions and studying. Paul studies hard, and goes regularly to the gym, but he contributes of necessity and quite willingly to the housework; he undertakes a variety of household tasks voluntarily and routinely 'to keep a lot of stress off my mum'. He is mindful of neighbours' surprise that he, a young man, does housework, and he recognises but does not criticise his father's declining to do so.

He has little time for those girls of his age who hold stereotypes about Middle Eastern men. Paul is participating in the active construction of new forms of masculinity, at the same time as he is part of the collective construction of new combinations of ethnicity. Both these 'intersecting' sets of social relations are powerfully inflected by the class relations in which Paul must make his life history. This is shown clearly in his desire to marry a 'hard working woman' and not a 'racist snob'.

Paul and his contemporaries are active: they are not 'caught'. They are navigating with pretty serviceable maps of their social surroundings: they are not lost.

Elsewhere we have written of a different type of ethnic masculinity, a 'protest' form which is constructed in opposition to the racism which young second-generation immigrants find directed at their cohort, their fathers, their 'brothers' (Poynting, Noble & Tabar 1999). This involves asserting what for them constitutes their Lebaneseness in Australia, and doing so with a good deal of male aggression, often directed at authority figures from the 'mainstream' culture which are implicated in institutional racism (Poynting et al. 1999; Collins et al. 2000). What the protest masculinity and Paul's new form of masculinity have in common is that they are being constituted by the young men's experiences of being, and ways of being, men of a minority ethnicity in a racist society. Their disposition towards their parents' ways of being Lebanese, and the elements of these which they adopt, exaggerate, transform, downplay, negate or reject, depends largely on the social context in which they find themselves and how they move to assert their interests and their dignity.

We have elsewhere called these cultural manoeuvres 'strategic hybridity' (Noble et al. 1999). This is almost the opposite of being trapped between cultures; it involves appropriating elements of parents' homeland culture and the 'dominant culture' in creative and quite fluid ways, shifting according to circumstances. What the various hybrid forms share is that they are misread and deprecated both by the traditionalists of their parents' generation and those of the dominant culture who feel threatened when (only) elements of it are appropriated by 'others', who stubbornly remain *other* by refusing to assimilate unconditionally, and who feel just as threatened when other elements of it are rejected, undermining the singularity and exclusivity of what they see as 'their' Australian cultural heritage: 'one nation'.

The young Lebanese Australians are operating — we will not say 'caught' — within a double contradiction. Their parents want them to succeed in the new country. The younger generation knows that this necessarily entails a degree of strategic adoption of dominant cultural forms: what Ghassan Hage (1998) calls 'accumulating whiteness'.[2] To the extent that they do this, however, they experience a sense of reproof for abandonment, neglect, disregard, or even perhaps betrayal, of their parents' culture and their own origins.[3] On the other hand, to the extent that they become fluent in the dominant cultural idiom, they are never judged to do so enough to attain the equality that they seek. They always do so imperfectly from the point of view of the cultural arbiters; they always have a cultural 'accent', as it were, which serves as a marker and a pretext for discrimination.

So, while the myth of being caught between cultures does not accurately represent how second-generation Lebanese Australian youth live their lives, it does contain elements of how they are at times made to *feel*. Like all ideology, it reflects aspects of reality which are presented in distorted form as appearances.[4] We are not suggesting that this myth is simply propagated by liberal journalists and community workers and conservative ethnic community leaders. Rather, it comes to frame the wider perceptions and public debates. As Angela McRobbie suggests (1994:214), folk devils are often defended by welfare and other progressive interest groups in order to contest stereotypes, yet in so doing they frequently take for granted, and thus help reproduce, the very frames that are problematic. Thus the myth of two separate cultures, with conflicting values and demands, producing directionless youth lost between them, accepts the premise of 'culture clash' and leads to the conclusion that one or the other culture is the source of the problem. We take up this argument in Chapter Six in relation to the politics of ethnic communities and ethnic leadership. We would also note here, in passing, that it is in many ways the local-scale analogue of the 'clash of civilisations' thesis criticised in Chapter One. Ideologues can take either side, can champion the one civilisation or the other as more 'civilised', humane, moral, and so on, while assuming that the clash is inevitable and that one or the other of existing contenders must be championed. Fortunately, the world of the young people whom we interviewed is not at all like a 'clash of civilisations' writ small. So, we will suggest, perhaps it is through such creativity as can be found in their lively, nuanced, struggle-produced culture-in-the-making, that history might be made for the better.

'I am divided up into two'

George was born in Australia. Both his parents were born in Lebanon and migrated to Australia some 'fifteen or twenty' years ago, according to George. He was 15 years old and in Year 10 at a local Catholic high school in south-west Sydney when he was interviewed.[5] His father is a labourer and his mother a housewife. George says he talks to his parents in 'Lebanese', and to his brothers in 'either Lebanese or English'. 'My dad doesn't speak that much English; it's not good.' His mother understands English better — she had somewhat more formal education in Lebanon — but he speaks Arabic with both his parents, 'so they can understand better'. There are exceptions. Almost all of our second generation interviewees told us that they spoke English to their parents when angry and that their parents spoke Arabic when angry. George said, 'If I am angry I would be either shouting or speaking English; the next sentence I would change to Lebanese. I'm a bit of a mix there'.

George defines his identity as 'Australian-Lebanese':

> It means like inside I'm Lebanese, but I'm Australian-Lebanese because I'm living in Australia as a country. So that's what I have to follow, but it would be a different story if I was Lebanese-Lebanese. If I was born in Lebanon, that's what I'd describe myself as.

We were interested to know what the *content* behind these identity labels was for the young people we interviewed. What do they mean in practice?

> *PT*: Can you tell me more about the Australian part of your identity? I mean what things do you feel that you do because you are Australian-Lebanese?
>
> *George*: Well firstly Australian-Lebanese. Australians over here, if they feel like it they go for a drive, they just like to show off. For example you can go down to a beach here, and just keep showing off in your car. In Lebanon I don't know whether it's really done or done at all. That's what I follow, and me and my friends follow. We go out and hang out and do that. I'm not sure whether it's done in Lebanon, but that's what we follow, because everyone else does it in Australia.

Asked about the Lebanese component of his identity, George then starts talking about being divided. Curiously, moreover, he reinvents the meaning of place of birth in order to assert his Lebanese 'half':

> *George*: I am divided up into, one side of me is Lebanese, and one side of me is Australian, because I was born in Lebanon, but I am living in Australia. So I want to do a bit of both.
>
> *PT*: You weren't born in Lebanon, you were born here, you said.
>
> *George*: I was born in Lebanon — I've got Lebanese parents, plus Lebanese background. I still follow Australian, because I am living in Australia. So you can say I am divided up into two. Half Lebanese and half Australian.

We asked all our young interviewees if they thought their parents had the same idea as they did about what it means to be Lebanese-Australian (or whatever identity combination they volunteered):

George: Because they were born in Lebanon, and you can say they brought the tradition of the Lebanese from Lebanon, and they still continue it here. They've got a bit of Lebanese-Australian, but there's mostly Lebanese-Lebanese. And they follow and have never changed tradition.

George is not lacking in confidence, in either his identity or his demeanour. He repeats: 'I am proud of being Lebanese. I am not showing and telling people I'm Lebanese. I'm proud of it. Like I'm proud of being Lebanese. It doesn't bother me in any way'.

What does bother George is racist portrayals of Lebanese in the media; he feels personally 'put down' by this. He refers to an event in 1993, when there was a fracas labelled as a 'riot' between police and participants — especially young men — at an Arabic Day carnival in an inner-western Sydney park. According to the subsequent Ethnic Affairs Commission inquiry (Ethnic Affairs Commission of NSW 1994), male police had allegedly manhandled some Lebanese Muslim women, in attempting to intervene in an altercation between them, and there arose scuffles with male youths which escalated into a large-scale confrontation with the calling of many police vehicles with reinforcements and equipment, followed by the inevitable arrival of the media. The inquiry identified what amounted to institutional racism, and recommended many improvements to police training in cultural diversity and ethnic relations, and further suggested that the media should show more responsibility in such matters.

George says:

Sometimes when you hear on the news, bad things that Lebanese people have done. Like I'm put down — like this person is like me ... I remember I think it was about two years ago. Every year they have a Lebanese carnival, and it was in Tempe. There was a big fight there with police, and on the news all you heard was Lebanese doing this, doing that. It puts me down, because that's when Lebanese get the bad name ...

Differently from his parents' generation, George's sense of his Lebaneseness, that part of his identity, is constructed from the beginning in the environment of 'white Australian' ethnocentrism. But being 'put down' is not the same as being 'lost'.

Ali, at twenty-two years old, gives an articulate account of the same process. He is Sunni Muslim, born in Australia of Lebanese-born parents. He is bilingual, speaking 'mostly Arabic' at home. He counts himself as 'an Australian with Lebanese background', though in common with most of our interviewees, when he uses the word 'Australians' without a qualifier he usually means Australians of Anglo background:

> They [the media] describe us as troublemakers, as coming from a country where there was war and in their minds ... it automatically means that they are troublemakers. It's not like that; most of us, the youth, have been born here. We are raised just as the Australians are, we are taught exactly what they are, we are like identical to one another except we have a different colour in our skin. We speak the same language but we know a different language. Some Lebanese boys don't know Arabic; they just speak English[6].

Ali's response to the 'put-down' is to reverse its meaning for him, by taking on the label and acting the part:

> I have come to realise I am an Australian but I am not treated like an Australian. I do not act like an Australian. I am more Lebanese. I am treated like a Lebanese, so I will stick to what I am treated like (Collins et al. 2000:165).

John, a sixteen year old Maronite Christian attending the same Catholic school as George, says that his parents' culture and his are 'two different worlds'. John was born in Australia; both his parents in Lebanon. At home he speaks 'Half-half: English and Lebanese', though with his parents he talks 'mostly Lebanese', but when he misses a word, or when he gets angry, he switches to English. He speaks English with his sisters and brothers. His parents will change to English if he doesn't understand something they say in Arabic. 'When they are angry, they say it in Lebanese'. This is quite typical of our second-generation interviewees.

John describes his identity thus: 'Like first I speak Lebanese. I am Lebanese. I am half Australian as well, because I was born in Australia. And I do live in Australia. So I'm half Australian as well'. Unlike Ali, John takes for granted some of the portrayals shown in the media, of Lebanese as troublemakers. He says he doesn't really like the neighbourhood where he lives in south-western Sydney, because 'there is a lot of Lebs. Don't get me wrong. I like socialising with a lot of Lebs, but I like socialising with other cultures. And there is a lot of trouble in this area'. He 'accumulates whiteness' (Hage 1998) by deploying his Christian identity to distinguish himself from the troublemakers:

PT: How do you feel about Muslim Lebanese?

John: Oh sometimes they are all right. Most of them are troublemakers you know. I've had a lot of bad experiences with Muslims.

PT: Like what?

John: They'll argue.

PT: Over what do you argue?

John:They just want to pick a fight. They pick some thing out of their head like 'what are you looking at me for?' They just want to pick a fight. I hate it. I don't like it when they do that. I just keep walking. Stuff them!

PT: Do you think they do it because of religion?

John: Sometimes they pick a fight, but most of the time it could be of religion.

PT: How could they tell that you are a Christian?

John: I don't know. I have no idea. I know some Muslim guys, and they're good. Good friends.

John is describing what we have identified as an ethnic form of protest masculinity constituted in opposition to racism. His antagonists are unable to accumulate as much 'whiteness' — national cultural capital — as he; they are not Christian. These moves in the formation of John's identity were taking place at a time in Australia where the racist right was beginning to reassert the cultural politics of 'white Australia' which had been virtually eradicated from the Australian political landscape for almost thirty years. As will be analysed in Chapter Five, the right-wing, assimiliationist, anti-immigration, anti-multiculturalist One Nation party and its supporters oppose immigration from 'non-Christian lands', and express their offence at immigrants who keep their distance, retain their cultural differences and form 'ethnic' enclaves. John's statement, 'I like socialising with a lot of Lebs, but I like socialising with other cultures', was made in that context. It is a manoeuvre which highlights his own 'whiteness' in contradistinction to others such as Lebanese Muslims who are thus positioned as more 'different', less civilised and inassimilable: a process which we have examined in Chapter One. One Nation and their supporters claim that immigration produces increases in crime, that many immigrants are lawless, and that alien lawbreakers should be deported. John's distancing himself from the Lebanese Muslim 'troublemakers' should also be seen in that light.

Asked whether his parents have a similar view to his about what it means to be a Lebanese Australian, John replies:

> Oh, a very different view! 'Cause they were born in Lebanon, and they came over in their Lebanon tradition, and they did everything Lebanese do. I came after, and I saw the Australian world. So it's two different worlds.

John is familiar with 'two different worlds'; he is not lost. But the cultural-political landscape in which he has to find his way conditions the way he forms his identity.

Mohammed is the sixteen-year-old son of Lebanese-born parents, who own and work in a small family business. They came to Australia about twenty years ago, and Mohammed was born in Australia. He attends the local coeducational state secondary school. He says that he speaks 'Lebanese' with his parents, and English with his two brothers and three sisters. He says that is it very important to his father that he speak Arabic, though his father will sometimes speak to him in English when he is working on something. His father will always speak in Arabic when he is angry and when he is talking about behaviour.

Mohammed defines his identity primarily by his religion: 'I am Muslim, but [an] Australian citizen'. Note the 'but': Mohammed is aware of an opposition. It reappears when he is asked to expand on what he means:

> My religion is Muslim, but my citizen[ship] is Australian. I'm half Australian and half Muslim. I believe in my religion but I am Australian. I've been born here, and I wouldn't say I was pure Lebanese.

He has experienced stereotypes about Lebanese from teachers (they're dumb) and from girls his age (they're dishonest). He finds that teachers treat 'wogs' — he includes Greeks and Italians with the Lebanese here — with lower expectations and give them less time. He responds with lack of respect. He finds a commonality with the Greek and the Italian girls: 'You can relate to them, you can talk to them … Because they have the same traditions. Their parents are strict. Their brothers like to face things'.

None of this alters the fact that he sees himself as Australian. He contrasts himself here with his parents:

> If I ask my mum and dad which country you would like to live in, they would say Lebanon. I would say Australian. They would say Lebanon is your homeland. I was born here; I am an Australian citizen. Only my religion is Muslim. Everything else apart from that is Australian.

Ghassan is a sixteen year old Australian-born student in a Catholic school in south-west Sydney. His father is self-employed in a small business; his mother is a full-time housewife. Ghassan cannot remember when they migrated to Australia from Lebanon. The family speaks mostly English at home. Ghassan says:

> I mostly speak in English with my little brother or my mum, but sometimes my dad will speak with me in Arabic. So I just reply in Arabic … Sometimes I can't express what I'm saying in Arabic, so I put it in English.

His father, for his part, can speak English but there are some things he can only say in Arabic.

But there are other reasons for his father sometimes speaking to his son in his mother tongue: 'Sometimes ... he'll say to me, "Speak Arabic". So if he just wants to keep the language together — so I won't forget. Or just to keep the language and culture alive'. And then there's the issue of respect:

> I sometimes switch because, like some people, like my grand-parents, some people who don't understand English very well. I speak with them Lebanese, just through respect. So they know what we are saying.

Like a lot of other teenagers, Ghassan has arguments with his parents over issues such as going out and the amount of study he ought to be doing:

> My mum wouldn't let me out without someone like my cousins or her like after six, because that's when it gets dark. She's got a phobia of the dark I think. Yeah, she wouldn't let me go to nightclubs — too young ... Some of my friends would go out with girls at this age. Like the girls would actually come to their house and say, 'Let's go', or whatever. But my parents, or my mother or father or whatever, wouldn't like that. They would tell me to concentrate on my studies.

As with many second-generation immigrant families, however, these disagreements appear to both sides as clashes of Australian and Lebanese ways:

> *PT*: Do you think about this matter, your parents are —
>
> *Ghassan* [interrupts]: Lebanese. Yes, they would say to me, 'When we were small, we didn't do that'. I have sort of adapted to the Australian way; I would say, 'That's nothing.' Some people, ice-skating sometimes, under 18s nights for people to go to nightclubs sometimes on Fridays. See my mum thinks it's all 18s and over like. So you still have to study. Like it was in Lebanon, everyone used to study. Well everyone here goes out.

Ghassan sums up this way the values and traditions his parents pass on to him:

> Like treat others how you want to be treated ... First study and get your future like set, then you can sort of have a good time.

> You should get married first before any sexual relationships.
> Marry a Lebanese girl, because it is easier for any marriage.
> Traditions basically. They taught me stuff like Lebanese
> traditions. Dancing and stuff.

Likewise, George saw having to obey his parents over the issue of girlfriends as a key part of his identity. Asked about the things which comprise the Lebanese component of his Australian-Lebanese identity, George offered, 'Like I said, if I want to do something that I like, and I speak to my parents about it, they might not agree. They might not think it's appropriate'. Asked for an example, he responded:

> I will never have a relationship. This was, I think, two years
> ago. I will never have a relationship with a girl. My parents
> didn't approve of her, because they thought I was too young,
> and they said when I get older, when I get in my teenage years,
> late teenage years. I should start dating then, but you see that
> was something that I would never do. I chose; my parents
> wouldn't approve.

Ghassan, while he disagrees with his parents about the issue of girlfriends, agrees that there are limits: 'As long as it's nothing too serious'. Sexual intercourse before marriage doesn't come into the question: 'I'm a Catholic person. So that's beyond — [stops in mid-sentence]'.

This pattern was repeated among the second-generation Lebanese teenage boys we interviewed almost as much as the girls[7]. They saw it as constitutive of their identity. And the pattern persisted across religious creeds. A seventeen year old male Ala'wite Muslim assessed the market with some signs of experience:

> If there is a pretty white girl Australian, she would have to pick
> from Lebanese or Australian. A guy, no matter how good-
> looking a Lebanese guy is, she would go for an Australian ...
> Because we're discriminated, that's why.

His response is to say that he respects Lebanese girls more than 'Australian' girls. He says that he finds Anglo girls:

> very easy, you know what I mean? ... Like you can do anything
> with them. I like to have something inside that I hold back like.

You know what I mean? I can't do it, because religion into it. Some people don't have their morals. They just do it. With me I can't. I have morals.

He said that he would 'flirt around', but 'when it comes to doing the sin, that's when I stop'. He mused:

A friend said that to me the other day, he said, 'I think I know why girls go out with Lebanese guys'. I said, 'Why is that?' He goes, 'because youse don't lose your virginity; it's a sin for youse, but for us we do it anyway'.

Another seventeen year old interviewee, whose mother is Lebanese and father Syrian, describes himself thus:

You can say I am Australian. I was born here, so I'm partly Australian, and my background is Lebanese. But I don't really say that. I mostly say that I'm Muslim, 'cause that's the main thing.

He says he has had girlfriends from Lebanese, Greek, Italian and Australian backgrounds. He says that he wouldn't stay more than two weeks with a Lebanese girl, because they tend to get too serious. 'I just stop it'. With Italian and Greek girls, 'Some of them have to be home early. It's all family things'. He says many 'Australian' girls are prejudiced about Lebanese boys and he doesn't have much in common with them and doesn't like going out with them; he has more in common with Lebanese, Italian and Greek girls. When it comes to the question of sexual relations, he says he would not have a 'full relationship' before marriage. 'It's me. It's my religion. I wouldn't go all the way with a girl'.

'Olive-skinned homeboys'?

Another timeworn point of conflict of the teenagers with parents, about which there is nothing peculiar to immigrants or Lebanese — is the matter of clothes and dress codes. Ghassan, for example, spoke of one such disagreement with his parents:

I had a bit of a hard time last year or the year before that. When I was sort of getting to teenage years, when you start to wear fashionable clothes and that. And they were telling me that's

not right, or it doesn't look good. I would say that this is what
everyone else is wearing. To wear baggy jeans, like it took me
a month to convince my dad, because he was saying it's for the
gangsters.

For Ghassan and his friendship group, the dress code was part of
belonging. It was fashion. To his father it was a fashion redolent of
North American gangs, and to be avoided. To the *Daily Telegraph*,
and to many older Anglo people in the south-western Sydney
suburbs, according to our police service and community worker
interviewees, it marked the wearers as a Lebanese gang.
'Punchbowl Homeboys ... ape the black homeboy gangs in the
United States — they wear the same baggy jeans, sportswear such
as Fila and adidas, and listen to rap music' (Casey & Ogg 3/11/98).
An Arabic-speaking background female Police and Community
Training Officer interviewed in 1999 described the dress code:
adidas, track suits with stripes, a beanie or a cap. '... when you get
the average Arabic group who stand on the corner wearing the
adidas and not doing much, they look threatening', she explained.
Yet she conceded, 'Most of our teenagers who hang out on the
street wear that kind of stuff' (Collins et al. 2000:173).

There is nothing particularly new in a youth dress code being
taken as a sign of deviance. What is interesting here is the way
that it is ethnicised. The young people themselves use the dress
code to identify as members of a subculture adopted by their peer
group, not to signal their membership of a criminal gang. Those
who rely on illicit business for a livelihood rarely seek to identify
themselves so visibly, and when interviewed those who 'used to'
do so will disparage those who so draw attention to themselves as
'wannabes' or 'tryhards'. It is significant, moreover, that the
'uniform' of the subculture has the cachet of the cultural metropolis,
the United States, while being identified with minority and
marginalised groups (Afro-Americans, Latinos) with whom
Lebanese-Australian youth can feel some commonality. (This
'appropriation' from subcultures of the Other in another national
culture means that there are already more than two cultures at
stake. The notion of fixed cultural borders, between which one can

be trapped or lost, is just not applicable here.) In any case, Anglo-Australian youth tend not to adopt this style; not being marginalised, they have no need to reappropriate the symbols of the cultural resistance of the marginalised.

Towards the beginning of this chapter, we quoted the *Australian* as reporting, 'Confronted with the sight of a bunch of them in Nike caps and Fila jackets, many other Australians seem to see an olive-skinned apparition of a bunch of homeboys from South-Central Los Angeles' (Wynhausen & Safe 7–8/11/98:13). We did not there emphasise that this was a statement about how *many other Australians see* the Lebanese-Australian young men on the streets. The journalists, of course, mean *Anglo* Australians. Yet parents of the young men sometimes also have reservations about their dress code, which they share with the respectable Anglos fearful of 'gangs' and with police responding to these.

An Anglo male police officer in his late twenties, said to one of the authors in an interview:

> The major problem is, I think, they are too heavily influenced
> by the American rap culture. They are still running around
> thinking that they are MC Hammer, they are living in East LA
> (Andy 18/7/99 cited in Collins et al. 2000:178).

To risk labouring the point: the young men know exactly where they are running around. If United States rap music speaks to their experiences, then perhaps we should look for the commonalities which it expresses. 'Racial profiling' by police is just one experience which Lebanese-Australian youth share with Black United States youth (Poynting 2001). Institutional racism in schools is one more (Poynting, Noble & Tabar 1999). Labour market segmentation is another such commonality (Collins et al. 2000). As is lack of resources and adequate public space in neighbourhoods. The phenomenon of 'Lebbo rap', a hybrid music form emerging among this second generation in Australia, shows the creativity of their youth culture and the permeability of its ethnic boundaries. Such hybridised cultural forms are expressed by the Lebanese Australian singer of the 'young multicultural rap band, South West Syndicate', whose song 'Equal', says:

> I've got a new story but it ain't no throwback
> I ain't got not time for no racism bro
> I'm too busy I got people to see and places to go (excerpted in Stani 2000).

Caught between two policies

What are the consequences of seeing young Lebanese-background men's being caught between cultures as the cause of social problems? The first consequence, to blame and to punish these young men and their communities for the problems, has been discussed at length elsewhere (Collins et al. 2000). A further consequence is that 'solutions' are logically presented in terms of the purported cultural divide which is supposed to be experienced by these youth.

One imagined solution is a return to the mythically untroubled past, 'before the war' when young working-class men did not intimidate and offend respectable citizens on the street with bad language, outlandish clothes, idleness, and a threatening demeanour. No such past, of course, existed (Pearson 1983). For those sectors of — especially older — working-class or petit-bourgeois Anglos who are themselves experiencing feelings of displacement or disorientation, and very real economic disadvantage, through the effects of globalisation, a convenient apparent cause is presented by the new racist politics of One Nation and the like: it is non-Anglo, non-white and non-Christian immigration. They look back fondly to the time when suburbia was marked by neat white picket fences and all the shop signs were in English and they were not threatened by the ebullience of young people because they were young themselves. They demand that immigrants assimilate to what, for them, used to be Australian culture, or they want some sort of white Australia policy restricting immigration to the right kinds or the right numbers. In this way, we would have no cultural divisions, because there would be one culture, one nation. According to this account, multiculturalism has been the cause of untold social divisions, inequities and tensions. This past is mythical, the culprits are imagined and the solution is a fantasy. We shall return to this fantasy, in relation to fear, in the final chapters of the book.

Nevertheless, it is a fantasy that has appeal and effects. Populist politicians like Premier Carr, with an eye to this appeal (as will be shown in Chapter Five), will make damaging public pronouncements about getting tough on 'ethnic gangs' (Poynting 2002), and will purge 'ethnic affairs' from the state's policy vocabulary.

Another equally imaginary and reactionary solution is propounded by conservative spokespeople who present themselves as the representatives of whole ethnic communities. For example, the Mufti of Australia, Taj Al Hilaly, responded to the racism of the media outcry about 'ethnic youth' being 'out of control' by blaming the laxity of western culture and western laws, as will be detailed in Chapter Six. Often in the absence of any evidence as yet presented by police and tested in court, he seemed to be accepting the police, media and politicians' assertions that the perpetrators of the high-profile crimes of 1998, the Lee killing and the Lakemba shooting — and the pack rapes two years later — were Lebanese-Australian youth. He simply downplayed their Lebanese identity (or rather Arabic and Muslim identity, which had become blurred together in the mainstream media discourse), because it was not properly, traditionally, Lebanese (read Arabic and Islamic). The young people being talked about were really Australians, he said in several instances, as they were born and educated in this country. He complained about restrictions by the State on parents' disciplining of their children, and urged legislators to 'go back 25 years' and to introduce curfews for young people to keep them off the street. Similar rhetoric issued from spokespeople from Lebanese Christian communities.

The Mufti was right that the young people being targeted on the streets were Australian — by birth, by citizenship, and by important elements of their identity. Yet to ascribe their purported criminality to some essential Australianness or Westernness which they have adopted is just as irrational as to blame it on an essentialised Lebaneseness which they have inherited. It leads to policy prescriptions which are just as ineffectual. Going 'back 25 years' or imposing curfews is hardly likely to appeal to the young people or to work for their parents. Moreover, our interviews with the young second-generation Lebanese Australians indicate that what they see as being Lebanese is indeed important to their identity, and comes into relations with police, teachers, journalists and other bearers of institutional racism. As we have shown in our interviews, it might not be the same as their parents' or their religious leaders' ideas of Lebaneseness, but the young people are not about to adopt the latter as a neatly wrapped package, whatever the level of complaint or moral pressure.

In contrast to these reactionary approaches, liberal pluralist discourses favour 'Harmony Days' and talk of 'building bridges' between cultures. Yet they tend to accept the same assumption that there is a rift between cultures; they differ in believing that it is bridgeable in and their well-meaning objective of bridging 'it'. Yet they too often ignore the reality of the young people from various ethnic backgrounds that are building myriad cultural connections in their everyday lives. They are unconsciously ethnocentric in deprecating hybridity or blendedness of cultures, seeing it as mere imitation of something(s) which properly belong to distinct cultures. They underestimate its creativity and its potential for struggle and change. We have attempted to convey some of these intercultural connections, the permeability of cultural boundaries, and the creativeness in constantly shifting them, in the lived experience of the second-generation youth whom we interviewed. Liberal pluralist discourses also pronounce all cultures equal and then assume that they are. They thus ignore the reality of the racism that looms so large in the lives of the young men we interviewed. In policy terms, they are useless in confronting or overcoming racism.

These prescriptions are futile because the premise of two neatly bounded cultures with second-generation immigrant youth trapped in between does not accurately represent the lived reality of the young people. Ethnocentrism in education and criminal justice systems is part of the problem. These young people need educators who do not assume that they are academically uninclined and interested only in pursuits such as muscle-building or fashion. They also need schools which recognise the language development needs of bilingual immigrants with parents who are often illiterate in their first language and have little formal education. The second generation shift, as they need, between languages, tending to hide this need, and leaving the appearance to their teachers of being 'unacademic' and to their parents of being well developed users of school English and thoroughly 'Australian'. They are not trapped between languages, rather their facility with both hides their educational needs.

Furthermore, the 'two cultures' discourse lends itself to 'welfarist' policy strategies in response to problems which are perceived to be inherent in culture. The culture of the disadvantaged is thus found to be wanting and in need of remediation, obscuring the real, fundamental causes of strife in the discriminatory processes of structural racism and class exploitation. The welfarist, soft approach is 'armoured', in Gramsci's language (1971:263), by the coercive moment of hegemony. In the policing of second-generation immigrant youth — especially young men — it needs to be recognised that the culture of resistance in the masculinities of the marginalised is only exacerbated by 'zero tolerance' over-policing. Teenage friendship groups of immigrants are not 'gangs' just because they are immigrants, and their youth subcultures are not a sign of being 'lost between cultures' — they would not be labelled as such in the case of young people from the cultural backgrounds of the dominant.

It is necessary to deal with the realities of class inequality, including unequal means and power in the production and valorisation of hybridity. It is vital, then, that social researchers, social policy-makers, community representatives, journalist representors of society to itself, political 'representatives' and others come to see that second-generation Lebanese immigrant young people are not 'lost'. They are making their lives, constructing their identities and finding their way in what is currently an abidingly unequal society. This recognition is an important step in the cultural struggle to overcome the structural inequalities of race and class.

In the following chapter, we detail and analyse a moral panic which arose in 2001–2, after a series of group sexual assaults in Sydney, for which a number of working-class young men of Lebanese Muslim background were eventually convicted. Most were second generation immigrants. The crimes were highly racialised in media and political commentary, presented as 'ethnic' gang rape. We shall see here how relations of class and gender (masculinity) inflected by racism are given the appearance of race, ethnicity or religion, to which causality of the crimes is ideologically ascribed.

Notes

1 For a very good analysis in the case of Germany, see Eckert, 2002.

2 The term 'whiteness' here is used by Hage as a metaphor for a form of *national* cultural capital, tied to belongingness and ownership of nation.

3 This is somewhat analogous to the process of abandonment of one's *class* culture in order to appropriate a new class culture on the path to upward mobility, which has been well documented, especially in the sociology of education.

4 Ghassan Hage (2002) has some interesting comments to make about the pertinence of the *camera obscura* metaphor and the classical Marxist theory of ideology in the current conjuncture.

5 The interviews with George, John, Mohammed and Ghassan (pseudonyms) were conducted in 1996 by Paul Tabar, as part of a joint project between him, Greg Noble and Scott Poynting.

6   This interview was conducted by Michael Kennedy in 1999, as part of a collaboration with the authors. These tracts of the interview with 'Ali' have been published in Collins et al. (2000:150–165).

7   This chapter focuses on the interviews with the boys. For the material on the young women, see Poynting, Noble and Tabar (2001).

4

'You deserve it because you are Australian': the moral panic over 'ethnic gang rape'

Around August 2001 and again in August 2002, there were some 20 lurid front-page headlines in the Sydney daily and weekend tabloid newspapers coinciding with the trials and re-trials of a group of young Lebanese-Australian men for several particularly degrading and callous group sexual assaults in Western Sydney in the year 2000. The number was nothing like the 70 alleged by the *Sun-Herald* nor the 30 claimed on Radio 2GB, but they were brutal, violent and frightening as such crimes always are. They were apparently seen as good news copy as well, as such crimes also often are, but this time the news was racialised. Hundreds of news articles gave saturation coverage to the trials and issues that were associated with them, along with scores of opinion columns, editorials, letters to the editor, radio talkback discussions, television news and current affairs items. The racialisation of these crimes has been briefly outlined in Chapter One in connection with the 'Othering' of Arab and other Middle Eastern immigrants and asylum seekers and also Muslim Australians as: illegal immigrants, people-smugglers, criminal gangs, terrorists, rapists. This chapter will now analyse the ideological elements of the 'ethnic gang rape' moral panic which centred on Sydney in 2001 and 2002. The inter-connected threads in this ideology involve common-sense 'orientalism' of the Arab/Muslim Other's masculinity as deviant, immoral and dangerous; it is racialised and criminalised. These contradictory racist themes include: Lebanese/Muslim men's purported disrespect of women in general; Lebanese/Muslim men being allegedly brought up to regard 'White', 'Western', 'Caucasian', women as 'sluts' and thus 'fair game' as distinct from their own women who are respected or at least valued as property; 'ethnic gang rape' as an expression of anti-'Aussie', anti-White, anti-Western hatred which is supposedly encouraged in Muslim communities at large; Muslim and 'Third-World' cultures as barbaric, uncivilised, violent and misogynistic in their law and their morality; condemnation of laxity and indulgence in the Australian legal and political system towards transgressors and calls to mete out 'their own medicine'. We also see, a fortiori, the metaphor of war analysed in Chapter Two: Australia's race warrior journalists leave us in no doubt that this is 'race war' being waged.

'Caucasian women the targets'

From the beginning, newspaper reports undoubtedly sourced from NSW police (see Wockner 25/8/01:4) couched the story in racial terms. The *Daily Telegraph*'s crime reporter, Charles Miranda (13/9/00:14), for example, wrote: 'In a chilling racial development, some of the victims said they were asked if they were true Australians before being attacked by the youths, believed to be of Middle-Eastern extraction'. (This 'extraction' was in later public discussion to be recast as 'Muslim' and also at times associated with refugees, as we shall see below). All the alleged attackers came from 'the same ethnic community', wrote *Sunday Telegraph* court reporter Warren Owens (11/3/01:19), while 'all the alleged victims come from ethnic groups other than their alleged attackers'. (These ethnicities were later to be recast in terms of race as 'Caucasian' or 'white'). Nationality was also used as a descriptor: 'Several girls claimed their attackers had boasted of their "Lebanese" prowess, while others claimed their attackers had questioned them about their ethnic background' (Owens 11/3/01:19).

On 29 July 2001, the *Sun-Herald* had a front-page story which headlined, '70 girls attacked by rape gangs' (a fallacious figure) which was sub-headed 'Caucasian women the targets', and in which it repeated the phraseology that the alleged perpetrators 'are all of Middle Eastern extraction' and remarked that 'their alleged victims have all been Caucasian' (Kidman 29/7/01:1). 'Police are concerned that the acts may become culturally institutionalised', it recorded. The following day, 2GB radio talkback host Philip Clark (30/7/01) referred to pack rapes by 'Middle Eastern gangs' around Bankstown, canvassed the belief that the crimes were racially based, and suggested that members of the 'Arabic community' could be harbouring the criminals.

We see here the ideological themes which emerged during the 'ethnic crime gang' moral panic in 1998 (Collins et al. 2000): the observation that the alleged perpetrators share a particular appearance or ethnic background; attribution of causation of criminality to the supposedly shared culture of the offenders; and apportionment of responsibility for the crimes to entire ethnic communities. In addition, in these instances it is asserted by police, media and then politicians, that the victimisation is on the basis of race:

> Police said they were 'keeping an open mind' on possible links between Tuesday's attack and similar incidents in which teenage girls and women have been targeted by middle eastern [sic] men for being Caucasian.

> Insp. Johnson said there were no clear links between the latest attack [sic] but said the girl was of Caucasian appearance. The three attackers were all said to be of Middle Eastern appearance (Gee 9/8/01:1).

'There are suburbs in which the streets are not safe and young Caucasian women are at risk of rape', editorialised the *Telegraph*, which explained that the crime was associated with a lack of assimilation or integration into 'our' Australian society. 'Many of the members of these gangs declare they don't regard themselves as Australians even though they were born here, and this challenges the comfortable image of the society we have built' (*Daily Telegraph* 6/8/01:20). On commercial radio station 2GB, Alan Jones (26/7/02), following the further trials a year later, also attributed the crimes to immigrants' failure to integrate. Refusing to resile from what he reiterated was the truth, that gang rapists were raping girls for racial reasons, he continued, as if these claims were logically and inextricably linked, that if Lebanese Muslims wanted to live [in Australia] solely as Lebanese Muslims, then 'Australia is not going to take it'.

An opinion column in the *Daily Telegraph* remarked on the racism raging on radio talkback shows, and observed how the untrammelled racial vilification was linking the gang rapes with asylum-seekers. From being of Middle Eastern 'extraction' or appearance, or being 'Lebanese', the gang rapists were now being ideologically identified as 'Muslims':

> In this past week I have heard the most outrageous bile and venom coming from the mouths of [talkback] listeners, with the announcers making no attempt whatsoever to correct or bring balance to the diatribe. 'Ya mustn't let those Muslims in ... they breed like flies', said one caller, to which the announcer replied: 'Yes' ... Many callers have made the connection between the pack rapes which have received much publicity recently, and the MS Tampa boat people. To claim the Tampa unfortunates would, if allowed into Australia, rampage and rape through our suburbs is an obscene defamation, yet it has been peddled at will on some talkback stations through the week (Day 5/9/01:31).

Melissa Fyfe, reporting in the broadsheet Melbourne newspaper the *Age*, wrote, 'Like Pauline Hanson revisited, it has been a week of racist bile over Sydney's airwaves and in the pages of its tabloid press' (Fyfe 25/8/01:4). NSW Islamic Council Chairman Ali Roude concurred:

> Talkback radio had broadcast a stream of abuse and hatred over the past few weeks directed at Muslims and people from Arabic speaking backgrounds. 'It's like a war, if you listen to talkback radio,' he said (Tremain 16/8/01:1).

Alan Jones (30/7/01, excerpted in *Media Watch* 9/9/02), referred to 'attacks against ordinary Australian girls carried out by out of control Lebanese Muslim gangs who hold us and our police service in contempt'. He commented, 'Now they are showering their contempt for Australia and our police on these young girls', and described this as 'the first signs of an Islamic hatred towards the community that welcomed them' (Fickling 2002).

The *Daily Telegraph* also underlined the supposed racial causation of the crimes, hear-hearing with Premier Bob Carr against politically correct qualms about declaring the apparent conjunction of empirical factors to be a cause:

> After a series of gang rapes in Southwest Sydney, Mr Carr stated the irrefutable fact that groups of Lebanese youths were responsible for the attacks. It was important to make this distinction because the attacks against the women were racially based ... The accused in the rape cases brought to trial were Lebanese and the victims were 'Australian' women (*Daily Telegraph* 5/9/01:30).

The editor of the *Daily Telegraph*, Campbell Reid, stated the newspaper's position on this representation during an interview by Nadya Stani on ABC Radio National (27/8/02):

> Why did a group of men attack those women? What was it that brought that group of men together? To be involved in that pack rape, who did you have to be? And if the answer to those questions is that you had to be a young Lebanese Muslim man, then that is something our society should discuss and that is something I firmly believe and have evidence to support that that is indeed what happened.

Tabloid columnist Miranda Devine weighed in with a breathless argument, reprised a year later by Janet Albrechtsen (17/7/02), that it was *multiculturalism* which caused the rapes. 'How many girls and young women have been sacrificed because no-one wanted to offend ethnic sensibilities?', she asked rhetorically (Devine 12/8/01:15). Heaping hyperbole on the rhetoric, she wrote that it was no less than war being fought, in:

> a home-grown form of systematic ethnic cleansing by a group of men said to be of 'Middle Eastern' extraction ... [T]hey wage war on those they feel do belong. And make no mistake. It is a war, and one in which our laws are impotent.

Very similar claims were made in an anonymous, racist pamphlet handed out to school students at Bankstown railway station and a number of other sites in Sydney around September 2002, and bearing the name, postal address and website of the Australia First Party. Subheaded, 'Don't Be a Victim of Multiculturalism Gone Mad!', the leaflet asserted that misogynist Muslim culture caused the sexual assaults. Referring to the rapists (the convicted 'leader' of whom is pictured), it asks, 'Why Do They Do It?', and answers (falsely), 'They Quote From The Koran'. There follow three purported quotations from the Koran in English, which are summarised (again patently falsely) as follows:

> In other words, women can be taken by men as they will; men can control and dominate women and use violence against them; women who assert their physical beauty could be open to punishment. The victims of the gang attacks were so chosen!

The pamphlet continues with the familiar blaming of multiculturalism as a cause of the rapes:

> It is teachers and clergy, politicians and pop-stars, who preach the multicultural lie. These people make it possible for some girls to get into a situation where rape can follow. On September 11 [2002], school-kids were supposed to show tolerance to Moslems in their schools. Sadly, this tolerance rubbish, leads to letting the guard down (anon 2002).

A similar pamphlet was handed out in Young, in rural NSW.

Miranda Devine recounted the story of 'Steve', a Lakemba father and grandfather who had been a caller-in to John Laws's program on radio 2UE during that 'week of bile' on the airwaves, saying (among other hair-raising stories) that his attractive blonde daughter and her friend had been spat on and called 'fucking skips' by 'Lebanese' men in a southern Sydney shopping mall. Steve said (and Devine quoted in approbation), 'They just have no respect for Caucasian women' (Devine 12/8/01:15). 'Steve' , who had identified himself as 'a white working executive from the suburbs', had said on 2UE, 'We are not a soft touch, you can't rape our girls', and grimly predicted vigilante reaction, which of course he did not sanction (Fyfe 25/8/01:4). The ideological notion of Australia and (White) Australians being stood over or taken advantage of as 'a soft touch' also circulated during the 'boat people' crisis of 2001, promoted by conservative politicians including the Prime Minister and the Immigration Minister. It touched a chord which continued to reverberate. A talk-back caller, 'Stephanie', on Alan Jones's Radio 2GB program (19/9/02:8:50am) linked the gang rapes in her stream of consciousness with lack of assimilation or assimilability. People were not Australian just because they are born here, she said. She demanded that the rapists' names be published, and condemned Lebanese Muslim Association spokesman, Keysar Trad, for arguing against this. She said that she was angry about 'these Muslims' who constantly 'push their religion', and that Australia had been 'a soft touch' for too long.

Nor was ABC Radio immune from talk-back attacks on multiculturalism and recommendations of vigilantism. One caller to the morning program in Wagga Wagga in country NSW said, 'There's only one thing you can with these pricks, it's not right treating women like this, you just want to get 'em and string 'em up by their nuts ...'. Another said:

> It just hasn't been going on for a couple of years. This dates back to about 15 years that things have been going on with this multi-cultural rubbish up there and I think there has to be a minimum sentence, not just a maximum sentence (excerpted in *The World Today* 27/8/01:12:14 pm).

In the second half of 2001, the *City Star*, the local paper of Penrith in the outer west of Sydney was 'besieged by letters from angry, white males about "ethnic crime", especially rape'. The editor, Chris Hutchins, recounts to Andrew West, 'They would say these rapists were not real men ... Send them out here and we'll show them what a real man does — all that stuff' (West 18/11/01).

The tabloids and talkback demanded tougher sentences and Premier Carr (and, of course, the Opposition) promised tougher sentences. They reviled judges as soft and out of touch and they called for appeals on the sentencing, and the Director of Public Prosecutions indeed appealed against the 'ridiculously lenient sentences' (Morris 7/9/01:4). They pilloried 'ethnic leaders' to accept the blame on their communities, and, as we shall see in Chapter Six, some leading ethnic community figures were in fact bullied or manoeuvred into doing so (e.g. *Sun-Herald* 14/7/02:1). When Police Commissioner Peter Ryan referred to the rapes as 'racially motivated' (*Daily Telegraph* 18/8/01:11) and described the situation as 'to some extent a by-product of Sydney's recent huge immigration', Premier Carr headed off criticism with a populist swipe at 'political correctness' (Chulov 18–19/8/01:1). The *Daily Telegraph* noted:

> Mr Carr refused to apologise, saying he would not stop speaking out on international linkages with local criminal activity and was not embarrassed at identifying criminals by their ethnicity to help police tackle the problem.

Mr Carr elaborated, 'These acts are the responsibility of criminals — they can't be slated home to Australian society. I won't accept that for a moment' (Morris 22/8/01:4).

When being interviewed for the Sydney-based Arabic newspaper, *El Telegraph*, by a young woman journalism student questioning the Premier over his government's handling of the gang rape matter, Mr Carr became angry. The *Sun-Herald* reported (from a transcript) that he said:

> I'm sorry that I'm emotional because I met one of the victims yesterday, and I just find an appalling insensitivity in the questions you're asking about the plight of these victims ... She was held by these men for hours. They said disgusting things to her and some of them were out there committing this crime against other young women. You're saying that the Government is somehow responsible. The cause of the unease in the community, and you must face up to it, is what these violent rapists said when they committed the crime — that projected race into this argument (*Sun-Herald* 11/8/02:7).

Opposition Leader John Brogden, for his part, promised compulsory minimum sentencing should he be elected. He concurred on air with Alan Jones (2GB 18/7/02) in his criticism of Lebanese Muslim leaders for denying the racial aspects of the gang rapes, and (in this context) offered amendments to the *Crimes Act* for hate and racially motivated crimes.

Nicholas Cowdery, the NSW Director of Public Prosecutions, was critical of both the Premier and the Opposition Leader for encouraging racism:

> There is an element of racism in the community, and the politicians prey on these mindsets and make statements which are sympathetic with the prejudices of the people they wish to vote for them (Gerard 10–11/8/02:5).

One Nation MP David Oldfield called for a ban on the immigration of Muslims following the gang rape convictions:

> What we have seen with the latest offenders is just the tip of the iceberg, these people are not alone. There are others like them. Those 14 men did not come to the conclusion that Western women are 'sluts' and 'whores' by themselves, they were indoctrinated with these beliefs by Islamic leaders ... The socially primitive nature of Islamic society is evident ... in the way they treat their women and, surely now, in the way they treat ours ... such backward practices are not acceptable to Australian society (*The Torch* 24/7/02).

Two converse interesting ideological manoeuvres being effected here are the 'othering' of the perpetrators and the 'whitening' of the victims. The suspected and later convicted rapists were often referred to as 'Muslim' in contexts where this identity was contrasted with Australiannness. They were repeatedly described as 'Lebanese', notwithstanding their Australian nationality, residency and country of upbringing. By contrast, the seven victims of the rapes, invariably described as 'Australian', included two girls of Italian and one of Greek background. The victims were often collectively designated as 'Caucasian', and sometimes as 'white', despite the fact that one was of Aboriginal parentage (Fickling 2002).[1]

'The rapists mentioned race first'

There is a grain — and only a grain — of truth in the widely repeated claims that the gang rapes in question *appeared* to be racially motivated. It was reportedly asserted by at least one of the victims that the perpetrators made racial remarks and insults while the young women were held captive and sexually assaulted. These allegations, and what the police, media, and politicians made of them, will be discussed in the following section. What the judiciary made of them is something quite different, and therefore 'lenient' and 'out of touch' judges were excoriated for precisely that, at a time when a general onslaught of 'penal populism' (Totaro 27/1/03:1; Roberts, Hough, Stalans & Indermaur 2003) was coming into full battle cry, not least in NSW in the approach to yet another 'Law and Order' driven state election (Totaro 27/1/03:15). Other, later judgments, which fell into line with the 'public expectations' thus constructed, were in turn crudely applauded by populist media commentary (often presented as 'news'), as were political and administrative announcements of 'reform' to the criminal justice system, and especially to sentencing. Notwithstanding this, it must be recognised that there was also just a kernel of truth in the furore about failings of the justice process, as we shall see.

It should be stressed at the outset of this discussion that the mostly untested allegations of a few racist remarks do not remotely demonstrate the race-based motivation that was inferred or even assumed with such irresponsible abandon. Moreover, given the horrific humiliation and damage of the rapes, it is interesting that the relatively minor aspect of these comments should be so seized upon and emphasised — by certain media and populist politicians as a major aggravating factor of the crimes, with implications about their causality. Likewise, it is noteworthy that procedural short-comings identified in this particular moral panic both in the processes of charge-bargaining and in ignoring victims' impact statements — processes which had been in place for a considerable time — should have surfaced and arisen to such prominence in these very instances, laden as they were with racial overtones.

Neither, furthermore, do the convictions and the backgrounds of the offenders demonstrate culpability on the part of communities from which they come, and of which they are unfairly held to be representative. Still less can they be taken as evidence of endemic cultural wrongs and inadequacies of particular ethnicities and/or religions which are ideologically taken to be causes of the crimes under discussion. All of these ideological elements pervaded the moral panic about the 'ethnic' gang rapes.

In March 2001, the *Sunday Telegraph's* court reporter wrote, 'Fourteen youths from a Sydney suburb have been accused of raping at least seven teenage girls during a five-week rampage'. His sources were police. He continued, 'Several girls claimed their attackers had boasted of their "Lebanese" prowess, while others claimed their attackers had questioned them about their ethnic background' (Owen 11/3/01:19). Neither the 'Lebanese prowess' claim, nor that about questioning over ethnic background, is particularly surprising. Indeed, research by the present authors on masculinity and identity among second-generation Lebanese-background young men has documented how boasting of the supposed attributes of the manhood of their culture of origin is a common theme of their conversation, often advanced in the face of experienced cultural denigration (Poynting, Noble & Tabar 1998). Nor is there anything very culturally specific about that; the theme can be observed in boys' talk among any number of ethnicities, including Anglo Australian. It occurs in quite mundane, quotidian situations. The fact that the same topic then arises in the context of a horrific group sexual assault does not therefore imply that this sort of talk and attitude is causally related to the crime in any direct or ethnically specific sense. (Patriarchy and dominant masculinity *are*, of course, causally related to rape, irrespective of ethnicity). The inquiry about the ethnic backgrounds of the girls being targeted is hardly astonishing either. Because of the opprobrium it would cause (to those of both genders involved) in a close-knit community where strong sanctions apply against extra-marital sex, young men of this second-generation background often look for non-marital sexual partners outside of their community (Poynting, Noble & Tabar 1998). Again, this is the case in legal, everyday sexual encounters where no crime is involved. As Andrew Jakubowicz (27/09/01) argues:

> There are two questions then about whether these are racial rapes ... One is is there something about the general Lebanese Muslim culture that drives young men to rape Anglo Australian women? The answer to that is quite clearly No, there's nothing specifically cultural about it. Is it the case that adolescent thugs, looking for easy targets to play out their stuff on would pick women from outside their own community? The answer is Yes, they clearly would.

That is to say, there is no necessary causal link between such precautions and the rapes to which it becomes ideologically joined. The rapists said things claiming cultural superiority and expressing cultural put-downs at the same time, but they surely say them at other times, too, in common with their entire cohort. Many men say them who are not rapists. An empirical conjunction does not entail a cause-effect relation. The *appearance* of causality arises in the process of racialisation.

The issue of motivation goes to the heart of the characterisation of the rapes in question by a number of commentators, intent on attributing a measure of responsibility to the Lebanese community of the perpetrators, as racist hate crime. According to Byers (1999, cited in White & Perrone 2002:163), a hate crime:

> is a prejudice-based criminal offence *motivated* by the victim's membership within a particular social group. This could include, but may not be limited to, crimes *motivated* by the victim's real or perceived race, ethnicity, national origin or sexual orientation [emphasis added].

The evidence that some of the gang rapes in Sydney in 2000 involved abusive reference to the ethnicity of the victims, does not demonstrate such motivation. As columnist PP McGuinness surprisingly observes, '... gang rape is not the product of religious or ethnic factors'. He compares the recent sexual assaults with an infamous case in Sydney in 1886, the 'Mount Rennie Outrage'. Nine youths were sentenced to hanging for the offence; all had 'typical Anglo and Celtic names'. McGuinness concedes that, 'It is relevant that the perpetrators of the recent cases of gang rape had common identifiers', and also refers to the alleged race-based insults so emphasised in the recent moral panic:

> Any girl who is targeted by a bunch of thugs of any origin will be described by epithets which somehow make her inferior, and therefore fair game unlike their own women, who are protected by tribal or group loyalties (McGuinness 23/7/02:11).

In the first of the series of trials prominently reported by the media in August 2001, four youths, two of whom were brothers, submitted pleas of guilty: three men accepting two counts each of aggravated sexual assault and the fourth man pleading guilty to detaining for advantage. They further admitted a number of other sexually related crimes, which were to be considered in sentencing them. In September 2000 they had offered a ride in their car to two young women waiting at a railway station, then taken them to a house in western Sydney where they were threatened with a knife and forced to have sex a number of times (Temple 11/8/01:3). An effect of their pleading guilty, in addition to guaranteeing their conviction, is that the victims were spared the trauma of having to confront their attackers in court and to relive their experiences in a harrowing and drawn-out trial, and they also avoided the often humiliating and painful process that cross-examination can take in such cases. To encourage this preferable course, which also delivers savings of court time and expense for the State, sentences are routinely discounted for such pleas. This became one issue in the moral panic which ensued.

Another issue was also a matter of routine in the process of 'charge bargaining'. In order to secure a plea of guilty and obtain a definite conviction with minimal delay and cost to the State and (the cynical might argue, not so crucially, from the State's point of view) less suffering to the victims, lesser or fewer charges are usually proffered: ones which both prosecution and defence agree would be likely to be sustained in the event of a defended trial. Moreover, an agreed statement of 'facts' of the case is commonly in such instances negotiated between prosecution and defence, to go before the judge in determining sentence. Again, this avoids questioning and cross-examining defendants, victims and other witnesses in the process of an expensive and protracted trial which would also cause further pain for the victims.

A third issue in the subsequent moral panic was the length of custodial sentence initially determined, which fell within the usual range for such offences: a norm which came under sudden, strident and unrelenting attack in the media from commentators, journalists and politicians. The type of corrective institution — the prisoners were minors — also became a issue, albeit a subsidiary one, linked to the general ideology about judicial leniency.

Finally, there was a significant media campaign to have the names of the convicted released to the public: something normally precluded by law in the case of minors except where a judicial determination is made that it is in the public interest. (This very exception had been provided for as the result of previous moral panic and law and order auctioneering).

Two days after this case was adjourned for sentencing, and while the judgment was being awaited, the weekend tabloid *Sun-Herald* carried an article by its state political editor, Alex Mitchell, entitled 'Libs push life terms for gang rapists' (12/8/01:31). The story was based largely on quotations from the Liberal Party Opposition police spokesman, Andrew Tink, clearly intending to make political capital out of the case before the courts, and was plainly aimed by the newspaper at influencing the sentence. Tink complained that the Wran Labor Government had done away with life sentences for rape in 1981, and had defeated the Liberal Party amendment then proposed to its *Crimes (Sexual Assault) Act*, stipulating a maximum sentence of 'penal servitude for life'. Tink called for a major review of sentencing for sexual assault, following what Mitchell called 'an alarming increase in pack rapes, particularly in the Bankstown area'. The President of the NSW Police Association was quoted in support, saying:

> These predators are roaming around like a pack of dingos attacking young girls ... Every decent-thinking citizen will want to see them locked away for the maximum ... We have to make the penalty fit the crime and lock them away for as long as we can (Mitchell 12/8/01:31).

That same issue of the *Sun-Herald* carried an opinion column by Miranda Devine (12/8/01:15), reiterating that newspaper's supposed 70 rapes, and attributing racial motivations to the sexual assaults. It repeated from talkback radio the version of events with 'Middle Eastern' and 'Lebanese' perpetrators and 'Australian' and 'Caucasian appearance' victims. Devine (19/8/01:15), followed up in the next issue of the *Sun-Herald*, retelling the 'story of a neighbourhood under siege, divided between "skips" (Australians of Caucasian appearance) and "lebs" (Australians of Middle Eastern appearance)'. Every day between this weekend (Chulov 18–19/8/01) and when the sentence was handed down on 23 August in the case before the court (Toy & Knowles 24/8/01:1), the newspapers were replete with articles, letters, columns and editorials about the rapes.

The judge did not succumb to this campaign: the sentences ranging from 1 year for detaining for advantage to 6 years for aggravated sexual assault left the tabloids and the talkback opinion-vendors, and the politicians who are so much at their mercy — including both Premier and Opposition Leader — as well as the Police Commissioner, disappointed and outraged. Then, daily, editorials soapboxed, Votelines vox-popped, cartoons chided, letter-writers lambasted. Miranda Devine (26/8/01:15) devoted her third weekly column in as many weeks, weighing in with, 'Sorry, but the rapists mentioned race first'. For Judge Megan Latham had also fallen short of expectations by explicitly rejecting their unsubstantiated and irresponsible inferences of racial motivation. The written judgment included the observation, 'There is no evidence before me of any racial element in the commission of these offences'. Judge Latham also remarked therein, 'There is nothing said or done by any of the offenders which provides the slightest basis for imputing to them some discrimination in terms of the nationality of their victims' (*Daily Telegraph* 24/8/01:26).

Premier Carr reacted rapidly to the public criticism over the 'soft' punishment, announcing that he would meet with the Chief Justice to 'express concerns' over the supposed leniency of the sentences, 'passing on concerns of the public over the sentencing to Justice Spigelman and other legal bodies'. The Government had immediately referred the case to the Director of Public Prosecutions (DPP) for review (Jacobsen, Burke & Connolly 25–26/8/01:2). The outcome of the DPP's deliberations in the prevailing climate may well have been a foregone conclusion. As the President of the NSW Law Society Mr Nick Meagher was reported by the *Herald* as saying, 'Judges did reflect public opinion and the current debate would "probably influence what judges do"' (Jacobsen, Burke & Connolly 25–26/8/01:2). Indeed it did.

Journalist and lawyer Richard Ackland commented on the 'political posturing' in Premier Carr's hurried appearance 'on the doorstep of Chief Justice Jim Spigelman', with the result that the case, with the original sentence duly appealed by the DPP and with the benefit of the swiftly announced 'Aggravated Sexual Assault in Company legislation' making those convicted of this crime liable for life sentences, would be heard in the Supreme Court by a now severely chastised judiciary. Ackland remarked graphically upon:

> the unseemly haste with which the Chief Justice made his announcement ... within moments of his meeting with the Premier. One would have thought that if Carr wanted to scratch his fleas all over the Chief Justice, prudence would have dictated that at least the head of the judiciary could have left a decent interval before making any response (Ackland 8/9/01:10).

This posturing was taking place just prior to the state by-election in Auburn in western Sydney, in the campaign for which ethnicity and crime and law and order were key issues. The Law Society 'accused the government of politicising the sexual assault sentences because of recent media attention on ethnic related crime' (*ABC Online* 24/8/01). The Opposition, for its part, promised to introduce legislation stipulating life sentences for 'pack rape' (Videnieks & Leech 25–26/8/01:4; Jacobsen, Burke & Connolly 25–26/8/01:2).

As a matter of fact, the sentences under question were not especially light. John North, past president of the NSW Law Society, commented that the sentence was neither unusual nor lenient and that 'politicians should not meddle with the law' (*PM* 24/8/01). Judicial Commission statistics indicated that, of the 237 people charged with sexual assault over the previous seven years, the average minimum sentence was around 4 years and the average maximum 6 years. Almost half of those gaoled received sentences between five and eight years (Videnieks & Leech 25–26/8/01:4). Richard Ackland (8/9/01:8) compared the case here under discussion to *R v Rushby*[2] in 1999, pointing out that the offences in that case were almost in the 'worst category' of the new scale concocted by the Premier: 'forced vaginal and anal intercourse of a 13-year-old girl by an 18-year-old male and his 16-year-old male companion', who 'pleaded guilty and were given total sentences of six and seven years respectively'. Ackland reports that, notwithstanding 'certain aggravating circumstances, including the fact that the victim was tied up and left in a remote location', there was no intervention by the Court of Criminal Appeal. Nor, manifestly, was there a campaign by the tabloids accompanied by political grandstanding. This must surely lead us to ask, if there had been no outcry over such leniency for the preceding seven years, why did it suddenly emerge in this case? The obvious answer lies in the moral panic linking ethnicity to the cause of the crime in this instance.

As we have pointed out earlier, the moral panic over 'ethnic rape gangs' was preceded by, and then developed coterminously with, a more generalised moral panic in urban Australia, and especially Sydney, about 'ethnic crime gangs'. Both 'Middle Eastern' and 'Asian' gangs had been focused upon in this cycle of media frenzy. Front-page stories, also occurring in August 2001, included supposed recruitment of schoolchildren as drug runners and extortionists in 'Asian' gangs. (See, for example, the five pages of the *Daily Telegraph* of 6 August 2001, bearing: the front-page lead story, numerous articles on pages 4 and 5, the editorial and the main daily cartoon.) This story was promoted by a right-wing group consisting of: 'disgruntled detective' Tim Priest, the self-styled 'whistle-blower' who received much media attention for accusing the government and police hierarchy of turning a blind eye to problems of ethnic crime and gangs in western Sydney; psychological anthropologist Richard Basham, who claims 'far more in common with police than with academics' (cited in Dixon 2003:197) and presents himself as an expert on 'Asian crime'; radio personality Alan Jones; and Ross Treyvaud, a western Sydney publican and Cabramatta Chamber of Commerce chairman who has campaigned to clean up the streets of drugs and crime in his locality. One supposed exposé of such practices by a 'former gang member', which was highly publicised by this high-profile coalition, was demonstrated by the ABC program, *Four Corners* (6/5/02), to be a total fraud. The schoolboy 'James' had never attended the school in question!

Other front-page tabloid stories from within a fortnight's period also in August 2001, as well as 'Gangland' (McDougall, Lawrence, Morris & Miranda 6/8/01:1), included the gang rape story, 'Women told to beware' (Gee 9/8/01:1). 'Gang Force: 240 police to fight crime' (Gee 10/8/01:1) followed next — an 'announcement' later denied by the police hierarchy and 'adopted' after a top-brass police regime change and months of tabloid campaigning (Poynting 2002).

Then came 'How one family's campaign paralysed a police station' (Miranda 15/8/01:1) which vilified as vexatious and criminal an entire Lebanese Australian family whose members had complained about police harassment, then 'Guns for Hire: Red Army soldiers recruited to city gangs' (Miranda 16/8/01:1), and 'Gangs steal kids' future' (Wood 19/8/01:1). Aspects of this moral panic included themes of importing crime; an attack on multicultural 'political correctness', including blaming this for supposed official reticence to identify ethnic crime as such, and the associated failure to record ethnicity-based crime statistics; the related supposed indulgence towards the civil rights of ethnic minorities and criminals, making the job of policing impossible; the need for tough policing and crackdowns on (ethnic) gangs; and an attack on ethnic leaders for refusing to accept responsibility for, and to remedy, the alleged criminality of their communities.

In the context of this wave of moral panic, the DPP did decide, as expected, to appeal against the 'ridiculously lenient' sentences using, as a mechanism for appeal, the pending application for sentencing guideline which was instigated by the Premier. The Crown Advocate was to submit, on behalf of the Attorney-General, that there was a 'trend toward judicial leniency in the cases of rape and gang rape' (Morris 7/9/01:4). Upon appeal, the sentences were more than doubled, to 13, 14 and 13 years respectively for the three young men first convicted (Wockner 14/3/02:3). There was a further reference to the DPP, and a further outcry, when the fourth offender who pleaded guilty in this case was sentenced in November 2001 to four years' imprisonment. The type of corrective institution also became an issue: '"Why should this bastard ... have the rest of his sentence in a juvenile jail? He committed the crime of an adult, he should have the sentence of an adult," the mother of one of the victims said outside the District Court' (Connolly 3–4/11/01:5). After the determination of the NSW Court of Criminal Appeal, the two youngest of those convicted were ordered to serve the remainder of their sentence in an adult jail, rather than the juvenile detention centre previously stipulated (Wockner 14/3/02:3).

In the later, and more notorious case, the 'ringleader' of one group of offenders was sentenced, to a total of 55 years' imprisonment — more than most murderers receive. This was the effect of the new, tougher legislation celebrated by the *Telegraph*: 'Die in jail: Carr's new sentences' (Peterson 5/9/02). The tabloids 'applauded', to use Piers Akerman's term (18/8/02:83). 'Well done, your honor', the *Telegraph* (17/8/02:18) headed its congratulatory letters. To underline the point, and in a truly popular approach to justice, it contributed a 'Vote-line': 1060 votes for and 193 against the severity of the sentence (17/8/02:19). Miranda Devine (18/8/02:15) called it a 'sentence to smile about'. The Premier and Opposition Leader both endorsed the sentence, the latter saying 'he hoped the rapist would rot in jail' (Pryor & Totaro 16/8/02:2). Even the Prime Minister, not one to miss a populist gesture, gave tacit approval (*Daily Telegraph* 19/8/02:4). One victim gave a door-stop interview outside the court, saying, 'I'd just like to say thank you to all of the media for your support ... if it wasn't for your support it wouldn't be such a hefty sentence' (Crichton & Stevenson 14–15/9/02:30). Quite so.

As mentioned earlier, it was not only the severity or otherwise of the sentences that was in contention during the course of the moral panic. One of the issues canvassed especially by the *Daily Telegraph*, beginning while the young men were still awaiting sentence, was that the process of charge-bargaining explained to, and agreed to by, the young women victims, left them feeling that their story had not been fully told in court — as indeed it had not (Wockner 25/8/01:4–5). In particular, they expressed repeatedly in the media their experience of the sexual assaults as *racial* humiliation, and their perception that the attacks were racially motivated. They appeared to view the omission of this emphasis of theirs, which loomed large for them in importance, as somehow lessening the gravity of the crime for which the youths were being convicted. The *Daily Telegraph* clearly shared this view. It editorialised, in a column which railed against denial, selectivity and distortion, and suggested that Judge Latham may have gratuitously intruded a 'personal view' into her judgment:

> ... there is evidence that race has been a factor in a number of assaults, particularly on women. If law enforcement and the judicial process are permitted to obscure the truth — and no one speaks up to object — then we will all be complicit if racial crime does become a widespread problem (*Daily Telegraph* 25/8/01:16).

The victims further complained that their victims' impact statements, in which they also told of their experiencing the ordeal as racial humiliation, were not taken into account in summing up and determining sentences. Judge Latham said that she had disregarded the aspects of the Victim Impact Statement that went 'beyond the agreed facts upon which the offenders stand to be sentenced' (Connolly 25–26/8/01:2). This is apparently usual and proper legal procedure. Whatever discrepancy there may have been between the intention, the representation, and the actual legal status of victims' impact statements, it is clear that there is nothing unusual and certainly no bias involved, in the inability of these statements to become a vehicle for the telling of the girls' story. So they told their story instead to the very willing media, while the young men, without right of reply, were yet to be sentenced. The *Telegraph* could offer sympathy to the victims, and posture on the moral high ground, while gratuitously, incessantly picking over the sordid facts of the case which, along with the controversy it generated, doubtless garnered considerable profits for News Ltd.

The young women also protested that the 'agreed statement of facts', agreed between prosecution and defence lawyers, was never agreed to by them, the victims, and diminished the crime while making them appear foolhardy at best, voluntarily accepting a ride in a car late at night with a group of young male strangers, whereas they claimed they were forced at knifepoint. Neither the perception of motivation nor this version of events was ever tested in court or subjected to cross-examination; this is the effect of charge-bargaining to secure a plea of guilty and precisely to spare the victims the further humiliation and anguish of cross-examination. An agreed statement of facts is exactly that — a set of facts uncontested from the point of view of both prosecution and defence, that can be agreed by both parties. The naivete of the teenage girls in not grasping this is quite understandable, and a failure of the legal process. On the other hand, the *Telegraph* and other tabloid style media portrayed the process as one of censoring,[3] and linked this ideologically with 'political correctness' and reluctance to offend ethnic sensibilities. 'There is a tendency in our society to deny the truth instead of confronting it, on the basis that it may cause offence or challenge fashionable beliefs', pronounced the *Telegraph* editorial in criticising the legal process in the case heard by Judge Latham (*Daily Telegraph* 24/8/01:26). This portrayal was disingenuous, wilful 'dog-whistling' (a process we shall explore in the next chapter), and highly irresponsible.

Some of the damaging effects of this irresponsibility ironically involved both sexual assault and racial hatred: evils which the commercial media claimed to be exposing and opposing. Hind Karouche, a member of the Supreme Islamic Council of NSW, complained that women wearing the hijab 'had become targets' because of the reporting about the supposedly race-based sexual assaults being blamed on Muslim and Lebanese communities. She told how 'They are abusing them, they are threatening to rape them' (Morris 5/9/01:6). The *Sydney Morning Herald* reported that 'Muslim women and girls have become the targets of threats and abuse in Sydney's south-west following police reports that blame Middle-Eastern men for recent gang rapes of European women'. Keysar Trad, Vice-President of the Lebanese Muslim Association, said, 'They have been receiving threats of rape and also some ladies in our community have been spat on in the street'. He reported that an anonymous telephone call to a western Sydney Islamic school had threatened to abduct and rape pupils (Kennedy 17/8/01). According to Sheikh Al Hilaly, the Imam of the Lakemba mosque, such threats were not idle ones: he told of the rape by a 'Caucasian' man of an 18-year-old Muslim girl producing 'uproar' in the community and a very dangerous situation. The victim was a virgin, according to Keysar Trad, who said the case, though not recorded by the police, was known to elders of the community (Walker 26/8/01:10).

The *Telegraph*'s words, 'we will all be complicit if racial crime does become a widespread problem' (*Daily Telegraph* 25/8/01:16), though unintendingly, cannot have been more prescient. Complicit they were. 'Rape, hatred and racism' have never been accorded the column-inches and the air-time when suffered by subordinated cultures, be they Indigenous or immigrant. Now, if a 'racist giant awakes in south-west Sydney', to use Miranda Devine's own phrase (12/8/02:15), the *Daily Telegraph*, the *Sun-Herald* and the populist talkback comperes have coloured its dreams and aroused it in anger.

Unholy trinity: power, thuggery and silence

One case of comparison will suffice to show that the media furore about the process of charge bargaining and the overlooking of the victims' impact statements was determined by relations of racism and class.[4] This case in Sydney's inner west came to light in October 2000, at much the same time as the group sexual assaults in south-western Sydney, and went to trial in 2001. It involved at least 75 sexual assaults over a four-month period — 50 on one victim and 25 on another — often 'in front of "spectators"' (Connolly 21/12/00) who 'stood by and cheered them on and laughed as the victims screamed' (Overington 4/2/01). The perpetrators were teenage males from the same religious background, and police stated to the court that the practices of violence, humiliation and bullying were endemic to the subculture of these young men. The group sexual assaults involved elements of torture — a description Justice Finnane used about the rapes discussed above (Wockner 9/8/02) — tying up and beating were part of the ritual violence.

As in the case we have been concerned with here, charge bargaining took place, which shaped the course and outcome of the trials. The offenders agreed to plead guilty to lesser charges and the prosecution 'agreed to accept the pleas and drop more serious charges of sexual assault', in return for the guilty pleas which 'saved the victim the stress and trauma of having to give evidence ...'. (Walker 11/2/01). In one instance, 'two counts of aggravated sexual assault were reduced to one count of intimidation' (*Sydney Morning Herald* 24/2/01:2). In all, 'Twelve other charges were dropped in exchange for the guilty pleas' on the basis of this agreement. One other youth had already accepted the offer of a guilty plea in January, when the DPP:

> offered a plea to the boys of aggravated indecent assault, whereas in December, back-up charges (made on the advice of the DPP) included aggravated sexual intercourse and sexual intercourse without consent. (If defendants admit to a form of penetration they are allowed to plea to a lesser charge.) One said yes, the others no (Lawson 10/2/01).

Nevertheless, the story told by the agreed statement of facts was horrific. A children's court magistrate was reported as saying that there was an ongoing culture of bullying and abuse, in which victims were tied to beds and sexually assaulted in front of their peers (Connolly 6/2/01). In passing sentence, the magistrate 'said the offences were committed in company, were ongoing, and involved the use of implements "in a most degrading way for the victim"' (AAP/*Weekend Australian* 24–25/3/01:11).

As the victims did not give evidence at the hearings, when they became disappointed at and hurt by the lenient sentences, and felt betrayed by information management and denial, they told their story instead to the press. It involved racism and bullying (Walker 11/2/01).

Two 16-year-old offenders were given twelve-month good behaviour bonds and had no conviction recorded (*Sydney Morning Herald* 10/2/01:40; ABC News Online 24/3/01). The one youth who admitted using his school tie to bind one of two victims who had been sexually assaulted more than 75 times over four months, was found guilty of intimidation and released on a good behaviour bond of six months without a conviction recorded. A fourth boy was allowed to plead guilty to intimidation in return for the withdrawal of two charges of aggravated indecent assault, and was placed on a good behaviour bond of six months, with no conviction recorded (AAP 8/3/01).

Each young man had his own team of lawyers. These were ruling-class boys. They and their victims had been boarders at the exclusive, Anglican, all-boys Trinity Grammar School, in whose boarding house the sexual assaults routinely occurred.

There was no moral outrage expressed in the media about the charge bargaining process. There was no shock or disgust voiced by press or politicians at the leniency of the sentences. No change was proposed to the law. The same tabloids which, in the 'ethnic gang rape' case, campaigned stridently to have the offenders publicly named (e.g. *Daily Telegraph* 13/7/01:20), even though they were minors, seemed to accept as appropriate that the offenders not be named in this instance, in the interests of rehabilitation — certainly, there was no campaign for them to be identified. Nor were their families identified. In this instance, the media did not make an issue of the common religion of the offenders. The contrast with the media, political and juridical treatment of working-class, poorly educated Muslim boys speaks volumes.

Blind spot allows barbarism to flourish

In July 2002, as the young men convicted of the south-west Sydney rapes were awaiting their sentences in prison, the conservative *Australian* columnist, Janet Albrechtsen (17/7/02) wrote a provocative and misleading opinion piece entitled 'Blind Spot Allows Barbarism to Flourish'. The 'blind spot' was multiculturalism and the barbarism was 'racially motivated gang-rape' practised by 'Muslim pack-rapists' from 'a culture that can treat women as second-class citizens', 'a culture which places so little value on gender equality'. The article not only took racial vilification to new depths among Australian broadsheet newspaper journalists, it regurgitated borrowed and unacknowledged material, misrepresenting the original stories and 'verballing' sources (Australian Muslim Public Affairs Committee 2001). The piece is of particular interest, because of the extent to which exactly the same ideological elements, phrases, stories, comparisons, distorted logic and common-sense cultural-political conclusions were picked up and circulated widely on talkback radio and in everyday conversations; one can find some of the very same formulations in rabid, racist letters to the editor of tabloids. The fact that the article appeared in a 'quality' broadsheet, the Murdoch 'flagship' in Australia, gave authority and apparent credibility to the ideas. The same ideas, expressions and arguments did not have either this circulation in Australia, nor this cachet, when they appeared on a US neo-Nazi website a year earlier, below the swastika and the heading 'New multiracial sport: GANG RAPE!' (Francis 26/8/01). Both the author of this article, Sam Francis, and Janet Albrechtsen had picked up on a media story from France, about an allegedly cultural or racial practice there dubbed *tournante* (Francis) or *tournantes* (Albrechtsen), translated (by both) as 'take your turn'. Francis (26/8/01) wrote, on the white supremacist American web page, 'It consists in the ritual gang rape of white women by non-white immigrants', and further (referring to the *Sun-Herald*'s fallacious front-page story of 31 July 2001), 'France isn't the only nation to experience the pleasures of diversity. Reports from Australia reveal that racially motivated rapes are catching on there as well'. Albrechtsen described *tournante* as 'the French term for the pack-rape of white girls by young Muslim men'. Like Francis, she took a swipe at multiculturalism: 'For 20 years the French ignored the ethnic causes of these barbaric crimes for fear of offending multicultural man. Along the way, more innocent young girls were pack-raped'. She continued:

> Now it's in Australia. Last week two Muslim brothers were
> found guilty of the gang-rape of a young Australian girl ... She
> was invited for a drive but taken to a secluded park and gang-
> raped while 14 Muslim boys watched (Albrechtsen 17/7/02).

The main difference in the two accounts seems to be that Francis
is more interested in race (white/non-white) whereas Albrechtsen
focuses more on culture ('white' girls but 'Muslim' men) in the
mode of what has been called the New Racism (Barker 1981),
which in Australia is basically the form of racism of One Nation,
as outlined in Chapter Five. Both refer to the press statement of
French magistrate Sylvie Lotteau, undated but (northern) spring
2001, according to Francis. The latter refers to 'black male' rapists, Albrechtsen to the religion of the young men, both attributing
this meaning to Lotteau. Francis describes the typical victim as 'a
white female'; Albrechtsen (purporting to quote Lotteau directly)
as 'a white girl'. The French *tournante* story and its comparison
to the 'ethnic gang rape' crisis in Australia had already appeared a
year before Albrechtsen's effort, in the column of fellow critic of
multiculturalism, Paul Sheehan (29/8/01:20), three days after the
Francis piece, and also in Jackman (29/8/01:31).[5]

Albrechtsen reproduces a version of the 'caught between
cultures' myth, which we have critiqued in Chapter Three, and
presents it as a cultural cause of endemic gang rape: 'French and
Danish experts say perpetrators of gang rape flounder between
their parents' Islamic values and society's more liberal democratic
values, falling back on the most basic pack mentality of violence
and self-gratification' (Albrechtsen 17/7/02). *Media Watch* (9/9/
02) argues convincingly that she lifted this story without citation
from an article by Adam Sage in the *Times*, some 16 months earlier:
'Caught between their parents' Islamic values and societies [sic]
Christian and social democratic values, some youths appear to have
fallen back on the most basic instincts of violence and pleasure'
(Sage 5/12/01, cited in *Media Watch* 9/9/02). Albrechtsen falsely
ascribes to the 'French and Danish experts' the identification of

the rapists as Muslim and the victims as 'white'. Sage's original article had quoted French Psychotherapist Jean-Jacques Rassial as saying that, 'gang rape had become an initiation rite for male adolescents in city suburbs'. In Albrechtsen's rather more creative version, 'male adolescents' becomes 'a small section of young male Muslim youths', and 'gang rape' of unspecified victims becomes 'pack rape of white girls' (*Media Watch* 9/9/02; Australian Muslim Public Affairs Committee 2001). The Danish expert, criminologist Flemming Balvig, receives similar treatment, with Albrechtsen, still referring to the 'young male Muslim youths', claiming that he corroborated 'the French experience of this barbaric rite of passage into manhood for some of these young men' (*Media Watch* 9/9/02). When Balvig was presented by *Media Watch* with Albrechtsen's misuse of his work, he rejected this interpretation indignantly: 'The citation is completely wrong. What I have said is, that the main explanation of gang rape probably is social, and not cultural or religious' (*Media Watch* 9/9/02).

Not only did Albrechtsen add to the European academics' accounts her own supposition that the rapists were Muslim, she also omitted that some of the victims whom she (but not the academics) described as 'white' were themselves Muslim. Scott Johnson's *Newsweek* report of August 20, 2001 is quoted on this by Australian Muslim Public Affairs Committee (2001):

> There are increasing reports of gang rapes called tournantes by bands of adolescent boys, some no older than 14. The victims are often young Muslim girls, doubly victimized by depressed socioeconomic circumstance and the fury of the boys who haunt the abandoned buildings where the rapes take place.

We have seen some stark examples in this chapter of how racial or ethnic profiling of a particular type of crime, and the dominance of racist mindsets in the social context in which it takes place, can 'bleach' victims to 'white' and 'blacken' offenders to 'non-white'.

As magistrate and Aboriginal woman Pat O'Shane wrote in her letter to the *Australian* (19/7/02), this way of looking flies in the face of history:

> Janet Albrechtsen does not let Australian history stand in the way of a few prejudices. Her comments about racially motivated gang-rapes, and that this first hit in the last 12 months, ignore 200 years of such events. Indigenous Australian women have been subject to such criminal behaviour by Anglo-Australian men, many of them in positions of control over the women and their communities, without a single bleat from the likes of Albrechtsen.

We wish to make a methodological point about appearances and ways of looking, empiricism and causality, and a political point about 'correctness', before concluding this chapter with a cautionary tale about how the assumed 'non-whiteness' of a crime can produce false conclusions about suspects.

'Open eyes to ethnic crime'

Albrechtsen's, Sheehan's, Devine's and Duffy's (17/8/02:16) tirades about the supposed ethnic causes of gang rapes were each inter-woven with an attack on 'political correctness' in relation to multiculturalism. Both the July-August 2001 and July-August 2002 rounds of this story coincided with a media campaign to have 'ethnic crime' named and dealt with as such, in the face of the suppression of this 'truth' by misguided liberals and academics and the stubborn refusal to recognise it on the part of purblind 'ethnic leaders'. An aspect of this campaign was the push to have 'ethnicity data' recorded in crime statistics in NSW.

In 2000, the present authors agreed — with reservations — with the suggestion then being floated that ethnicity data be gathered and recorded in the criminal justice system of NSW. The reservations had to do with the practical difficulties of obtaining accurate data (what would count as ethnicity and who would count 'it'?), as well as its possible ideological misuses (Collins et al. 2000). In the end, we were convinced by the arguments being put forward by Don Weatherburn of the Bureau of Crime Statistics and Research, and others, that such data would be useful in determining whether there was over-policing of certain ethnic groups, or overrepresentation in arrests, convictions, incarceration, and so on, as indeed analogous statistics had demonstrated with Aboriginal people, especially young men (Cunneen 2001). If the data were objective and 'true', why, indeed, should social scientists or the people in general fear their being known? In retrospect, perhaps we should have had more reservations about *why* the data and why these particular data were being demanded. What ethnicities and what crimes were focused upon in the popular label 'ethnic crime' or in the practical labour of data collection to which it gave rise? Imagine if, because of a few high profile cases and longstanding cultural stereotypes, the demand were raised to keep statistics on, say, Jewish businessmen in white collar crime? The proposal would rightly be rejected, with contempt and outrage, as racist. Why then, Lebanese car theft, Muslim rapists, Middle-Eastern appearances?

Even the ABC's *7:30 Report* became caught up in the ethnic labelling and attacks on 'political correctness'. Journalist Maxine McKew, leading into the piece with comments about 'squeamishness' over 'crime and ethnicity' and 'political correctness', put to NSW Director of Public Prosecutions, Nicholas Cowdery, that 'what makes this [the "brutal gang rapes"] case unique was a particular ethnic group targeting another exclusively' (*7:30 Report* 15/7/02). Apart from the 'particular ethnic group' coming into focus in a certain way of looking, we have also seen that the exclusive targeting of 'another' ethnic group was more folklore than reality — just as it was in the French cases. McKew made clear who that other targeted group is: '... there were seven women and all Anglo-Celtic'. Wrong.[6] Cowdery assents both times. The first time, he replies:

That was certainly the case in the recent series of matters that have been dealt with. And that of course makes it doubly relevant. How can you say it is not relevant when it seems to be a factor in the motivation of the actions of the perpetrators of offences' (*7:30 Report* 15/7/02).

Seems. Appearance is everything. What causal mechanisms have been proposed and tested? We have seen no explanations beyond the sorts of folk prejudices rightly dismissed by Pat O'Shane. What tests, beyond the market research of the successful manufacturing of 'public opinion'? Beyond social-scientific knowledge, was the purported motivation ever proven at law?

In the same interview, Keysar Trad, Vice President of the Lebanese Muslim Association, makes a telling argument, going directly to the question of causation and refuting its (ideological) link with ethnicity. McKew Asks him, '… what about this crime? This was a particular group targeting western women, non-Muslim women'. Trad replies:

> This is the issue that I'm getting at. That I've received reports from Muslim women who feel that they were also targeted by rape, sexual harassment, so forth. Now, the issue in this case is that the lady who came forward and reported the complaint happened to be an Anglo-Celtic woman. I believe that if we follow the case further, you will find that the motivation itself of these people, even though they are making derogatory, racist slurs, that their motivation was the object of their gratification rather than the race of the object of their gratification.

Cowdery then concurs:

> I think that's right. I think the criminality of the crime of rape, as we used to call it, was the primary motivating factor and I think the rest was just regarded as an embellishment by the people who were involved. I have difficulty accepting that this was some sort of ethnic offence by one ethnic group against another ethnic group. I think it was delinquent male behaviour (*7:30 Report* 15/7/02).

How did the papers report this? The *Herald* headlined, 'Open eyes to ethnic crime: DPP' (Stevenson 13–14/7/02:7); the *Telegraph*, 'Racism a factor in gang rapes: Cowdery' (Hilderbrande & Morris 16/7/0:4). Racism was indeed a factor, but not the way the *Telegraph* meant.

'Gang wrongly jailed for rape'

Empiricism — the leap from the observable conjunction (say, statistical regularities) of particular ethnicities and given crimes to the assumption that the ethnicity is a causal factor in the crime — is not the only difficulty, but it is a besetting one. We also need to be especially alert to the ideological ladenness of the observations, and we need to take into account the impact of the social relations of racism pervading the State which is doing the policing, charging, trying, sentencing, incarceration, along with the intimidation, harassment, humiliation and sanctioned violence, as well as doing the statistics, objectivity, recording, reporting. We need theories which can grasp this.

The authors were impressed by the analysis of James Messerschmidt (1993), who attempts — as is in our view greatly needed — to grasp theoretically the complex interplay of class and gender (masculinity) relations in crime. In fact, we are still impressed, though chastened with a salutary lesson. In his groundbreaking study of masculinity and crime, Messerschmidt postulates that racial subordination can be ideologically inverted in acts of sexual violence, in a process by which the less powerful (racialised minority) men are made to feel more powerful in a collective practice of violence expressing momentary but significant power over women victims who come from a more powerful position in the prevailing class and ethnic relations. He may be right. It is an open question, to be tested, like all theory of any use, empirically.

The embarrassment of those of us impressed by this analysis — and doubtless now also of Messerschmidt — is that he used the 1989 New York Central Park 'wilding' case to instantiate his theory.

Five black and Latino youths were jailed for up to 13 years for the rape, brutal bashing and leaving for dead of a middle-class white woman jogger in Central Park. The viciousness of the violence was a factor to be explained. The 'gang' of young men had been identified 'wilding' in the park, that is, carrying on in a wild manner, skylarking and scaring people. The five matched the ethnic or racial profile fitted by the police to the crime. They were interrogated and they confessed, and their confessions were recorded. Their conviction was a matter of course. The American media called them 'animals', and the rapes were invariably reported in terms of race. They fitted the profile. They were, however, innocent of the crime. Recently, another man has confessed to the rape and near-fatal beating, and DNA evidence has shown him to be the offender and the five who were convicted to be innocent (Gordon 7/12/02:28; *Weekend Australian* 7–8/12/02:15; Sauiny 21–22/12/02:13).[7] So, in addition to the questions about the inexplicable violence of the assault, we now need to explain why and under what circumstances the five convicted but innocent men confessed. We have no answers, but the question takes us back to the point about racism within the State. We also need to ask why Messerschmidt — and, reading him, why we — did not raise these questions then.

The point of this example is not to suggest that those convicted of the gang rapes in Sydney in 2000 are innocent. It is to say that, until proven otherwise, it is scientifically prudent and socially responsible — not merely 'politically correct' — *not* to *assume* that their culture is an accomplice, that their ethnicity is a causal factor in the crime. It remains an open question, and one to be investigated empirically, what interrelations were at work between the masculinities of the perpetrators and the class relations and social relations of racism in which they were constructed and in which the young men lived.

The poverty of tabloid 'sociology'

One unnamed 'Sydney sociologist who has worked extensively with the Lebanese community' was quoted in the *Weekend Australian* as saying, of the western Sydney gang rapists:

> They want to impose themselves, albeit in a perverse way, over a culture that they feel has done them wrong ... And that culture could be a Christian culture or perhaps any culture that is non-Muslim. There are few worse sins for a young Muslim youth than to sleep with a girl outside of marriage, so they find strength in numbers (Chulov & Payten 13–14/7/02:23).

This is sheer speculation. Where is the evidence? What is the theory, the explanation for the articulation of reaction to racism (or is it class exploitation, or both?) to sexual violence? This is exactly the sort of glib formula much sought-after by busy journalists with tight deadlines, little time for investigation and less for reflection, and pressure to publish saleable copy. Sydney University anthropologist, Richard Basham, was a key source for two tabloid 'Gangland' beatups: one in the *Sun-Herald* (Walker 8/4/01:1,6–7) and one in the *Daily Telegraph* (McDougall et al. 6/8/01:1,4–5). The latter cited him thus:

> Anthropologist and crime researcher Dr Richard Basham believes the gang problem has spread in Sydney and become more entrenched: 'The most powerful [gangs]nes [sic] are ethnic [and] the Chinese the most structured'.
>
> But the crime and violence does not just happen between the gangs. It has already affected the broader community through the pack rape of more than 30 Caucasian girls and drug dealing on a huge scale ...
>
> Dr Basham believes the gangs have little fear of Australian police.
>
> 'It's part of their culture and it's being imported here,' he said (McDougall & Miranda 6/8/01:5, original parentheses).

Alec Pemberton, a senior lecturer in sociology at the University of Sydney, wrote in the *Daily Telegraph* that 'Black Panthers targeted white blonde women for rape during the Black Power movement in the 1960s'. He did concede that 'we don't know if this is happening here', but immediately followed this with the (non-) sentence:

> The persistent suggestion that fundamentalist Islamic attitudes, married to feelings of marginalisation and devaluing of Lebanese youth, might well have led to an explosive mixture and specific targeting of Caucasian women (Pemberton 22/8/01:4).

It might not have, too! Whose persistent suggestion was it? What motivated this persistence? What corroborated the suggestion? To reproduce the folklore about the Black Panthers in this context — irrespective of the slander to them — is plain silliness. Beyond that, it is exactly this sort of racially framed common sense, and irresponsible attribution of criminality to cultural causes, which led the five Black and Hispanic youths, innocent but convicted of the Central Park 'wilding' rape, to be targeted by police, to have false confessions extracted, to be taken to be guilty, to 'rot in jail' for 5 to 13 years. To this must be added the untold damage suffered by the rest of the communities of blame, which are assembled by such assumptions and the associated profiling.

The argument has been canvassed in Chapter One that the discourse of orientalism began among academic 'experts' and filtered into everyday common sense. This is one moment of a two-way, developing process. No doubt there is a dialectic at work, as Antonio Gramsci (1971) has argued, whereby the folklore of the 'masses' is picked up by intellectuals, worked up into more coherent form, and fed back into popular circulation. In any case, the sorts of letters to the editor of tabloid newspapers which reflect everyday lay conversations, contain the same myths about Arab/Muslim/Lebanese masculinity. Jennifer Whaite, writes to the *Telegraph* (24/8/01:28) that 'many years ago' she 'spent some time in the Lebanon'. The natives were friendly, she reports, but the men incessantly:

> made ... the obvious assumption that, as a European woman, I
> was a whore who would welcome any sexual advance ... This
> sort of behaviour is at one end of the spectrum whose other
> end is gang rape.

Irene Lesley, in the same edition (*Daily Telegraph* 24/8/01:28),
writes of 'the misogyny that one specifically associates with Islam'. She instances 'young women here in Sydney who have repressive dress restrictions imposed on them that do not apply to
their brothers, or other Australian women'. She is clear that it is
the masculinity in the culture that is the problem: just 'ask female
high school teachers how Muslim boys treat them'. Jodi Farr, on
the same page, concurs; it is the boys who are problematic: 'If lack
of discipline is the problem', she replies to Sheikh Taj el-Din Al
Hilaly, 'then why don't we see gangs of Arabic girls cruising the
streets causing pain and suffering?' (*Daily Telegraph* 24/8/01:28).

We have enumerated the ideological elements of the racialisation of deviant, 'Arab Other' masculinity as its supposed:
deprecation of all women, oppression and subjugation of their own
women, denigrating 'western' women as immoral and sexually
promiscuous, sexual violence towards 'white'/Caucasian/western
women as a manifestation of bitterness and hatred towards the
'west'. Arab and Muslim cultures are thus ideologically represented
as backward, brutal and misogynistic, and their masculinities present
a problem to be firmly rectified.

Such folk prejudices should not be elevated to the level of
scientific pronouncements. They cannot be superseded by social-
theoretical critique alone, but must be confronted in practice. Well
informed social-scientific alternatives will need to be empirically
based, and the authors intend the previous chapter (Three) to be a
modest contribution to that project. Chapter Five will now examine
what happens when racist folk prejudices lead, beyond social-
scientific pronouncements, to social policy announcements.

Notes

1 The authors are grateful to Ruth McCausland of the NSW Anti-Discrimination Board for this reference. The point is made in NSW Anti-Discrimination Board (2003:82n).

2 [1999] NSWCCA 104 (24 May 1999).

3 The Warren cartoon in the *Daily Telegraph* of 25 August (25/8/01:19) depicts censorship, confusing the charge bargaining process with the victim's impact statement. It shows bewigged woman judge reading a document headed 'Victim's Impact Statement' in which most of the text is blacked out, leaving only, 'On ... and then ... again ... repeatedly'.

4 This case is traced in detail, and analysed in terms of ruling-class masculinity, in Poynting and Donaldson (2002).

5 An earlier article in the *Daily Telegraph* by Christine Middap (21/8/01:6), reporting from London, drew on the French *tournante* story from *Le Monde*. Though it did not explicitly compare events there with the Sydney rapes, the story was juxtaposed with two other pieces on the page, which did deal with the latter.

6 Or, at best, raising some very sticky questions about 'objectively' identifying ethnicity, as alluded to above.

7 The authors are grateful to Michael Stutt, of Justice Action, for bringing the re-opening of this case to our attention.

5

Dog-whistle politics

The dog-whistle election

'Dog-whistle politics' was the subject of considerable discussion around the 2001 Australian federal election campaign (e.g. Barkham 10/11/01; Green 6/10/01; Oakes 13/11/01:18; Goot 30/8/02). The notion involves sending a particularly sharp message which calls clearly to those intended, and goes unheard by the rest of the population, like the dog whistles advertised in 1960s comic books.

Prime Minister Howard's 'We will decide who comes to this country and the circumstances in which they come' conveyed to a particular 'we' a message that deliberately went beyond the words. Ostensibly it was an impeccably reasonable statement about national sovereignty which almost goes without saying in a contemporary nation state. At the inaudible level, it spoke to those disaffected, disoriented and displaced by local effects of globalised economic restructuring — those whose insecurity and ignorance leaves them susceptible to populist claims that their relaxed and comfortable past had been stolen away by cosmopolitan, 'politically correct' elites and the 'multicultural industry', by favouring Asian and Middle-Eastern immigrants, refugees, and by privileging Aborigines. Thus it silently but successfully promised barriers against the unassimilable, the irrevocably different races or cultures — non-Christian, non-white, non-'western' — against whom the previous supporters of One Nation had raised their voices, once the consensus of bipartisan multiculturalism had been ruptured in the mid-1990s (see, e.g. Manne 29/10/01:16; Oakes 13/11/01:18; Ramsay 27–28/10/01:40; Hogg 2002:139; Simms 2002:99–103).

In 1996, the assimiliationist, anti-multiculturalist Pauline Hanson was elected to federal parliament for the Queensland seat of Oxley as an independent MP following her expulsion from the Liberals after unguarded comments about 'handouts to Aborigines' and other racist remarks. The One Nation party which she founded attracted huge media attention and garnered up to ten per cent of the vote in several subsequent state elections in addition to the federal one, by opposing immigration and rearticulating the racism of the old 'white Australia policy'. Their supporters object to immigration especially from 'non-Christian countries', and accuse immigrants of bringing unemployment, crime, corruption, communal strife, disease, among a list of social ills.

While these 'White Australia', assimilationist principles could be enunciated explicitly by mainstream politicians and newspapers in 1901, they could not in 2001. The right of the Coalition parties had railed against 'political correctness' before the 1996 election, as an imposition against freedom of speech and suppression of genuine debate. They were not only the province of Ms Hanson; they opened up a space for the ideas which she represented to be aired with some sort of respectability and taken seriously. In the light of the electoral impact of the re-emerging popular racism, the backlash against multiculturalism was partly adopted by both Government and Opposition. Only partly, however, for the two major parties wanted to retain the 'ethnic vote' and that of the small-l liberals among the middle strata, while courting the disaffected minority which had turned to One Nation. Hence the strategy of sending different messages to each cohort on distinct wavelengths, as it were. In the event, the dog whistle worked for the government in the 2001 federal election, in the context of a moral panic over the Middle-Eastern 'queue-jumpers' rescued by the MV Tampa off Western Australia in August and the fear and insecurity induced by the airborne terrorist attacks of September 11 in the USA.

In August 2001, before the fateful date in September and before the federal election, there was a meeting between NSW Premier Bob Carr and the federal Minister for Immigration Philip

Ruddock after Mr Carr 'had called for tightening of immigration policies to reduce ethnic crime on Sydney's streets'. Mr Carr remarked that ethnic crime gangs were 'causing mayhem on the streets' and announced that the federal-state plan devised at the meeting was to address 'problems ... because of decisions about immigration made decades ago' and was 'about making it harder for criminals to get into Australia and about making it easier for us to kick them out' (O'Malley, Jacobsen & Kennedy 2001:3; Morris 2001:8). Mr Carr's whistle was sounding the same note as Mr Howard's.

While immigration policy and 'border defence' are federal responsibilities in Australia, law and order are by and large matters of state jurisdiction. State politics in Australia, especially in the leadup to elections, have been redolent in recent years of 'law and order auctions'. New South Wales in late 2002-early 2003 had its third such election campaign in a row (Poynting 2002). Premier Bob Carr appears as attracted as Mr Howard by the campaign tactics of dog-whistling. He advocates tighter limits on immigration — ostensibly on environmental grounds. He vociferously opposes further expansion of Sydney through immigration — because of want of infrastructure and impact on amenity, he argues (Lipari & Skelsey 26/2/02:8; *PM* 25/11/02; Wainwright 26/11/02:4; *Daily Telegraph* 26/11/02:2). He names cultures and communities in association with criminal gangs or delinquent youth cultures: not blaming, he says, but facing stark reality and bravely standing up to the politically correct (e.g. Chulov 2001:1). It goes down a treat in the tabloids and with the talkback populists whom he allows to vet his police ministers and his police commissioners (Wilkinson 21/11/01; 24/11/01).

Dog-whistle journalism

Meanwhile, there is some dog-whistling about cultural minorities in the tabloid press, with the shrill becoming deafening in subsequent reverberation on talkback, in letters columns and pay-as-you-voice 'vote-lines'.[1] A seeming good news story about a Muslim women's gym, for example, provoked a predictable backlash from those who resent any space for the unassimilated (Murray & Morris 13/8/02:10; *Daily Telegraph* 16/8/02:26, 23/8/02:22; Murray 22/8/02:21; Puplick 22/8/02:21). Why was it full-page news? Could it be just for that reason? The story was about a women's-only gymnasium in south-west Sydney which catered exclusively to Muslim women, as a place where they could exercise within the dress constraints of their culture without being made to feel uncomfortable or the objects of scrutiny. The proprietors had taken the precaution of checking their entry restrictions with the NSW Anti-Discrimination Board, which approved them (Murray & Morris 13/8/02:10). The report was situated among strident stories about the heavy sentencing of several of the much-publicised gang rapists, which made much of their Muslim background. A backlash followed, in talkback programs, opinion columns, letters pages. The story melded with another myth aired in dial-in and tabloid complaints, about a public swimming pool proposing to close to the public for several hours to allow for the exclusive use by an Islamic girls' school 'in all their clobber' (Alan Jones program 22/8/02, cited in Duffy 14/9/02a:18; also in *Media Watch* 9/11/02 and Anti-Discrimination Board 2003:71). Despite school hire being a longstanding normal practice, the pool was forced by the furore to revoke its agreement with the school (*Media Watch* 9/11/02). The *Daily Telegraph* 'Vote-line' for 14 September 2002 asked, 'The Anti-Discrimination Board has granted an exemption for a muslim (sic) women-only gym. Does this discriminate against others?' Some 471 replied 'Yes' and a mere 11 'No'. The question for the day, above this reported 98% to 2% breakdown, was: 'The ringleader of the south-west Sydney rape attacks has been sentenced to 55 years jail. Is this penalty too severe for his crimes?'. Was the juxtaposition a coincidence, or was there some dog-whistling involved?

Another seeming success story, this one about halal hamburgers, in which there was nothing new at all, blew up into a major controversy. Why was it 'news' at this time? A rival fast food chain has been serving halal food in the same Sydney neighborhood for several years. Nevertheless, an apparently positive article occupying most of a tabloid page in the *Daily Telegraph* was published in September 2002 (two days before the well-publicised anniversary of the Islamic fundamentalist terror attacks), accompanied by a pleasant photograph of a smiling young woman eating one of the burgers in question: 'McDonald's is a mecca (sic) for Sydney Muslims' (Saleh & Hudson 2002:11). Predictably, the letters pages resonated on following days with outrage about special provision for Muslims, lack of choice for non-Muslims (in a city with dozens of non-halal outlets of the same 'family restaurant') and the prospect of being defiled by unwittingly eating food over which such heathen rites had been performed. The *Daily Telegraph* 'Vote-line' for 11 September 2002 recorded that 75% of voting readers responded 'No' to the question: 'A McDonald's restaurant in Punchbowl now serves only halal meat in its burgers. Is this practice fair to other customers?' (*Daily Telegraph* 11/9/02:33). The result was printed under the question for that memorable date: 'Some readers are concerned about media coverage of the September 11 anniversary. Is it important to remember the tragedy?'. The momentous debate resounded for several days on talkback radio and in opinion columns, and numerous letters to the editor were positioned alongside those discussing the morality or otherwise of the sentence under Sharia law to death by stoning of a young Nigerian woman convicted of adultery.

Another example is the report about a Muslim man suddenly threatened with the sack for praying at work, where he had previously done so without problems for many months. The story at first appeared sympathetic, but the paper could anticipate the response it would provoke from readers well primed for the game. 'Stop praying or be sacked' (Denholm 10/10/02:3) appeared to take the part of the threatened worker, in a full-page article with coloured photographs of the man, in traditional garb, kneeling with the Koran in hand, and another picture of the man in the grounds at lunch hour, along with an unnamed woman co-religionist in hijab —

the usual media cliche for Islam. Again followed the tirade of letters to editors, of calls to the shock jocks, and a plethora of press articles both tabloid and broadsheet (see also Nixon 10/10/02:3, 11/10/02:4; Karvelas 11/10/02:5, *Daily Telegraph* 14/10/02:17). Once again these were interspersed with reports about the gang rape sentences with headlines like 'Wild Animal' (Knowles 11/10/02:1; *Illawarra Mercury* 11/10/02:1). The *Daily Telegraph* 'Vote-line' reported on 12 October 2002 that 612 (87%) of readers' votes responded affirmatively to the question, 'A Muslim computer technician has been threatened with the sack for praying during working hours. Is his employer acting fairly?'. Only 88 (13%) answered 'No'.

All this was before the Bali bombing. For about four years, Sydney has been treated to an irrational and ignorant, but powerful formula from populist columnists and opportunist politicians, equating terrorism, ethnic crime gangs, Islam, misogynist violent crime, Muslim ethnic-religious leaders, Middle-Eastern asylum seekers. This ideology is now becoming frenzied. The dog-whistling provokes racial vilification, which incites attacks.

The fire last time

From early 1991 in the context of the Gulf War, there was an outbreak of racist hate crime in Australia against Arabs, Muslims, or those who apparently seemed so to the attackers (Poynting 2002b). The Hawke Government response urged 'tolerance' towards minorities under its policy of multiculturalism, though it did little to act effectively against racial vilification, and neither did state governments (Human Rights and Equal Opportunity Commission — hereafter 'HREOC' 1991; Newell 1990; Hage 1991).

Many Muslim women wearing their *hijab*, or traditional headscarf, in public places, were assaulted, abused and had strangers of both genders, but usually men, grabbing at their scarves to tear them away. Most of the victims were not Iraqi; some were not even of Arab, but rather of South-East Asian background; but such confusions of the object of racial hatred are not unusual in the history of Australian racism. There was an outbreak of incidents of people in Islamic dress or of 'Middle Eastern appearance' being spat upon or more violently assaulted in the street, of incidents of arson, vandalism, threats, harassment and other racist attacks directed by 'white-thinking' people against these newly discovered enemies within. It was as if, as Ghassan Hage has recently put it, there were now manifold 'borders' internal to the nation rather than around its edges to be patrolled against the non-Christian, non-western, 'third-world looking' outsiders who might endanger the good life from within (Hage 1998; 2002). The Prime Minister's appeal during the Gulf War for 'us' to be 'tolerant' only served to underline who was in a position to tolerate and who was to be magnanimously tolerated (or not) (Hage 1991). 'Tabloid' media, and especially their 'personalities' on commercial television and talkback radio, demanded that Arab-background migrant leaders declare their allegiance to Australia and that they simultaneously renounce and apologise for the evils of Saddam Hussein.

Can these latter verbal attacks, these media discourses of what amount to racial vilification, be causally linked to the physical attacks just outlined? The case for such connections would be strengthened if a repeat cycle of this sort of media attack were accompanied by another round of racist hate crime in the streets, shops and workplaces. The case would be further fortified if similar ideological elements could be found between the attacks of the tabloid and talkback rants and the attacks of the street. If this similarity were repeated in more than one cycle of xenophobia and racism, then the case would be even stronger. All of these conditions obtained in Australia in 2001 — before and after the airborne terror of 11 September.

Having experienced the fire last time, the Community Relations Commission for a Multicultural New South Wales established a bilingual (English and Arabic) Anti-Racism Hotline as early as 12 September 2001, to enable persons experiencing racial vilification to report such incidents and to be referred to other agencies as appropriate. Already by the end of September, the Hotline had logged well over 300 calls (Brown 2001:2); by the time it finished operation on 9 November, there were about 400 responses recorded. Another such Hotline was opened immediately after the Bali bombing in October 2002 (Community Relations Commission 2002). It needs to be recognised that the number of incidents actually tallied in this way is a measure only of the 'tip of the iceberg': those with knowledge of the Hotline and with the most motivation and means to complain. Other official bodies, such as the New South Wales Anti-Discrimination Board (ADB), also received and recorded a plethora of such complaints, and community organisations, too, such as the Sydney-based Australian Arabic Communities Council (AACC) and the Lebanese Muslim Association kept logs of telephone and mail complaints of racist attacks. The Melbourne office of the Australian Arabic Council (AAC) has maintained a Racism Register since the time of the Gulf War, and also reported a rapid and twenty-fold rise in the rate of incidence of anti-Arab racial vilification immediately after 11 September 2001. This organisation itself received ten threatening letters and 14 abusive telephone calls in just a few days following the plane attacks in the United States. One normally quiet community welfare office alone had 20-odd instances of racist harassment by phone (Australian Arabic Council 2001).

So just as during the Gulf War Arab and Muslim communities in particular experienced a marked rise in the incidence of racial harassment and attacks (HREOC 1991:362); community organisations across Australia reported a similar increase immediately after the airliner attacks in the United States on 11 September and also after the bombing in Bali on 12 October 2002. This upsurge was widely reported in the media (Jopson 2001; Brown 2001; *PM* 2001; Burke 2001; *Daily Telegraph* 17/10/02:11; Lipari 2002:6). In each case, there was an intensification of existing, ongoing and everyday forms and patterns of vilification. The AAC's records of an increase of twenty times virtually overnight indicates an existing base level of incidence of such attacks and an underlying tendency waiting for an immediate cause to realise it. The range of types of racist attack, moreover, remains continuous: only the intensity surges.

The pattern repeated

At the time of the Gulf War, the brunt of racial attacks was disproportionately borne by women, notably Muslim women and girls wearing the hijab (Newell 1990:21). This pattern continued following the events of September 2001 and October 2002 (Burke & AAP 2001:8; Rath 2001; Jopson 2001:18; *Daily Telegraph* 16/9/01:9; *Daily Telegraph* 26/11/01:13; AACC Racism Register 2001; Poynting 2002; Donald 21/11/02). For instance, a middle-aged housewife recorded on the Australian Arabic Communities Council Racism Register on 17 September 2001 an attack by 'a group of Australians' on her and her daughter in a south-west Sydney supermarket:

> She had the veil taken off her and her daughter's head. Then [they] had dragged both of them to the floor and beaten them up, at the same time yelling obscenities. The daughter's arm was broken (AACC Racism Register 2001).

A number of the recent attacks were explicitly sexualised, involving, for example, indecent exposure and offensive sexual suggestions. For example, on 17 September in a south-west suburb of Sydney a young 'Australian' male on a bicycle confronted S, a woman, between 45 and 60 years old, wearing hijab:

> She was coming back from the shop when she was stopped by someone on a bike. He asked her a question, which she thought he is asking her about a place. She referred him to the shop, then he said, 'What I want is to fuck you', and he showed her his penis. The woman now [finds it] difficult to go outside the house. (AACC Racism Register).

HREOC (1991:362) notes that, in 1991, 'There were also reports of violence and harassment against people of Middle Eastern origin who are neither Arab or Muslim'. The recent round of attacks included assaults on people who were neither, such as Sikh men wearing turbans; and others who were not Muslim, such as painted swastikas and racist graffiti and arson attacks on Orthodox Christian churches that bore signs in Arabic script such as in Western Sydney's Merrylands (Rath 2001; *Daily Telegraph* 14/9/01:8). In Lidcombe, a Russian Orthodox church was vandalised with racist slogans, according to the *Telegraph* (15/9/01:10).

Schools, places of worship, workplaces, shops and streets were all sites of racist attack. Vilification came by internet as well as radio, telephone and mail. A busload of Muslim schoolchildren was attacked with stones and bottles in Brisbane. An Islamic school in Adelaide at first hired 24-hour security guards and later was forced to close down for about a fortnight (ABC 12/9/01; Phillips 2001; *PM* 14/9/01). A school in Melbourne's south-east was graffitied with 'death to Muslim scum', and a 16 year old male student was verbally threatened there. The AAC's Racism Register records that a schoolboy was set upon by 3 men 'of Australian descent' aged 20–25, and had his legs slashed and was punched and kicked while racist abuse was shouted at him (AAC 2001). Australia was far from unique in this respect: five schoolchildren with Arab-sounding names were assaulted in Oakville, Ontario, for example; and Kuwaiti embassy workers had to counsel terrified Kuwaiti children subjected to vilification in schools across the United States. A mosque was subjected to an arson attack in Kuraby, Queensland. Another mosque in Mirrabooka, Western Australia, was defiled with human excrement (Burke & AAP 2001:8; AAP 13/9/01). Some 1000 worshippers were evacuated from a Turkish mosque in western Sydney's Auburn after a bomb threat on 14 September (*Daily Telegraph* 15/9/01:10). Similar attacks on mosques were also occurring overseas: incendiaries were also thrown at mosques in Chicago and Montreal (*Guardian Unlimited* 13/9/01; *PM* 14/9/01). While George Bush visited a Washington mosque 'to calm anti-Muslim sentiment', and Prince Charles later did the same in east London, Prime Minister John Howard declared himself 'too busy' to accept an invitation to a mosque in Sydney[2] (Clark 2001:2; *Sunday Telegraph* 25/11/01:89). Like former Prime Minister Bob Hawke who had called for (White Australian) tolerance towards Arab Australians during the Gulf War, Mr Howard 'appealed to Australians to show tolerance to Australian-Lebanese and other people of Arab heritage in their midst' (Grattan 2001:6).

The Internet was not immune from anti-Muslim and anti-Arab racism. In a discriminatory (and probably illegal) reaction to the political climate, a number of private sector employers proscribed Muslim employees from sending or receiving emails in Arabic and from accessing Arabic websites (*Daily Telegraph* 9/10/01:7). By 20 September, the level of racial hatred expressed on 'Sydney's most trafficked Web site', Ninemsm, became so intense that its online discussion board was closed down, though a censored condolence book remained available (Needham 2001:3).

The spate of racist attacks continued long after September 2001. For example, the Melbourne Magistrate's Court was told that on 6 March 2002 a South Yarra man had threatened a Muslim taxi driver with a 26 cm knife and forced him to drive around Melbourne while he scolded him over his religion and the September 11 attacks (Calvert 2002). It bears repeating that this outbreak of racial vilification was but an upsurge, albeit a dramatic one, against a background of anti-Arab and anti-Muslim racist attacks that existed in Australia well before 11 September. As Ghassan Hage (2001:241–2) puts it, with the recent racism directed at Middle Eastern 'boat people' and so-called 'Lebanese rapist gangs', '"September 11" happened right after "June, July and August 11, 12 and 13"'.

Again after the Bali bombing on 12 October 2002, mosques were attacked in Australia; a Muslim cleric in western Sydney was even besieged in his house by an angry and violent mob (Cameron 16/10/02:3). The office of a Liberal-voting, cricket-playing, small businessman Muslim Australian of Tanzanian origin suffered a smashed window, and his household was the subject of an arson episode after he applied to build an Islamic meeting hall in middle-class Baulkham Hills (Cameron 28/11/02).

Women in hijab were once more singled out for assault and vilification (*Daily Telegraph* 17/10/02; *Sydney Morning Herald* 17/10/02; Donald 21/11/02). A letter-writer to the *Sydney Morning Herald*, M Ferrie, recounted:

> I was on the train when the peace was suddenly shattered. From the other end of the carriage a booming male voice was verbally abusing someone at length, apparently blaming him, or her, for the bombing in Bali ... When I went to get off the train, there, in the end compartment, was a young woman, trembling, and being studiously ignored by the other passengers. She was wearing a headscarf (17/10/02:16).

The vilifiers included fundamentalist Christian MP, Rev. Fred Nile, who even proposed in the NSW Parliament that women be banned from wearing the Islamic head-to-toe chador in public gatherings, to prevent the possibility of concealing terrorist weapons (*AM* 21/11/02; ABC News Online; *PM* 21/11/02; Riley & Burke 22/11/02:1). ABC journalist Annie White suggested that shopping-centre santas might share the same fate (*PM* 21/11/02). Nile later said that only 'extremist' and not 'normal' Muslim women wore the chador (Riley 23–24/11/02:10). One Nation MP David Oldfield joined the controversy, objecting to the presence of a veiled woman in the public gallery of the NSW Parliament, and calling for body searches of women in such traditional dress (Hornery & Wyld 25/11/02:18). ABC reporter, Annie White (*PM* 21/11/02; see also Riley 23–24/11/02:10; Howard 21/10/02) recorded Prime Minister Howard's dog-whistling 'apparent equivocation' thus:

> JOHN HOWARD: I don't have a clear response to what Fred's put, I mean I like Fred, and I don't always agree with him, but you know, Fred speaks for the views of a lot of people.
>
> On the other hand, I feel it's very important at the moment that the Islamic people don't feel they're being singled out.

The *Sydney Morning Herald*'s front page the following day (Riley & Burke 22/11/02:1) reported more equivocation from the PM's press office, 'clarifying' that Mr Howard 'neither ruled in his support [for the ban] nor ruled it out'.

'The PM stole my boat people'

We have discussed in Chapter One the moral panic about 'boat people' which reached a crescendo in 2001 with the 'Tampa Crisis'. Here dog-whistle politics came to the fore. On the day the Tampa departed from Australian waters, an 'e-talk' letter to the editor of the *Telegraph* by a reader from Queensland quipped, 'Sorry, Pauline, we don't need you any more, John Howard is doing your job' (*Daily Telegraph* 4/9/01:19).

The One Nation party founded by Pauline Hanson espouses a zero nett migration policy and links this ideologically with stopping illegal immigration:

> Economically immigration is unsustainable and socially, if continued as is, will lead to an ethnically divided Australia. Current policy is encouraging large numbers of illegal migrants and it is time Australia, while recognising the contribution made by migrants in the past, send to the world the message that mass immigration has passed its use by date (Pauline Hanson's One Nation 2001).

One Nation and their supporters oppose immigration by those who are not 'assimilable'; they rail against immigrants who keep to themselves, remain different and form enclaves in 'ethnic ghettoes'. They claim that immigration produces increases in crime, that many immigrants are lawless, and that alien lawbreakers should be deported:

> It is no good having a rich country if it is falling apart because of violence, gang warfare and ethnic separatism. We do not want little ethnic islands separated from the rest of the Australian community. We do want migrants who can integrate into Australian society, not congregate in just a few areas.

> If I am allowed to decide who can come into my home, we Australians should be allowed to decide who can come and live in our country.[3] Migrant crime gangs have flourished over the last 20 years, with drugs and money laundering, something we rarely used to hear about.
>
> ... The present situation is just not good enough. Criminals convicted of serious crimes should be deported if not Australian citizens and, if they are, there should be harsher penalties to deter this sort of crime (Hanson 1996).

It is One Nation policy that refugees be offered only temporary protection, rather than given the right to immigrate (Pauline Hanson's One Nation 2001). Amnesty International argued in 1999 that the federal government's Border Protection Bill and new refugee visa regulations introduced at this time in fact 'mirror ... Pauline Hanson's policies and receive the support of the Opposition and the press' (Head 1999). Robert Manne (10/6/02:15) likewise refers to the government's temporary protection visa policy as 'Hanson inspired'.

During the 2001 election campaign, Ms Hanson herself claimed that the Prime Minister had embraced her policies (Scott 31/10/01:10), in turning away boats of asylum-seekers and sending 'boat people' to other countries:

> I am pleased to see they have listened to what I've been saying.
> ... A lot of people are actually saying I'm John Howard's adviser because he's picking up a lot of the policies and issues I have raised and spoken about over the years (Clennell 2001).

Howard wanted to whistle up support from One Nation supporters; in fact, he probably shares many of their views. Certainly, in defending Pauline Hanson's right to make racist public statements, he has called them 'an accurate reflection of what people feel' (cited by Kitney 23–24/11/02:10). Notwithstanding the recent media opprobrium when an Opposition spokesman recalled the matter to public attention (Kitney 22/11/02:13), John Howard in 1988 deliberately made controversial comments about too much Asian immigration to Australia. As Laurie Oakes (13/11/01:18) reminds us, Howard himself devised the slogan 'One Australia' long before Pauline Hanson's 'One Nation', and stated at a Young Liberal conference in 1988: 'Our national interest will be served by a migration program which preserves and promotes the unity and cohesion of Australian society'. Only recently, Howard declared that immigrants 'must understand that when they come to Australia, they make a decision to accept, they can't cherry pick the Australian way of life' (Banham 25/11/02:4). While Howard sought to garner the votes of One Nation sympathisers, he could not afford to alienate those of well-meaning white liberals (nor the 'ethnic vote') by explicitly and unambiguously espousing the views which Pauline Hanson expresses. His response to them, therefore, was akin to that of a rightwing talkback radio announcer when taking an on-air call from a rabid racist: allowing them to rave on radio and then (ever so slightly, equivocally) distancing himself by declaring the views interesting, not ones that all would share, of course, but ones strongly and sincerely held by many in the community who have a right to express them (*Media Report* 7/11/02). Dog-whistle politics and dog-whistle journalism go hand in glove.

'Jihad declared on Australia'

On 1 November 2001, during the US/UK bombardment of Afghanistan, a persistent Australian reporter goaded the Taliban ambassador to Pakistan into saying that Australia would be included in their holy war being declared on their attackers. (Some days earlier, the same spokesman had scoffed at the suggestion that Australian involvement had any importance, remarking that the superpower arraigned against his country hardly needed such help.) In the federal election campaign becoming coloured 'khaki' (Hogg 2002; Simms 2002:99–103), this became front-page fodder for the tabloids and a fillip for the campaign of the incumbent government (McPhedran 2/11/01:1). The same page one of the *Daily Telegraph* which bore the headline, 'Jihad declared on Australia', also had the headline, 'Suspected terror camp raided in NSW'. Now 'we' were at war, there was also an enemy within (Callinan, Targett & Marx 2/11/01:3).

Divided or questionable loyalties can become tantamount to treason in times of war or crisis. Over a decade ago, during the Gulf War, there was widespread popular worrying about whether 'we' had traitors in our midst. Saddam Hussein was the then current 'face of evil', before most Australians had heard of Osama bin Laden, and many national worriers held fears that Iraqi immigrants — or perhaps all Arabs? — or was it Muslims? — in Australia were harbouring secret support or sympathy for the enemy: a fifth column allowed in by non-European and non-Christian immigration and indulged by multiculturalism. Arab Australian community leaders had microphones shoved in their faces by self-righteous media 'personalities', accompanied by demands that they pledge their true allegiance to Australia and give such commitment on behalf of their communities. And the more the well-tamed of the community leaders performed this trick, and the ratbag misfit ones rejected the demands, the more white-thinking Australians just *knew* there was ingratitude, disloyalty and indeed treachery in these communities. Iraqi, Arab, Muslim: it doesn't much matter in the confused logic of racism.

Such media vilification virtually demands heavy-handed action by the State against the 'enemy within' (Centre for Contemporary Cultural Studies 1982:23), and incites vigilante style violence and individual acts of racist hatred. At the same time, the State's repressive measures invite 'where there's smoke there's fire' arguments: why should people object to covert surveillance, ongoing harassment, secret police, heavily armed dawn raids, and the like, for 'our' protection, if they have nothing to hide? Moreover, State terror of this sort seems to be interpreted by outraged pikestaffers as some sort of moral licence for their own violent racial attacks.

In late September 2001, the Australian Security Intelligence Organisation (ASIO), accompanied by the Australian Federal Police (AFP) and NSW police with 'intimate local knowledge', raided 30-odd suburban households and workplaces in south-western Sydney. Some of the families raided stated that they brought the media with them (Trad 2001; Kidman 30/9/01:4–5). Certainly, the front page of the *Sun-Herald* of 30 September had a large front-page colour photograph taken over a suburban paling fence of such a raid being conducted, with two uniformed federal policemen talking to a man and a woman, apparently residents, while a man in a dark suit talked on a mobile phone. The page carried the banner, 'War on Terror Exclusive' and the headline, 'Sydney raid: Suburban home searched as ASIO and police hunt Bin Laden connections' (*Sun-Herald* 30/9/01:1). The faces of the residents and the besuited officer were pixelled out, but not in the identical but smaller photograph, which additionally identified the suburb, accompanying Miranda Devine's column in the same newspaper on 11 November. Headed 'Where security counts, tolerance goes two ways', this opinion piece encouraged Muslims to cooperate with authorities in 'having to contend with their homes being invaded at dawn by armed police' for it 'helps make us all a little safer' (Devine 11/11/01:28).

Devine explains eloquently why it is those targeted who must pay 'the price of such vigilance'. Citizenship does *not* go 'two ways':

> The perpetrators of the September 11 attacks were young Middle-Eastern Muslim men. Bin Laden's followers are young Middle-Eastern Muslim men. So it is young men of Middle-Eastern Muslim background who will be targeted in Sydney, many of them Australian citizens, who were born here (Devine 11/11/01:28).

Whatever other purposes were intended, the raids were clearly meant to be a public gesture. They were also plainly designed to intimidate. In one case, 'five heavily armed officers stormed the house', forced a man to lie on the floor at gunpoint, and conducted a body search. His wife was escorted downstairs by a male and a female AFP officer, without time to cover her body adequately according to her religion. The house was thoroughly searched. The man was told, 'You have small children, you would not like for them to not see you for ten years'. (Another man was similarly told, 'You have a beautiful daughter, I believe that you want to keep your daughter happy'). He was told that they would be back and would be searching again. The family was traumatised by the incident. The photograph of the wife appeared in the newspaper, and the couple found this picture stuck on their window, and the windows of their house were spat upon over the next few days. At the time of the interview, they were seeking to rent a house elsewhere, but fearful of not being able to do so, now that their pictures had been published in the press (Trad 2001).

The *Sun-Herald*, in pages tagged with the 'war on terror' caption, dutifully characterised the raids as 'the first proof that the US's global anti-terrorist campaign has reached Australian shores' (Kidman 30/9/01:4). The reporter affirmed that his newspaper was on hand to observe one of the raids at a home unit in Lakemba. The woman resident, a mother of two young children, complained (as did others raided) that a gun was put to her head and she was made to lie on the floor. She said 'police turned the residence "upside down" and interrogated her in front of her family'. 'Senior government staff' denied that the firearm had been 'used' (Kidman 30/9/ 01:4; *ABC News Online* 2/10/01). The *Sunday Telegraph* added that the raids were 'backed by armed teams of the State Protection Group' and that there were dozens such raids around the country (Watson 2001:15). The article was similarly signposted, 'War against terror', accompanied by a little picture of the United States flag.

The reasons people were targeted for the raids, apart from the 'ethnic profiling' suggested by Devine, may have included, according to those raided in various cases: spending two and a half months in Pakistan the previous year when returning from a haj; spending five months at a Qur'an school in Pakistan many years ago when learning the Book by heart, not having left Australia since; travelling to Syria to visit a sick father after his stroke six weeks earlier, and staying for one week, not having exited Australia for years prior to this; and simply being active in Muslim organisations (including youth organisations) and having to answer questions about whether one could fly a plane or had studied aviation (neither of which was the case) (Trad 2001; *Daily Telegraph* 5/10/01:9).

Some two years later, there has not been a single arrest or charge arising from these raids. Computers, papers, bank records, passports and mobile phones were confiscated. Cash was also taken. None of these was returned, and officials do not answer phone calls at the number they left (Trad 2001; Kremmer 2002). In terms of intelligence-gathering, such methods can only be seen as ham-fisted. In terms of intimidation, social control, repression, they may well prove quite functional. One ASIO officer left an inter-rogated man a card with a contact name and number, in case he should come by 'any information as to who is behind the bombing'. This was after his home was 'visited' and he was obliged to be interviewed at his workplace in front of colleagues, during which interview his daughter was mentioned in what the man took to be thinly disguised threats. One Muslim community member, after his home was raided, said to the ASIO officer, ' I thought you had come to discuss ways to protect the Muslim community, as the Muslim community has been attacked, mosques have been damaged ...' and so on. The officer replied that this was a secondary concern (Trad 2001).

'This is going to exacerbate problems the community has been facing since the terrorist attacks', said Ahmad Ali Mehboob, Chief Executive of the Australian Federation of Islamic Councils (Labi 2001:3); and so it did.

'Hunt for faces of terror'

On 30 October 2002, eighteen days after the Bali bombings, ASIO and Australian federal police operatives again conducted a series of raids on a score of suburban homes of Muslim citizens — this time mainly Australians of Indonesian origin in Sydney, Perth and Melbourne (Karvelas & Chulov 30/10/02; Dunn 1/11/02; Powell

& Chulov 31/10/02:1; Morris & Cameron 31/10/02:1; Morris, Cameron & Cornford 1/11/02:7; Banham 1/11/02:1). Under coloured identification drawings of suspects in the Kuta attacks, the *Australian* had the front-page headline, 'Hunt for faces of terror', followed by 'ASIO raids target JI sleeper cell' (Powell & Chulov 31/10/02:1). Perhaps 'sleepers' are families who are slumbering in bed at 5am when the security organisation and police break down their doors and burst in with machine-guns. Certainly, as with the 2001 raids, there have (at least 11 months later, as this book goes to press) been no charges laid and no arrests made on terrorism-related matters — though there was an arrest over a visa infringement. Neighbours of one home raided at dawn in Perth's working-class suburb of Thornlie reported the timber door being splintered with sledge hammers and windows being smashed by a gun-bearing squad wearing black helmets, balaclavas, goggles and flak jackets, issuing from two four-wheel drive vehicles (*Daily Telegraph* 31/10/02:7). A 17 year old, whose home in Perth was invaded, told of the trauma she experienced along with her three brothers and sisters, one only four years old, who 'saw balaclava-clad officers thrust their machineguns in [their] faces' (Dunn 31/10/02):

> We heard windows breaking, including my bedroom window, we were all sleeping when these men with sub-machineguns came barging into our house ... They pushed my dad on to the floor, they handcuffed him and one of the police officers stepped on his ear and told him not to move, he cannot hear properly out of that ear. They grabbed my mum, they told us to get on the floor and pointed guns at us' (Yulyani Suparta, cited in Dunn 31/10/02).

In a simultaneous operation in Sydney's Belmore, some fifteen operatives confiscated mobile phones, computers, disks, passports, bank statements, and personal documents such as marriage and birth certificates, just as in the raids the previous year, along with — bizarrely — a copy of the *Daily Telegraph* reporting the Bali attack (Morris & Rowlands 31/10/02:7). One Sydney family was 'effectively held prisoner for five hours' (ABC News Online 31/10/02) according to those held captive. In bursting into the home of a businessman in Greenacre in south-west Sydney, one of the agents said to him, 'You are one of JI'. The man said that he had not heard of Jemaah Islamiah, the group being blamed for the Bali terrorist attacks, until the Kuta nightclub bombings occurred. ASIO seized computers, documents and business records (Morris, Cameron & Cornford 1/11/02:7). A man whose home in Sydney's south-western Lakemba was also raided by some fifteen officers with guns and a sledgehammer, said that he had no connections whatever with Jemaah Islamiah though he had attended two or three speeches made by alleged JI leader in Sydney (Karvelas 31/10/02:7; Morris & Rowlands 31/10/02:7). ABC Radio's *AM* program (31/10/02) reported that 'What appears to have been a key to the raids ... is that men in the target families had been to lectures given by Abu Bakar Ba'asyir, the alleged spiritual leader of Jemaah Islamiah, suspected in the Bali bombing'.

The front page of the *Sydney Morning Herald* of 5 November had an article telling how the previous week's security service and federal police raids were justified by the seizure of the Muslim equivalent of a parish newsletter denouncing Hollywood and promiscuity, laden with double meanings and expressing sympathy towards Osama bin Laden (Morris & Thompson 5/11/02:1). The newsletter was called *Al Haq* which 'translates as Truth'. So, incidentally, did *Pravda*. Just as many labelled as 'communists' and 'fellow travellers' during the Cold War had not the slightest connection with the Communist Party nor with Stalinism, so not everyone branded a Muslim terrorist (or terrorist supporter or sympathiser) will prove to be one. Most will not, as in the armed ASIO raids in western Sydney over a year earlier, when citizens were forced to the floor and had guns pointed at their heads — a perfectly proportionate precaution, some will say, in the 'war on terror', a small price (for others) to pay for the defence of freedom, civilisation and democracy. Nevertheless, the suppression of 'terrorists' serves an important function in the maintenance of the prevailing hegemony. The effect goes well beyond those raided. It, too, is a form of terror, as is the gentler form of persuasion in the form of fear of the ubiquitous enemy, propagated by the repressive arm of the State and purveyed by its ideological apparatuses, above all the mogul-dominated media and those who mirror them.

The Moir cartoon in the *Sydney Morning Herald* of 1 November makes the point eloquently. A family is in bed as the security forces break in with sledgehammers and automatic weapons; 'Don't be alarmed', their leader shouts. The cartoon is captioned, 'Terrorism in Australia'.

As with the raids of the previous year, the widely publicised appearance of strong and decisive action seems to have been a major goal of the State forces in these swoops. The President of the Council for Civil Liberties, Terry O'Gorman, said:

> For police and ASIO to turn up in combat gear, heavily armed, breaking open gates and so on is simply a stunt ... There is absolutely no justification for the public way in which this raid was done (ABC News Online 31/10/02).

Intimidation of the communities concerned was certainly a major function of the action. According to the *Age* (1/11/02), Muslim leaders said the raids had 'caused hysteria and fear that anyone in the community could be targeted'. The *Age* quoted Sheikh Fehmi Naji, Imam of Preston Mosque, as saying that many Muslims were upset about the blaming of their community.

Governments — federal and state — were unapologetic. Foreign Minister Alexander Downer, for example, said in an ABC Radio interview:

> Well, obviously most Muslim homes in Australia are not going to be raided. I mean there are hundreds of thousands of Muslims in Australia. This won't affect hundreds of thousands of people. There are a handful of people that the intelligence services, the police have some particular concerns about and you've got to remember that we have now proscribed in Australia Jemaah

Islamiah and where there might be links with an organisation like that, we have just got to, in the interests of the country's security, do what we can. If you know that there is a threat to security, or you're worried that there might be a threat to security, you can't just turn your back on it and ignore it. You have to be effective, maybe even a little ruthless in addressing it, you really must. It's all been done within our law and, well, I think the Australian public expect us to be tough on the issue of security and we are being (*AM* 1/11/02).

Though these state actions were claimed to be within existing law, federal and state governments saw the need for further legislation effecting anti-terrorist measures. The *Australian Security Intelligence Organisation Legislation Amendment (Terrorism) Bill* 2002 provides for the capacity hitherto unknown under Australian Commonwealth law to arrest a person merely for interrogation. According to Justice John Dowd, a judge in the Supreme Court of NSW, people could be held for a maximum of seven days under the pending new legislation, and when released, 'can be detained on a new warrant as they stand in the lobby of the building as they leave' (*Lateline* 26/11/02a). The whole family of a 'person who may have information that may assist in preventing terrorist attacks or in prosecuting those who have committed a terrorist offence' could be detained in this manner (*Sydney Morning Herald* 28/11/02:12; *Lateline* 26/11/02a). 'People of interest' may be so held for a week under the legislation, without charge, without legal representation, without appearing in court, and without the right of silence (Morris 27/11/02:9; *Lateline* 26/11/02b). The 'safeguards' regarding the issue of warrants were virtually valueless, in Dowd's experience:

All of the so-called safeguards are there means it doesn't mean to need a very intelligent officer of ASIO to put together a case, quite well meaning. It may well be that he or she believes the material that's put before them to put out a case for a warrant to be issued ... they almost invariably are, not always (*Lateline* 26/11/02a).

Justice Dowd argued that in 'an atmosphere of hysteria', 'Muslims stood to become the first victims of the new laws' (Morris 27/11/02:9). Terry O'Gorman, of the Australian Council for Civil Liberties, concurred:

> I think there's a very big risk that there'll be racial stereotyping in respect of these new ASIO laws. Keep in mind the warrants are not issued by a court. They're issued by the Attorney-General, who's a politician (*Lateline* 26/11/02b).

Similar and related legislation was introduced in the NSW Parliament by the Labor government of Bob Carr. This politician responded to the criticism of the civil libertarians and the International Commission of Jurors represented by John Dowd: 'Can't John Dowd get it into his thick head that Bali occurred, that we have a problem here, that these threats are real?' (*Lateline* 26/11/02b). Of course, conservative newspaper columnist, Miranda Devine (28/11/02:13), chimed in:

> The way some people in Australia have been carrying on about new anti-terrorism laws you would think our government is more of a threat to the citizenry than the terrorists who murdered more than 80 Australians in Bali. For civil libertarians, human rights groups, lawyers and assorted interest groups, it is as if Bali and September 11 never happened.

Innocent Muslims targeted as terrorists (and terrorist supporters and sympathisers) would just have to bear the imposition on their human rights for the good of 'us' all, argued Devine, just as she had after the previous year's raids[4] (Devine 11/11/01).

Premier Carr, however, prefers to dog-whistle the same tune at a higher, more subtle pitch. Thus he equivocates:

> Mr Carr warned against isolating the Australian Muslim community. He said making the Islamic community, particularly young people, feel isolated, would 'produce conditions of paranoia' which would produce 'a recruiting ground for extremists' (Banham 1/11/02:7).

At the same time, he endorsed the raids: 'I think ASIO and the Federal Police would be criticised if they weren't investigating people with alleged [Jemaah Islamiah] links. I feel somewhat reassured that they've done that ...' (Banham 1/11/02:7). ASIO are not targeting Muslims; they are targeting terrorists: just as the cops are not targeting Lebanese; they are targeting criminals.

Mr Carr announced that Australians with 'suspicious lifestyles' ought to expect attention from the State's security apparatus. Civil liberties would have to be sacrificed. Those who had written pamphlets praising bin Laden or had published websites bearing his picture ought to be under investigation. Yet, the *Telegraph* put it well: 'Mr Carr warned against singling out Muslim Australians for the wave of terror'. Because of respect for their human rights, their civil liberties? No: 'Because that will drive young Muslims over time into the hands of extremists' (English & Morris 20/11/02:5).

Conclusion

This chapter has traced a number of cycles of attacks on Muslim and Middle-Eastern background people in Australia. These included racist media panics which criminalise whole communities, racist vilification for political advantage, physical assaults and property damage such as arson which are arguably provoked by the foregoing, and police and security service raids which trample on civil rights, just as the human rights of refugees are being quashed with the aid of cynical political opportunism and the manipulation of the media.

The burden of this chapter has been to demonstrate the common ideological patterns and to infer the existence of causal connections, however complex, multi-causal and indirect, between populist politics exploiting xenophobia; in symbiosis with manipulated and largely supine media; and repressive arms of the state responding to and dependent upon both of these. Thus raids at dawn are conducted by secret services in conjunction with tabloid journalists. Politically opportunist and sensationalist paper-selling 'attacks' in headlines lead to and give ideological licence to racist attacks in shops, streets and workplaces. Both these types of attack took place in Australia before 11 September 2001, which marked but a dramatic upsurge in such incidents. Nor was this the first such rise. The recurrence after 12 October 2002, sadly, will not be the last.

Notes

1 Indeed, according to the Executive Council of Australian Jewry, talkback racism targeting Muslims has been so prevalent since 11 September 2001, that there has been a marked decrease in anti-semitic racism on the airwaves, with Muslims bearing the brunt of radio racism (Burke 25/11/02: 5).

2 Some five weeks after September 11, however, on the very day he announced Australia's joining the military intervention in Afghanistan, the Prime Minister did belatedly visit the Preston mosque in Victoria, 'to extend the hand of "Australian mateship" to a community under siege' (Gordon 7/11/02). There he told Sheikh Al Imam that Australians 'have no argument with his community' (*PM* 17/10/01).

3 Compare John Howard's slogan during the 2001 election campaign: 'We will decide who comes to this country and the circumstances in which they come'.

4 Devine used here exactly the same logic that she had earlier deployed when she argued that whole Muslim communities blamed for rapes in which they had no part, had to accept the shame for the good of 'us' all:

> Yes, it is unfair that the vast bulk of law-abiding Lebanese Muslim boys and men should be smeared by association. But their temporary discomfort may be necessary so that the powerful social tool of shame is applied to the families and communities that nurtured the rapists, gave them succour and brought them up with such hatred of Australia's dominant culture and contempt for its women (Devine 14/7/02: 15).

6

'Our shame':
ethnic community leadership and self-criminalisation

In the first two chapters of this book we analysed the construction of an 'Arab Other' in contemporary Australian political discourse and media representations. This involved not just the conflation of diverse groups into a homogeneous category, but also the racialisation of crime and the criminalisation of the various cultures seen to be described by that category. These processes rested on a perception that crime and violence are an endemic, even pathological feature of those cultures. In previous chapters we saw how this frame was largely shared even by sympathetic accounts of the situation of young non-English speaking background people, and how it informed 'good news' stories through what has been called 'dog-whistling', which we extended to include media discussion. We have not said much, however, about how communities of Arab or Middle Eastern or Muslim ancestry responded to this construction. In exploring how criminal acts of specific individuals and groups become emblematic of whole ethnic communities, a central facet must be the ways those communities, and especially their leaders, respond to and negotiate the symbolic processes at work. This chapter is a case study of the responses by the political, religious and cultural leaders of the various Arab or Muslim groups, and especially what is seen to be the 'Lebanese community' and their role in the criminalisation process in the years since the killing of Edward Lee in south-west Sydney in October 1998.

Constructing an Other, like any form of symbolic practice, is never just a case of ideological representation; it involves *addressing* particular groups of people. An act of representation — as an act of communication — speaks to a certain type of reader or viewer in its mode of address, as contemporary communication and media theory has demonstrated. Yet in the act of addressing them, a message implicitly *inscribes* specific subjects in which certain readers or viewers recognise themselves, it *hails* them, it gets their attention and draws them into the act of communication. In doing this, it calls them into being. The mechanism of this process is best described by the concept of interpellation introduced by Louis Althusser (1971), and widely deployed since then in cultural analysis. Interpellation is basically a communicative act that involves the positioning of a person or a group of persons in a particular power location and the construction of their subjectivity according to the interest of the interpellator (or interpellating discourse). If the interpellator is a representative of the dominant social order, its terms of interpellating subordinate groups will be subservient to the interest of that order.

A problem with Althusser's notion of interpellation, however, is that it does not deal with the process whereby social actors respond to the act of interpellation — in Althusser's theory it is required structurally, so it tends to be assumed. There is, of course, no guarantee that the 'right' person will receive the message, and there is no guarantee that they will 'decode' it in the way that the message is intended. However, the inscription of a reader or viewer tends to circumscribe the kinds of messages received, and circumscribes the extent to which these messages can be accepted, negotiated or opposed (Hall 1993). In a complex, mediated culture like Australia's, different audiences process the same coded message in different ways. As we saw in the previous chapter, the construction of an Arab Other is largely directed towards a white community, tapping deep reservoirs of racism. However, these representations also address the communities that are being imagined, and especially their political and cultural leaders.

We argue that, in responding to the ways they are interpellated by political and media discourses during the 'ethnic gang' crisis and the recent local and international events discussed in this book, leading members of Lebanese communities participated, by and large, in the processes of racialisation and criminalisation. There was no single response, of course, just as there is no single 'Lebanese community'. As we have shown elsewhere, this 'community' and its leadership are themselves fashioned in response to the socio-cultural, economic and political forces at play in Australia, and especially in relation to the structures of political patronage that emerge out of the model of multiculturalism arising from the Galbally Report in Australia in the 1970s. Fundamental to the recent experience of this 'community' and its leaders was a sense of victimisation which allowed for a 'community of suffering' to arise as a rallying point and point of resistance. At the same time, this network of alliances is strung across significant differences — of national, regional and cultural origin, religion, class and political allegiance — and is also caught in the paradox of community politics, beholden to political patrons 'above' and claiming to voice the interests of those 'below' in the desire to attain the recognition of both political authorities and community constituencies (Collins, Noble, Poynting & Tabar 2000:199–222).

Unsurprisingly, community leaders have responded in different ways to current events. Some leaders rejected the burden of community responsibility for these crimes. Yet many responses betrayed a complicity with the racialisation of crime by the dominant culture under pressure from government and media, who criticised the leaders for not facing up to 'reality'. These responses range from outright 'self-criminalisation' — or the acceptance of community blame — to attempts to blame others within the category of the Arab Other, to attempts to blame 'Australian society'. Across these divergent strategies there is a common tendency to echo the dominant paradigm of the 'cultural' explanation of criminal acts that frames the social understandings of these events, and to reproduce the way of seeing which allows crime to be seen as emanating from cultural background. In doing this, prominent community leaders accept the location of the Lebanese migrant community in a subordinate position and the shaping of its subjectivity by the dominant white culture.

Blaming the community

We have, both in *Kebabs* and in the early chapters of this book, detailed the ways in which crime has become increasingly identified with particular ethnic groups, and especially with those of 'Middle Eastern' or Muslim backgrounds. We do not want to go over that ground in detail, but it is useful to return to this material and begin to think of the ways in which it addresses not just a dominant white culture in Australia, but also interpellates Australian citizens within the targeted communities.

Soon after the 1998 fatal stabbing in Punchbowl and the drive-by shooting at a police station also in south-west Sydney, Premier Bob Carr and the then Police Commissioner Peter Ryan identified the presumed perpetrators as being members of a 'Lebanese gang' (English & Walsh 3/11/98:4). In 2000–2001, after the gang rapes and during the subsequent trials, politicians, senior police and influential journalists again consistently referred to the offenders as 'Lebanese Muslims' belonging to a 'Lebanese gang of rapists' (Chulov 18–19/8/01:1). The identification of the offenders by their ethnicity was the first step towards the broad social acceptance of the racialisation of these crimes. Talkback callers and letter writers in mainstream newspapers provided abundant evidence indicating the extent to which Lebanese ethnicity was implicated in criminal activities. A large number of letters accusing Lebanese culture of criminality can be found in the *Daily Telegraph* and *Sydney Morning Herald* in August 2001 and between July and October 2002, coinciding with the trials of the pack rapists. The following are typical:

> While many Muslims would be genuinely appalled at these attacks, there is a widespread perception in the Muslim community that non-Muslim women, Western women in particular, who are free to drink, dance and engage in premarital sex, are immoral — which, to some young men, makes them fair game.
>
> In fact, the victims were the sort of young women these young men would be likely to date — while virtuous (and often

> identifiably headscarved) Muslim women would be expected
> to remain at home. The fact that the attackers were invariably
> Muslim, their victims invariably seen to be non-Muslim, speaks
> for itself (Alam 27/8/01:11).

> These boys may be born in Australia, but they consider them-
> selves Muslim enough not to rape other Muslims. Their parents
> teach them to respect only Muslim women, making these boys
> believe Aussie women do not deserve respect (Gartside 26/8/
> 01:90).

In addressing the issue of crime, representatives of the white
community — political leaders, journalists and ordinary citizens —
imputed to Lebanese migrants a number of attributes to 'explain'
the purported causal link between Lebanese culture and crime —
the kind of attributes we canvassed in earlier chapters. In the midst
of the 'gang crisis', in late 1998, and again during the 'ethnic rape'
panic in 2001–2002, many Lebanese leaders rejected the claim
that ethnicity was a causal factor in the apparent rise in ethnic
crime. However, some ethnic community leaders (whether they
represent Arabic, Lebanese or Muslim groups) participated in an
ideological process which we could call 'self-criminalisation'.
Further, the creation of a sense of community blame shifts much of
the responsibility for these crimes and their prevention onto community leaders themselves.

'The good name of Lebanese Australians is … under threat'

Influential 'numbers man' in the NSW Labor Party and Minister
for Fisheries in the Carr government, Edward Obeid, vociferously
defended Bob Carr's identification of the young offenders by their
ethnicity by arguing that even though most of the criminals were
born and raised in Australia, they identified themselves as 'Lebanese' (*SBS Radio* Arabic programme 1998). This assumption of
an unquestioned link between the crime and their ethnicity is
significant because Obeid is also a prominent Lebanese community

leader whose family own *El-Telegraph*, the largest Arabic news-paper in Australia. In this instance, his loyalties to the rightwing leadership of the NSW Labor Party and his motivation to defend it against an 'ethnic backlash' following Carr's comments about 'Lebanese crime' take priority over his role as an 'ethnic leader', to represent the interests of Lebanese communities in the political arena. His ability to 'deliver' for the communities concerned depends precisely on his leverage in the Labor Party, and much of his sway in the Labor Party right wing derives from securing the particular 'ethnic vote' and from crucially targeted recruitment of Lebanese communities into specific party branches.

Similarly, speaking at the Australian Lebanese Association's annual youth awards in 2001, Marie Bashir, the NSW Governor and someone also of Lebanese Christian descent, did not hesitate from referring to these young criminals as 'Lebanese Australians'. She added that 'the good name of Lebanese Australians is itself under threat' because of the 'disappointing antisocial trend' among sections of the Lebanese community. On this very public occasion, the Governor did not question the legitimacy of perceiving the young offenders as 'Lebanese', but simply echoed the link that white Australians were making between the young offenders, their crimes and the Lebanese migrant community at large. Moreover, she accepted the implication that the solving of these problems was the responsibility of the Lebanese community: she called upon them to 'work out what exactly was driving some young Lebanese Australians to violence' (Morris 9/7/01:7). In making these statements, another prominent figure of Lebanese background in NSW reinforced the trend initiated by the leader of the Labor government and mainstream media whereby the criminal activities of young people were identified as being primarily the acts of 'Lebanese gangs', and, by inference, were caused by their Lebanese ethnicity.

Other prominent people of Lebanese ancestry also seemed to accept the foregrounding of the link between ethnicity and crime: Farouk Hadid, the president of the Lebanese Muslim Association

(LMA), the largest and most influential Muslim organisation in NSW, had no problem in naming the gang by its ethnicity (English & Walsh 3/11/98:5). Another (unnamed) leader admitted that 'We are all embarrassed by what's happening here' (Sofios 22/8/01:4) — and embarrassment implies culpability.

These leaders did not question here the validity of identifying 'gangs' by their ethnic background. Nor did they show any critical awareness of the racist impact this identification was having on the Lebanese migrant community. Bashir's attempt to separate 'good' Lebanese from 'bad' Lebanese only served to reinforce the link between the offenders' ethnicity and their crime. Their unquestioning identification of the offenders as 'Lebanese' contributed to the criminalisation of Lebanese ethnicity by facilitating the process of making a causal link between crime and the identifiable culture of the offenders.

This 'self-criminalisation' implies not the acceptance of personal blame, but the acceptance of some degree of community blame because of the assumed link between ethnicity and offence, and hence some degree of leadership responsibility for dealing with this 'ethnic problem'. When Sheikh Al Hilaly decided, after months of criticising the media and the Carr government for their rhetoric of Lebanese gangs and Muslim rapists, to visit the homes of the rapists' families, the *Sun-Herald* (14/7/02:1) reported that Al Hilaly was facing up to the 'reality' of ethnic gang rape and admitting to 'our shame'. This 'self-criminalisation', then, is an act of accepting one's interpellation by the political and media discourse of the dominant culture. But this acceptance is not simply an ideological process; it also entails practical incorporation into a political system.

Ethnic crimes: taking responsibility

As we have seen, the Labor government and the Liberal opposition have engaged since the mid-1990s in a series of law and order auctions, each offering stricter policing, stronger laws and harsher sentences as the most effective way of fighting crime in NSW

(Lipari 24/6/02:3; Walker 26/8/01:10). This 'tough' approach to crime was partly responsible for a sweeping victory for the Labor Party in the 1999 state election, and it was again in the 2003 state election campaign in NSW, with ongoing announcements about boosting the police presence in 'dangerous' parts of Sydney and promises to spend more money on fighting crime (Rehn 28/9/02:4; Horan 13/10/02:2). The implicit message to the wider community behind the law and order auction is that this approach is mostly needed to curb crime within ethnic communities because they are the main cause of youth crime in NSW. By joining in the auction, Lebanese community leaders have, in turn, reinforced the same message. Indeed, many leaders demanded even tougher approaches to crime.

In the wake of the shooting incident in Lakemba, Lebanese community leaders expressed their total opposition to the lenient character of the criminal law in Australia. Consequently, they called for tougher laws arguing that this 'Australian' leniency would encourage Lebanese-Australian youngsters to engage in anti-social and criminal activities. The Mufti of Muslims in Australia and religious Sheikh at Lakemba mosque, and Michael Hawatt, a Muslim-Lebanese Canterbury Councillor (English & Walsh 3/11/98:5) were both critical of the law in Australia for not supporting the exercise of tough parental authority over kids. In an interview conducted by one of the authors in 2002 with Khalil Harajli, a community leader with the Lebanese Community Council (LCC) and St George Lebanese Joint Committee (LJC), and a multicultural health worker in southern Sydney, similar views were expressed in the following terms:

> … there is a lot of freedom to kids in Australia, [parents feel] they couldn't discipline them in a way [because of that freedom]. And so the law [plays] a big role in bringing up the kids. Especially when the kid is aware that he can report his parents to the police if they're classified as abused. It doesn't mean that [parents] want to abuse him; they want to straighten him up (interview with Khalil Harajli 13/10/02).

Despite the emphasis given to the Australian criminal system, Harajli asserted that weak parental authority over kids was the 'number one' problem that the Lebanese community is facing when dealing with its youth. For him, as much as for the previous two community leaders, Lebanese youth would be less likely to turn into a criminal if the Australian legal system gave greater authority to parents to discipline their children. The drive for tougher measures within the Lebanese migrant community led Barbara Coorey, an independent Canterbury Councillor to call 'for a curfew across Canterbury in the wake of the Lakemba shoot-up' and for tighter security around the police stations in the area (Field 13/11/98:6).

In response to public outcry over the supposed leniency of the initial gang rape sentences in 2001, Lebanese community leaders expressed their support for the government's proposal to introduce maximum life sentences, and prided themselves that the punishment for rape in their country is even harsher than the proposed sentencing laws. Charlie Moussa, President of the United Australian Lebanese Assembly (UALA), condemned the 'soft' sentences, saying that 'the law should be changed'. He declared that punishments for such crimes should be harsh enough to deter others (Kent 24/8/01:5; Connolly & Kennedy 24/8/01:3).

Ethnic leaders' support for and participation in a political system which was targeting their community extended even to forms of self-policing. In the context of the moral panic over male Muslim youths, a group of young men from Lakemba mosque was formed under the supervision of Sheikh Al Hilaly, with the their aim of going out on the street and bringing young Muslims 'back' to the mosque. On the question of sentencing, one of them declared:

> In Islamic law the penalty for rape is execution, but Australian law gave these gangsters just 6 years … Instead, these girls' parents will be paying taxes for years to feed and clothe these criminals in jail. Whose law is wrong?

A second member of the same group was not only critical of the 'soft' punishment, he also blamed the Australian schools for abetting laxity: 'Kids should be taught ethics and proper behaviour at school. Instead, they are told they have rights and told to tell their teachers if their parents discipline them' (Walker 26/8/01:11). Around the same time, LMA President Farouk Hadid, echoed similar views:

> [Lebanese kids] have no respect for their parents, elders and teachers because the law and the schools tell them to run to [authorities] if their parents show them some discipline, no matter how hard. They don't obey their parents, they don't listen to their parents and they don't know anything about their religion. Here we can't touch them — just to hurt them a little to punish them and teach them (Sofios 22/8/01:4).

On the question of the rape crime, he added: '[The rapists] have social problems, they need help and we don't want to protect them. They should be caught and punished harshly'. Hadid is not simply distancing himself from 'bad' Lebanese; he is refusing the principle of protection and representation at the heart of community politics. In adopting this position, along with other community leaders, Hadid reinforces the view of the government and other representatives of white dominant society that youth crime is a Lebanese problem, and that harsh sentencing is the most effective measure to deter them from committing these crimes (Sofios 22/8/01:4). Al Hilaly expressed similar views (Morris 21/8/01:5).

One year later, when the Department of Public Prosecutions successfully appealed against the so-called 'soft sentences' received by three members of the 'rapist gang', Lebanese community leaders joined the government in welcoming the new sentences meted out to the offenders. Keysar Trad, the spokesman for the Lebanese Muslim Association, said: 'I hope that [the sentence] sends a message to anyone else that may be thinking of committing a violent sexual crime that they will be put away for a long time' (Totaro 16/8/02:2). The *Daily Telegraph* quoted Dr Jamal Rifi, a commissioner representing the Lebanese community with the Community Relations Commission for a Multicultural NSW, as saying: 'We have no problem with this sentence whatsoever. Our community has repeatedly called for the toughening of sentences ... anything, as long as it sends a tough message'. Philip Rizk, President of the Australian Lebanese Association, made similar remarks:

> We are very happy that the perpetrator of such an awful crime has received the full treatment of the law. If you commit a crime beyond imaginable human behaviour, you should be put away and thrown away. This [sentence] is not excessive (Clifton 16/8/02:4–5).

Even Hilal Dannaoui, a rising cricket star of Lebanese descent, who has voiced strong opinions about his own experiences of vilification, stated that the young men who received long jail sentences for their part in the rapes 'deserved what they got' (Sygall 6/10/02:93).

The message conveyed by the above statements is clear; Lebanese community leaders strongly support the state policy of getting tough on youth crime. Leniency in punishment will certainly lead to more youth crime. The unintended (or intended) consequence of this message, however, makes the position of these leaders even more interesting. In the context where dominant white society links youth crime with Lebanese ethnicity, calling for a tough punishment policy on youth crime would effectively mean getting tough on Lebanese background youth because they are perceived to be the main cause of youth crime in Sydney. While adamant that the young criminals are not representative of their community and that the whole community should not be tainted by their crimes, they are positioned to endorse a raft of 'law and order' crackdowns, part of which is the ethnic targeting of 'zero tolerance'. When Lebanese community leaders welcome this 'get tough' policy, they are indirectly welcoming its application on Lebanese youth who are accused by broader society of being the main perpetrators of crime.

Incorporation into this system goes beyond support for tougher sentencing and involves practical involvement in the machinery of decision-making and policing. After the incidents in 1998, the Premier called Lebanese community leaders to a meeting to tell them that their community had a serious problem with gang crime and they should cooperate with the government to overcome this problem. He warned them that they should break the 'wall of silence' that had been erected to protect the young criminals in their community from law enforcement agencies (Humphries 4/11/98:5; Crosweiler 4/11/98:1–2). On another occasion, when the Premier announced a government plan to stop what he called 'the spiralling gang violence that was going to engulf Lebanese youth', he declared that it was important not to shy away from identifying ethnic-based crime problems:

> We've got to be candid and say there is a concentration of this type of crime in Bankstown and Lakemba, we've got serious problems and the problems are spilling over on to the streets and on to public transport and we want to tackle them.

Two important community figures of Lebanese background, Bulldogs Rugby League hero Hazem Al Masri and Aussie Home Loans chief John Symond, were standing by the Premier when he was making these remarks (Morris, R 11/7/01:2).

In an interview with *El-Telegraph*, Premier Carr, commenting on the pack rape incidents, argued that:

> the community had to accept the ugly fact that the perpetrators of the crimes had made race a factor, not the media or the government. One rape involved 14 men and during the rape, the men said racist things. Moreover, some of the men were involved in successive rapes. You had a gang (quoted in Horan 11/8/02:2).

The community should not only acknowledge that the rapists were members of a Lebanese (Muslim) gang, but that they were racist as well. The entire Lebanese community was expected to share responsibility for the crimes, as the misogyny and the purported anti-'Aussie' racism of the sexual assaults were ascribed to the culture from which the offending youths came.

The government strategy to make the Lebanese Australian community take responsibility for gang crimes in Sydney has been shared by mainstream media. As noted in previous chapters, prominent journalists, such as Miranda Devine (*Sydney Morning Herald* and *Sun-Herald*), Cindy Wockner and Piers Akerman (*Daily Telegraph*) and Janet Albrechtsen (*Australian*) have written many articles suggesting that youth crime is the product of Lebanese ethnicity and Muslim culture (see in particular, Albrechtsen 4/9/02:13). The editorial of the *Daily Telegraph* addressed ethnic leaders directly:

> Leaders of [ethnic] communities have a responsibility to encourage members to observe the laws of this country and assist the assimilation of their former countrymen in their adopted home ... cooperation is expected when the law has been broken ...The central topic for discussion should be how leaders can co-operate with the police and other agencies to prevent this criminal behaviour.

> As leaders, it is time to live up to their titles (*Daily Telegraph* 22/8/01:30).

In criticising those members of the Lebanese and Muslim communities who rejected the association of ethnicity with crime, the *Daily Telegraph* argued explicitly that the legitimacy of 'ethnic leadership' hinged upon their cooperation with the state authority to force members of ethnic community to respect the law and help law enforcement agencies to catch the Lebanese offenders (Kent 24/8/01:5).

One year later, when the rapists were brought to court for a re-trial, the same newspaper stated in its editorial:

> While the sins of the 14 young men who have been found guilty of these crimes should not be held against the Lebanese Muslim community, it is important that their true nature be understood.

> In this manner, the community and families can work together to prevent a recurrence of such appalling offences. All must come to understand there is no tolerance of such behaviour — or the attitude that nurtured it — in our society (*Daily Telegraph* 17/7/02:28).

While it seems to say at first that the community should not be blamed, it suggests that the community should take responsibility.

Lebanese leaders participated in two events that openly contributed to the incrimination of their own community. The first one relates to the 'Partnership Plan to Prevent Violence and Crime Among Arabic Speaking Young People'. The project was designed to prevent crime among 'young people of Arabic speaking background'. When the Premier announced the plan on July 10, 2001, he stated that Lebanese community leaders suggested to him the partnership plan in two meetings that he previously held with them. The Fisheries Minister, Edward Obeid, was appointed to supervise the implementation of the plan, and the group looking after its implementation included three leaders of Lebanese background: Randa Kattan, Executive Director of the Australian Arabic Communities Council, John Choueifate, Chief of Staff at Channel 9 and Jamal Rifi who is a Community Relations Commissioner. To propose the idea of a plan designed to prevent crime among 'young people of Arabic speaking background' is in itself a serious acknowledgment that there is a 'Lebanese crime problem'. To act as a partner in the implementation of this plan showed that Lebanese leaders are prepared to take responsibility for tackling the problem (Carr 10/7/01).

The Mufti of Australian Muslims, Sheikh Al Hilaly, initiated another project that conceded the tendency towards criminal behaviour amongst Lebanese Muslim youths. As mentioned earlier, this project involved the formation of a group of young Muslims whose task was 'to come down hard on Lebanese gangs hanging around after dark'. In the words of Imam Al Hilaly, the Muslim community 'will mobilise people to walk the streets at night to reclaim the streets. We will go to areas where young people congregate. We want them off the streets' (Walker 26/7/01:11). When the tabloid press interviewed some members of this squad, they declared they were furious about what they called 'the bad name' the gang members were giving their religion. To them, their mission was to bring lost young Muslims back to the mosque. They further stated that they were working with the police without necessarily taking the law into their own hands. 'Bring them to us. We'll sort them out'. These were the words used by one member of this group addressing 'gang members who targeted non-Muslim girls' (Walker 26/7/01:11). Clearly, this group not only accepted responsibility on behalf of their community for the 'gang crimes', they also conceded that the rapists were targeting 'Australian' girls. They took further responsibility for policing their own community. Central to this acceptance of community and leadership responsibility are two things: first, the acceptance of the idea of being a community, which we have shown elsewhere to be central to the formation of ethnic politics in Australian multiculturalism (Collins et al. 2000). Second, a sense of honour — and its converse, a sense of shame — which is fundamental to the formation of community identity generally, but is crucial to Arab and Muslim cultures, is exploited in the processes of interpellation at work here.

A Councillor of Lebanese background in southern Sydney critically described the entire approach taken by Lebanese community leaders as follows:

> … they walk into the traps, the media traps, the political traps, walk in. They, as I said, have good intentions, good intentions to resolve some of the problems, but they walk into traps, and the media manipulates it so well

> … the community recognises there's a problem, the Government says there's a problem, the community has recognised it as a problem, and people should see it, yes the Lebanese community do have a problem. So it creates this vicious circle that the Lebanese community, the Australian Lebanese community can't get out of the argument. You've told us, you're co-operating with us, you've told us your youth is a problem, and we're not saying it, you're telling us. So it's a fantastic policy, and you'll see it as a policy of targeting particular communities, and playing on the prejudices of the wider community (Interview with Councillor Shawkat Muslimani 13/10/02).

Sharing with state authorities the responsibility for policing Muslim communities has re-emerged in the aftermath of the Bali bombings. Yasser Soliman, the head of the Islamic Council of Victoria, said:

> We've been accused of not standing up so many times against violence and terrorism and this and that … Australian Muslims were eager to prevent terrorist activities and as likely as others to report suspicious behaviour to authorities as had happened in Preston when the community reported a Saudi national and suspected al-Qaeda member.

Mr Soliman added that 'there were other instances where Muslims alerted authorities to 'suspicious characters' (Schwartz 2/11/02). The Board of Imams, Victoria, and the Islamic Councils of Victoria issued a press release in which they also declared that 'Victorian Muslims support and cooperate with security forces in their bid to rid the nation of terrorism' (n.d.).

Explaining ethnic gang crime

Self-criminalisation is most clearly expressed by some ethnic leaders who ventured into offering an explanation of youth crime. In this case, the ownership of the gang problem is already implicit in the explanatory remarks they made in public. Amjad Mehboob, Chief Executive Officer for the Federation of Islamic Councils, was quoted approvingly by Miranda Devine as talking to ABC Radio of: 'Muslims accepting responsibility that they may have failed to do things that would have prevented these things [the gang rapes] from happening' (Devine 14/7/02:15). Mehboob's acceptance of the Muslim community's responsibility rests on the acceptance that the Muslim community and its leadership failed to carry out its duty. Had the community done these 'things', they would have not produced Muslim criminals. The Muslim community is perceived to be the key to both the problem of gang crime and its solution.

Perhaps the undefined things that the community failed to do are what other community leaders have mentioned on different occasions. Sheikh Khalil Chami, Imam of Penshurst Mosque, categorically blamed community leadership for the crimes of the Muslim youth:

> There are a lot of younger people who don't want to be part of the wider community. It's because of the leadership. The leadership teaches them to hate the other and this is not the right way.

Sheikh Chami insisted that Muslim culture is 'insular' and it needs to be reformed (English 4/10/02:17). Leadership for Sheikh Chami includes Lebanese parents who:

> were refusing to teach their children about harmony and the need to love their neighbours, regardless of religion, creed or colour. Only when Muslim parents realise that this [teaching of harmony and love] is essential will our youngsters integrate, learn to accept and, in turn, be accepted (Duff 14/7/02:4).

UALA President Charlie Moussa made the point that the presence of young criminals in the community was the result of parents failing their families (Morris 23/8/01:7). The Governor of NSW, Marie Bashir, made a similar point by saying that parents should not spoil their boys and should teach them love and respect and offer them good education (Stephens 7–8/9/02:47). Furthermore, Sheikh Chami's eldest daughter Moufredi accused Lebanese Muslim families of nurturing in men a unique sense of superiority over others, which, when taken 'to an extreme', will breed rapists (Cock & Fynes-Clynton 15/7/02:6).

Ironically, unlike the tabloid journalists who believe that the problem is that Muslims haven't assimilated, these leaders see the problem being caused by these boys not being Muslim enough: a contradiction we explored in Chapter Three. But the perceived elements of the problem are shared — the insularity of Lebanese and Muslim culture, the lack of proper upbringing, the absence of love and respect. The claim here is that 'Lebanese rapists' exist in Sydney because Lebanese parents teach their children not to integrate in the broader community and to hate white Australians. They inculcate in them a sense of superiority over the Australian culture and of the inferiority of 'white' women, which could lead them in the future to commit rape against white female Australians. By accepting community blame for the crimes of a few offenders, Lebanese community leaders increase the susceptibility to being criminalised by the dominant white society.

The 'other' within the Other

Some Lebanese Christian leaders accepted the terms of interpellation by the dominant white community on condition that these terms are exclusively attributed to Muslim and not Christian Lebanese migrants. By taking this position, they rely on the belief that because they are Christian and white Australianness is defined as Christian, this will enable them to disown the Muslims from their Lebanese Australian community and count themselves as an integral part of the white Australian community. This echoes Dunn's (2001:303) analysis of conflicts around mosque development in Sydney over the last twenty years, which showed that Muslim groups with European heritage would frequently differentiate themselves from 'Arabs', effectively reinforcing the negative construction of the Arab Muslim. In other words, they are trying to prise themselves out of the Arab Other while leaving the structure intact. They can attempt to do this because this Other is already fractured by lines of difference and division, and because they see themselves as sharing some characteristics with a fantasised Australian identity. As Hage (1998) argues, national belonging is constituted by a complex array of elements of 'Australian characteristics', which he casts as forms of cultural capital. Accumulation and recognition of this capital allows citizens to attain symbolic power, as belonging to the nation. Migrants with more 'national capital' are perceived to be more Australian than those who possess less. This difference in the possession of national capital creates a hierarchy of 'others' in the nationalist imaginary of Australian society. Accordingly, Christian Lebanese migrants can feel more Australian than their Muslim counterparts because they share with white Australians a perceived nationalist characteristic of being Christian. Muslim Lebanese migrants, on the other hand, are not only 'Arab' with 'Middle Eastern appearances', they were also a 'Muslim Other' against whom the Christian identity of Australia is defined.

It was this distinguishing characteristic which enabled Christian Lebanese leaders to dissociate themselves from their Muslim counterparts and take part in the criminalisation of Islam. This is made possible by the relatively privileged position that Christian Lebanese leaders feel that they occupy in the hierarchy of others imposed by the dominant white community.

The criminalisation of Lebanese Muslims by Christian community leaders also relied on a deeply entrenched ideological tenet held by the Christian section of the Lebanese Australian community; the belief that since the inception of the state of Lebanon in 1920, Christians were the only section of the Lebanese population who identified with Lebanese national identity. In contrast, Muslims residing in Lebanon were always suspected of lacking a sense of belonging to Lebanon. They were accused of having allegiance to pan-Arab nationalism and to the broader community of Islam (Zamir 1985; 'Atiyah 1973). Against this background, Christian community leaders were able to disown gang members in Sydney because they supposedly had Muslim backgrounds. In their opinion, these gangs were not descendants of 'true' Lebanese citizens or the inheritors of Lebanese culture. The true Lebanese have always been the Christians in Lebanon and their descendants. The killers of Edward Lee, therefore, were not 'Lebanese gangs' as the Premier described them, but rather 'Muslim gangs'.

Some Christian Lebanese leaders implicitly used the same strategy to dissociate themselves publicly from any responsibility for the serious sexual assaults that occurred in south-west Sydney. This time, however, the incrimination of Muslims and their religion took a more naked and public form. On talk back radio, Joe Baini (n.d.), the ex-President of the Australian Lebanese Association, claimed that Islam entices its followers to degrade women and to rape Anglo women because of their 'footloose' behaviour and their belonging to an inferior culture. In addition, it was rumoured that during several meetings involving Lebanese leaders discussing their response, Philip Rizk insisted that Lebanese community leaders should acknowledge that the pack rapes were motivated by a racist hate that the Muslim rapists had towards their Anglo Christian victims. (It is worth noting that during the same meeting a Christian religious leader suggested that Lebanese community leaders should pay a sum of money to the rape victims by way of redemption. Another leader proposed that they also pay a visit to the families of the victims and apologise on behalf of the Lebanese community for what happened to their daughters). This leadership position on the radical distinction between the Christian and Muslim Lebanese communities is reflected in the words of a letter addressed to the *Sydney Morning Herald* by a writer who defines himself as 'a proud Australian of Lebanese background':

> I would like to make it clear that there are Australians of Lebanese Catholic background who form a completely separate Lebanese community and are the victims of generalisations.
>
> I believe that everyone who lives in this country should integrate into the Australian family.
>
> Multiculturalism has not proved successful in history, yet multi-ethnicity under one cultural umbrella, on the contrary, is very productive (Reston 24–25/8/02:21).

In an interview with the Coordinator of the LMA, the Christian/Muslim divide over the rape issue featured very clearly:

> … both the Christian and Muslim community have a division, because everybody wants to have their name, or the community name as being clean. Maybe some of the Christians are saying 'look, these were Lebanese Muslims', so they can feel better about themselves and their community. I actually heard that on talkback radio, where they say 'look, these were Muslim kids'. They are Lebanese, but they're Muslim, they're not reflective of the Lebanese (Fawaz Derbas 24/9/02).

The response of the Howard Government to the 'boat people' crisis that occurred between the second half of 1999 and 2001, encouraged even more Christian community leaders to dissociate themselves from Muslim Lebanese migrants in Sydney. Following the arrivals of illegal immigrants from the Middle East in recent years, the Australian federal government forsook humanitarianism for deterrence, as outlined earlier. Consequently, the atmosphere was highly charged with feeling of hostility towards the so-called 'queue jumpers' who happened to be mainly of Muslim background. The hostility towards Muslim migrants further escalated after the events on September 11, 2001. In this context, Christian community leaders found further reason to distance themselves from Muslim Lebanese migrants and to encourage the association of Muslims with youth crime and terrorism.

In these responses Christian Lebanese leaders were attempting to shift blame away from themselves and their community. They acted as though they were being interpellated as 'ordinary' (white) Australians, and as though the construction of the Arab Other was directed exclusively towards Lebanese Muslims, hoping that by following this strategy they could protect Christian Lebanese migrants from being criminalised. They were, however, still accepting the terms of interpellation by the dominant white community.

'Muslim leader blames Australia'

Despite the fact that Lebanese community leaders ended up taking responsibility for the problem of 'Lebanese gangs', on some occasions, Muslim leaders responded to the racialisation of crime by disowning the young offenders and arguing that they were the product of Australian culture. When the 'gang' crisis broke out in 1998, for instance, Muslim community leaders were keen to prove to the white Australian community that the perpetrators of gang crimes were not representative of the Lebanese migrant community. They first described the criminals as being non-Lebanese and/or non-Muslim. Leaders such as Al Hilaly and Trad, repeatedly claimed the young criminals were not really Lebanese or Muslim, and that their crimes showed that they had no knowledge of Islam. 'Those responsible were born in Australia and educated and raised here', said Al Hilaly to the *Daily Telegraph*. About this, he was quite correct. He continued, however: 'They have probably never been to Lebanon. All this [the actions of the rapists] is not part of our culture. They do not know our culture because they were raised here' (Staff reporters 21/8/01:5). Trad echoed these words: '[The young criminals] have no association with the culture and no association with the religious teachings' (Chulov & Payton 13–14/7/02:19). The following day he was quoted as saying: 'Because of the vile, heinous crimes they have committed, these men have disowned their religion and their race' (O'Bourne 14/7/02:4).

Even when community leaders opposed the criminalisation of Lebanese and Muslim groups by reversing the blame and making the claim that these 'criminals' were Australian rather than Lebanese Muslim, they fell into the trap of ascribing criminality to cultural attributes and thus sustained the problematic link between culture and crime through which their communities could be criminalised.

In the wake of the Bali bombings on October 12, 2002, major Islamic councils in Australia issued a joint media release in which 'extremists of the world' were condemned and 'terrorism' was described as being against the teachings of Islam. The signatories of the media release began their statement by saying that '… never in our name or in the name of any religion or God, can you ever be aggressive, unjust or hurt innocent people'. Then they added that aggression and violence 'are against every religious teaching in spite of what [extremists] may believe' (Islamic Council of Victoria [ICV] 6/11/02). Not surprisingly, the Islamic Egyptian Society (IES) of NSW had also intervened in expressing its position on the Bali event because the culprit was Muslim and the Islamic religion was subjected to numerous attacks. The secretary of this organisation declared that:

> We also wish to state that Islam condemns aggression against
> innocent people; the killings of innocent people are acts that

contravene all the Islamic religion's values and human civilised concepts. Those who carried out this criminal act have
nothing to do with Islam (Helal 16/11/02:16).

Randa Abdel-Fattah, a writer from Melbourne, proclaimed that,
'As a Muslim, it appals me to witness people who dare to profess
allegiance to Islam while committing heinous acts of murder and
destruction'. At another point, she added, 'The point is that these
people are aliens to the Islamic faith, and the cumulative effects of
connecting such people to our faith and community has only ever
served to create suspicion, fear and resentment of Australian
Muslims'. Even the possibility of considering the perpetrators of
the Bali bombings as representing 'an unsavoury deviation from
the wider Islamic community' was rejected. Abdel-Fattah argued
that 'this offers the people who committed such abhorrent crimes
a legitimacy they don't deserve, for the black sheep still belongs,
the thorn is still attached' (21/10/02). Many letter writers joined in
this campaign, trying to depict the Muslim community as being
essentially against violence and fanaticism, 'The people about whom
you are fulminating are fanatics, not fundamentalists', declared one
of these writers (Lewis Usman 17/11/02). This defence falls into
the ideological trap of seeing the debate about what a religion or
culture is or isn't, and who is an authentic representative of that
religion or culture, or not. It stays within a racist problematic which
seemingly accepts the terms of the debate: that crime and terrorism
are to be explained by cultural characteristics, not the dynamics of
economic inequality, globalisation, social change or international
politics.

It is clear from these statements and many more (press
releases by various Muslim organisations on the Bali events are
available on the ICV website) that this racist problematic was
reinforced when Muslim leaders, including those from the Lebanese
community, attempted to save the reputation of the Muslim
community by using the strategy of denying that the perpetrators
of the Bali bombings in October 2002 were 'real' Muslims.

Accordingly, Muslims in Australia and abroad are depicted as a one homogeneous group that is inherently anti-violent. This strategy of essentialising the community as an entity is the same as that utilised by anti-Muslim racists to make exactly the opposite claim; that all Muslims as an undifferentiated mass of people are essentially violent and aggressive. In both situations the logic is the same despite the defensive character of the 'racist' position taken by Muslim leaders. The social, economic and cultural diversity of the Muslim community is negated for the purpose of ascribing to it essentialised positive or negative characteristics. The uncritical adoption of this problematic by Muslim leaders would also help indirectly in the propagation of the same ideological framework that is used by the white racists in the criminalisation of the Lebanese and Muslim migrants.

Self-criminalisation: the product of state patronage institutionalised by multiculturalism

As we have seen, the various positions taken by community leaders reinforce implicitly or explicitly the process of criminalising their own community, partly by accepting the cultural explanation of crime and violence and by participating in the political processes of ascribing problems and solutions. These responses derive largely from the patron-client relationship between the state and Lebanese community leaders in Australian multiculturalism, and from the emphasis on community politics built into this relationship.

To begin with, it is important to realise that an important outcome of adopting the policy of multiculturalism in Australia was the creation of an institutional setting for the state recognition of ethnic leadership as an intermediary force between the state and migrant communities (Jakubowicz et al. 1984). Special State organs were created to deal with the leaders of ethnic organisations, including the Multicultural Affairs and Settlement Branch in what is now the Department of Immigration, Multicultural and Indigenous Affairs (DIMIA) and, at the state level, the Ethnic Affairs Commission, now called the Community Relations Commission (CRC) for a Multicultural New South Wales. Essentially, these State organs have the function of assisting migrant communities in the process of their settlement in Australia and addressing the specific needs that are generated by this process. In principle, ethnic organisations are funded to provide settlement services to their communities, and ethnic leaders are consulted in matters concerning the needs and problems of their respective communities. In reality, however, this practice, whose origin could be traced back to 1978 when the recommendations of Galbally report on migrant services were adopted by the federal government, has resulted in the creation of a hierarchical system of patronage between representatives of the state and ethnic leaders. According to this system, those ethnic leaders whose politics would fall outside the ambit of the state policy on community relations, are denied the high status attached to the state recognition of their leadership, and are financially penalised by receiving insufficient or no state funding at all.

At the present time, Lebanese community organisations which receive Community Settlement Services Scheme (CSSS) grants from DIMIA include: the Lebanese Community Council (LCC, $219,725 for 2002–2004), the Australian Arabic Communities Council (AACC, $116,218 for 2002–2004), the St George Lebanese Joint Committee (SGLJC, $56,000 for 2002–2003), the Australian Lebanese Welfare Group (ALWG, $204,800 for 2001–2003), the Lebanese Muslim Association (LMA, $100,400 for 2001–2003), the Al-Zahra Muslim Association (ZMA, $168,324 for 2002–2005) (DIMIA, 2002; see CRC 2002 for its funding measures). Social capital — the endowment of high status and prestige — is conferred upon compliant ethnic leaders through their selection for consultation on 'community relations' and their appointment in consultation committees sponsored by the federal and state governments. Jamal Rifi, a medical doctor of Lebanese background, for instance, was appointed by the NSW Labor government as a part-time commissioner with the CRC. He is well known in defending Carr's policies on Lebanese gangs and youth crime. Similarly, Dr Moustafa Alemeddine, who is an ex-president of the LCC, was accommodating in his relationship with the federal government. He was subsequently appointed by the Liberal federal government as a member of the Council for Multicultural Australia.

In order to retain the privileged treatment they receive from state officials, Lebanese community leaders were very cautious not to take a position that would effectively challenge the racialisation of youth crime by representatives of the state government. This was manifested in dropping their campaign to take legal action for racial vilification against NSW Premier, Bob Carr, for identifying offenders by their ethnicity in 1998 (Collins et al. 2000:210–212) and, a few years later, by implicitly or explicitly participating in the criminalisation of Lebanese ethnicity in the wake of the gang rapes. When Premier Carr insisted on the official use of 'ethnic descriptors' in identifying suspected criminals, despite the initial demand by some leaders to abandon these descriptors in NSW as in most other states, they never succeeded in forming a united position on the matter, nor did they take real action to press on with the demand to withdraw 'ethnic descriptors' from public circulation.

Similarly, the emerging focus on cultural identity in Australian multiculturalism (Hage 2002:110) not only has a class aesthetic which diminishes an initial emphasis on social justice, access and equity, it frames community politics with a cultural fetish that sees all customs and relationships as emanating from an essentialised cultural origin. The rationale of the leadership of ethnic communities derives then from an assumption that all behaviours are rooted in culture. Here the political appeal to responsibility and the cultural appeal to honour merge.

Shame, grief and yearning for belonging

The continuous fear of being held guilty of condoning the gang rapes has led many Lebanese community leaders to use every opportunity to express publicly their 'shame' over the incidents and voice their sympathy towards the victims. Sheikh Khalil Chami believed that the rapists 'have heaped shame on Islam'. Trad considered that the rapists have brought 'disgrace' to his community (Devine 14/7/02:4). Embodying a sense of collective guilt, leaders of the Australian Federation of Islamic Council (AFIC) made a statement in which they expressed their sympathy for the victims:

> … [We] feel strongly for the victims who have suffered immen-
> sely. We offer our condolences and warm words of support for
> the great courage that they have shown in standing against
> these sadistic and misguided youth (Tsavdaridi 18/7/02:2).

The fact that they felt obliged to issue a statement at all indicates the extent to which they are implicated in acceding to the criminalisation of their own community, and the racialisation of certain crimes.

Similar views were expressed in the aftermath of Bali bombings. A series of statements and press releases were issued by Muslim community organisations which expressed sorrow and sympathy towards the victims of the bombing. Two days after the tragic event, the president of Australian Federation of Islamic Councils (AFIC) publicly stated: 'Australians don't deserve this and without reserv-ation we condemn this attack. We extend our heartfelt sympathies to the families of the victims' (Mehboob 14/11/02). The Australian Arabic Council (AAC) reiterated similar views in a statement released on the same day. The IES of NSW wrote that their members convey their 'sorrow and grief for the innocent lives that have been lost during the barbaric and brutal bomb attack in Bali. We extend our sincere condolences to the families of the victims and those who are grieving' (Helal 16/11/02:16). On the national day of mourning for the victims of Bali bombings (20/11/02), a special prayer service was held by the LMA at Lakemba mosque. Two days earlier, Mufti Al Hilaly stated: 'We share the pain and grief, our sincere prayers go to the victims, we ask God to grant comfort to the grieving families and to all Australians to help get through these difficult times'. The spokesperson of the LMA, Keysar Trad added: 'Our heart-felt condolences to the families who lost loved ones' (LMA 18/11/02). Hassan Moussa (23/10/02:34), the chairperson of AACC, claimed in a letter to the *Daily Telegraph* that:

> Australia's National Day of Mourning (Domain Sydney) was a true reflection of a society united at a time of grief and sorrow. The emotional atmosphere was deeply moving and I felt pride in being part of this great nation and honourable society.
>
> The Bali tragedy was a horrific experience for every Australian and will leave deep feelings of pain and anger for a long time to come. It is beyond belief that the barbaric senseless killing of innocents would happen so close to our own backyard.

On November 15, 2002, the Prime Minister, John Howard, and the Minister for Citizenship and Multicultural Affairs, Gary Hardgrave, thanked AFIC for donating $22,000 to the Bali Appeal (2002).

The fact that they felt the need repeatedly to express 'grief and sorrow', while other community organisations did not felt the need to do this, reflected the acceptance of community blame by Muslim Lebanese and non-Lebanese leaders; an acceptance which buttresses the criminalisation of Islam, predicated on the entrenched belief that they were guilty of complicity with the terrorists because they share a religion. Muslims in Australia are required to denounce publicly and condemn the acts of 'terrorism' to demonstrate their innocence. It is precisely because their cultural ancestries are criminalised that Lebanese and Muslim leaders are expected to pronounce their innocence every time a person of similar cultural or religious background commits a crime (the 'ethnic gang' crimes in 1998, the pack rapes, September 11, 2001 and the Bali bombings in October 2002). When Lebanese and Muslim leaders publicly condemn 'gang' and 'terrorist' activities, they are at the same time reinforcing the criminalising of their own community precisely because their condemnation is motivated by accepting a measure of the guilt.

The subordinate position occupied by ethnic community leaders in the patronage system of multiculturalism makes them also continuously worried about their acceptance as 'good' and integrated members of the host society. During a function at Canterbury Leagues Club celebrating the initial implementation of the government-funded Youth Partnership Project mentioned previously, Hazem Al Masri, one of Australia's highest-profile Muslim athletes of Lebanese background, made a direct plea to Premier Carr — who was present and who also addressed the meeting:

> to help put an end to the isolation our community is suffering. … We do not condone rape … this is how we are being portrayed. Today the Muslim community is the most hated community in the nation.

He also revealed to Carr that he hated to use the label 'Lebanese community' when speaking about his community. 'I would prefer to be thought of as Australian … so that we all feel part of one family' (Morris 8/8/02:7). Al Masri's comments reflect the sense of exclusion of the Muslim community from the 'mainstream' of Australian society. They also reflect a recognition of the devalorising effect that the criminalisation of Lebanese ethnicity was having on the status of his community and its leadership. The social capital of leadership is predicated on the recognised and honourable reputation that the community and its leaders can attain. To be responsible in relation to these incidents is to disown the criminals (as bad Muslims), but this response sustains the link between ethnicity, religion and crime, rather than disavowing the link in the first place. Further, it is predicated on recognition from the political and cultural authority which identified the community as prone to crime and violence in the first place.

On another occasion, when Al Masri was awarded the Ken Stephen Medal for his 'outstanding work' for the community, his concern with the respectability of his community in the eyes of the dominant white society featured very prominently: 'There are a lot of good people in our [Lebanese] community and a lot of good developments happening and I want to let people know about this'. This award gave Keysar Trad the opportunity to emphasise 'the appreciation and acceptance of the broader community' (Haig 8/10/02:1). Not only did Lebanese leaders appear anxious to secure the good name of their community, they effusively expressed their gratitude at any opportunity afforded to them by the dominant society.

If the 'gang' crimes made white Australian society consider the Lebanese community as being against the 'Australian way of life', the Bali incident, on the other hand, made Muslims in Australia feel as if they were the enemy of the Australian nation. For this reason, the obsession with belonging to mainstream Australian society became much more acute among Muslim leaders immed-iately after the Bali bombings. The fear of being excluded lurks behind a number of statements made by Muslim Lebanese and non- Lebanese leaders. On November 3, 2002, Sheikh Al Hilaly with the spokesperson for LMA, Mr Trad, issued a press release indicating that 'tens' of Muslims will go down to St Vincent Church in Redfern to 'celebrate' their respect for diversity in Australia. In this press release, Al Hilaly stated:

> The greatest attribute of Australian society is the respect for diversity and the ethos of 'fair go'. In support of this great ethos, we share in this great Sunday meeting ... We are Aus-tralians promoting and protecting Australia and we here to work together to make Australia the greatest country on earth...

In the same statement, Trad declared his community's belief in 'God' and their 'commitment to the values of peace, love, compa-ssion and the security of our great country, Australia'. He then added that the Muslim community 'reject the present atmosphere of fear and apprehension', and they 'stand united as one society under God with expressions of love and peace for all' (Al Hilaly & Trad 2002). In his comments on the national day of mourning, Sheikh Fehmi Naji El-Imam from Melbourne said: 'We are Australians, we belong to this country and we are doing exactly what is expect-ed, just like anybody else' (Williams 21/10/02). More recently, Al Hilaly, in a *Telegraph* piece entitled 'Visiting Muslims 'a threat' (31/7/03:4), is reported as admitting that a large number of 'foreign extremists' are 'targeting' young Muslims in Australia, preaching 'social disharmony and intolerance'. The division between Christians and Muslims, noted above, is replicated in the division between moderate and 'extremist' Muslims, such as those associated with the Islamic Youth Movement (Morris 21–22/6/03:36). Once again, Lebanese and non-Lebanese Muslim leaders express their yearning to belong to Australia precisely because they fear being expunged from the Australian nation, which is derived from accepting the guilt of complicity imposed on them by the racism within 'mainstream' Australian culture. Paradoxically, these statements would reproduce the exact opposite of their intended message. They make the relationship of Muslims in Australia with mainstream society increasingly tenuous.

After the outbreak of the 'gang' panic in 1998, the 'ethnic rape' crisis of 2001–2 and the Bali bombings in October 2002, Lebanese and Muslim ethnic leaders undertook a number of steps designed to protect the good name of their communities and oppose their marginalisation by white Australian society. Their overall objective was to retain the recognition of the state and all the symbolic benefits (social capital of prestige and respectability) and material benefits (state and federal funding) that come with it. However, as we have seen, the response of these leaders intentionally or unintentionally contributed to the criminalisation of their communities and reinforced their marginal status in relation to 'White Australia'.

7

'Paranoia in the lucky country':
the fear of everything, everywhere

Fear finds its voice

> A 5-year-old says to his mother after listening to the latest
> report about bushfires in Sydney in December, 2002: 'Mum! …
> Something funny! There was an attack and then a fire last year,
> and there was an attack and a fire this year. They must have
> been done by the same person!'
>
> A *Telegraph* reader asks why we are sending troops overseas
> when we need them 'to combat terrorism in our own back yard':
> the terrorism referred to here is the 'mindless acts of terrorism
> perpetrated by arsonists' (Oloman 9/12/02:20).

It was not just Sydney where this association took hold: in the
bushfires in Canberra just a few weeks later one victim said 'I feel
like I've survived a terrorist attack', and referred to the threat
from Iraq or North Korea (Wynhausen 20/1/02); another compared
it to a bomb blast in Beirut (Channel 9 20/1/03). Prime Minister
John Howard commented that what we had seen was 'the national
capital under attack from the summer terror' (Channel 9 20/1/03);
and 'Summer Terror' was the *Australian*'s header for covering
the fires not just in the Australian Capital Territory, Sydney and
rural NSW, but in Tasmania, South Australia and Western Australia
as well (*Australian* 22/1/02:4–6). In a reversal of the metaphor,
Piers Akerman (26/1/03:111) opined that we need to get the 'global
firebugs' of terrorism:

> Images of Canberra's smoking suburbs, and the fires that are
> ravaging bushland across the nation provide a strong argument
> for those who suggest the case for bringing an end to Saddam
> Hussein's monstrous regime in Iraq.
>
> For Saddam Hussein is a proven arsonist on a global scale.

There is nothing logical in the association between the bushfires in the summer of 2002–3 and the threat of crime and terrorism, but logic is hardly the issue here. They are experienced as cognate, constituting the same environment of fear. In the same fortnight that the comments about Canberra's fires are made, there is further panic about armed robbery and rising violent crime, (ethnic) gangs and guns (Kamper 8/1/03:1), and one about the failure of the legal system to impose bail appropriately, allowing offenders to continue to commit crimes (Lipari 6/1/03:1). At the same time, detention centres are set alight by asylum seekers, and Sheikh Al Hilaly arrested on various charges supposedly based on surveillance 'intelligence', in circumstances which raise the threat of racial violence (Morris & English 7/1/03:1). The tangible threat of fire is thrown into the mix of crime, violence, gangs, refugees and terrorists. The summer of 2002–3 brought to a head those fears arising from the events we have described in this book. These fears ignite in all directions; they feed upon small scrub fires of anxiety, and burst into flame in tinder-dry Australia. It was not just the fires that gave these fears materiality: journalist Paul Sheehan describes the 'water crisis' as 'the greatest threat to Australia, an unfolding collapse that makes the incursions of al-Qaeda, the bombings in Bali and the prospect of war in Iraq all look trivial' (7–8/12/02:4–5).

It has become almost a truism amongst commentators that we are living in a time of great fear and anxiety. Media commentators and politicians, and not just academics, glibly talk about the pervasive 'fear of crime' (Cameron 7–8/12/02:3), 'Fears of cultural rift' (Millett 18/3/02:1), the 'politics of fear' (Newman 18/12/02:36), 'worry about war' and terrorism (Robins 21–22/12/02:4). There is talk of anxiety, insecurity, safety, uncertainty, and even paranoia (Mackay 26–27/10/02:30). Surveys demonstrate that this is not just media hyperbole: one survey showed that the threat of terrorism is the number one issue of concern in Australia, with 62% of respondents seeing Australia as a target (Shepherd 17/12/

02:12). The *Sun-Herald*, screaming 'TERROR THREAT GRIPS A NATION' (29/12/02:1,4), reported that 60% of Australians believed their 'relaxed way of life' had been changed forever, while more than a quarter suffered 'general paranoia' in the 'lucky country' (West & Walker 29/12/02:4). Australians responded by assuaging their paranoia in various ways: they attended church in record numbers (Moses 27/12/02:5), as they had done at Anzac Day earlier in the year, looking for spiritual and national community; they stayed at home and away from public New Year celebrations but attended sporting and cultural events in record numbers searching for the 'feel good factor' (Signy 9/1/03:1); they swapped rumours of pending terrorist attacks (Cornford 30/12/02:1) and rang the federal government's terrorist hotline reporting 'suspicious behaviour' (Allard 7/1/03:2), while stocking up on gas masks and other survival equipment (Morris & Murray 10/1/03:1). This climate of paranoia also licensed and gave credence to behaviour that is normally policed carefully, or ignored. The Government's 'terrorist hotline', for example, received numerous calls from 'bigots and hoax callers', and ASIO director-general Dennis Richardson revealed that many of its 'tip-offs' came from the mentally ill: 'Some of it is able to be put to one side fairly clearly as coming from a nutter', he admitted (*Daily Telegraph* 31/12/02:4). Sometimes these 'nutters' aren't so harmless, however, and engage in campaigns of race hate against Muslims (Morris 30/5/03:21).

A *Herald* article from November 2002 discusses how Sydney has become suspicious of strangers, producing rising intolerance as we 'learn to live with fear' (Allard, Cameron, Stevenson & Wainwright 23–24/11/02:27). The title of this article — 'The party's over' — implies that the euphoria and international bonhomie associated with the Sydney Olympics in 2000 is but a dim memory. It documents a number of incidents where sightings of suspicious containers and people have led to police responses. It likened this current mood with the Cold War and warned that psychiatrists have predicted an increasing incidence of anxiety and depression.

Other commentators have rehearsed the idea of the 'politics of fear' — the manipulation of human fears for electoral gain which we discussed in Chapter Five — especially as it has been used domestically by the Liberal Party (MacCallum 2002), while others have linked it to the international economics of oil and commodity trading (Newman 18/12/02:36).

This 'politics of fear', while not an inaccurate rendering of conservative campaigns and international politics in recent years, is nonetheless an inadequate tool for making sense of the current waves of panic experienced in Australia, and especially Sydney. It too easily collapses complex social phenomena into the cynical manipulation of those phenomena, and it too easily conflates the specific fears related to international terrorism with more pervasive and less well-defined social anxieties. Most media discussions of these fears fail to analyse in any sustained way what it is we actually fear. Nor do they consider the conditions of possibility of these fears — how it is possible for them to arise and be harnessed to specific political agendas. You cannot have a politics of fear unless you have a culture of paranoia; a paranoia built into a nation's anxieties around its racial and ethnic dimensions but deriving from a range of wider social, economic and political factors. The article by Allard et al., to give them their due, contains the recognition that this fear and anxiety are not just the result of specific terrorist acts per se. In claiming that 'fear found its voice ... on September 11', and got stronger with each incident, the article implies that fear was already present. It quotes one psychiatrist who suggests that it was an accumulation of events over the last few years that was the fundamental factor, each event 'priming and re-priming our anxiety'. It also hints at what the object of those fears might involve: it mentions one psychiatrist who argued that government warnings have shrunk the distance between Australia and world-scale tragedy, narrowing our 'comfort zones' and eroding our belief that Australia is a 'safe haven' in this globalised world (Allard et al. 23–24/11/02:27).

As we have already argued, moral panics are never just about single issues but are layered, complex phenomena, suturing a series of events, over time and operating at various levels of social reality, and giving them a focus. They articulate these events to broader social experience and structures of power. What makes the current situation so powerful in demonising the Arab Other was that events occasioning panic fed upon each other, and became inseparable, so that even minor incidents can become part of the larger ideological landscape via dog-whistling. We also suggested that what was at stake was not simply a specific concern — regarding crime, for instance — but a complex of issues and anxieties. The criminological literature has consistently shown that fear of crime involves the blurring of private and public concerns, personal experience and social problems (Hollway & Jefferson 2000:32), although this has rarely been extended to explore the links with larger questions of ethnicity and national belonging. In this chapter we want to unpack the fears and anxieties that have emerged in recent years and explore them in their complexity, to suggest that we are increasingly living in a broader culture of 'paranoid nationalism' (Hage 2002), in which the relations between national and ethnic identity are structured by international and domestic concerns around security and safety.

'The fear outside everyone's door'

In 2001, we conducted a survey of 825 people (380 adults and 445 youth) in Sydney that focused on social perceptions and fears regarding crime (Collins, Noble, Poynting & Tabar 2002). The research was undertaken before September 11, the refugee crisis and the widespread reports of the gang rapes, so it gives us some sense of the social mood as a result of the ethnic crime concerns. The survey was not a random sample representative of Australia's demographic make-up overall; instead it was designed to give a voice to Sydney's ethnic communities on the issues of crime and policing, and was stratified to target the most populous ethnic groups in seven Local Government Areas. Over 80% of those surveyed were from a non-English speaking background and lived in south-western Sydney. This is important, since more than half of those who live in Sydney today are first- or second-generation immigrants, with an increasing number from a non-English speaking background (Australian Bureau of Statistics 2001). Most of the adults were surveyed in their first language, and this was mostly a language other than English. Such voices are often ignored in the English-language based telephone polling of 'public opinion' that dominates contemporary Australian politics.

The research confirmed a high degree of fear of crime in Sydney, particularly among adults, in the wake of the ethnic crime panic. Paradoxically, however, the research revealed that most people we surveyed felt safe where they live, particularly those people living in the suburbs that have been characterised in media reports over the past four years as being the hot spots of 'ethnic crime'. The survey also suggests that ethnic minority youth are much more likely to experience crime as its victims than as its perpetrators and that reports of the level of concern over so-called ethnic youth gangs in Sydney are exaggerated — at least among the populations we surveyed.

Almost two out of three of the adults surveyed were *very concerned* about crime, with another 25% *concerned*. Only 12% of those adults surveyed were *mildly concerned* or not concerned at all about crime. In contrast, only one in five youth (21%) reported that they were *very concerned* about crime, though another 41% were *concerned*. Overall, females (45%) were more likely to be *very concerned* about crime than males (34%).

This fear of crime is linked to the firm impression that crime is on the increase in Sydney, a view held by nearly three quarters of adults surveyed and two thirds of youth. This seems to echo the findings of Don Weatherburn (2002), Director of the NSW Bureau of Crime Statistics and Research (BOCSAR), that Australia has a serious and growing problem with both property and violent crime;

but Weatherburn argues that, given that some crimes appear to be in decline, this does not constitute a 'crime wave'.

The research also probed the sorts of crime that were of most concern to the people we surveyed. It revealed that crimes related to drugs were perceived as the biggest problem by adults (41%), followed by violent assault (15%), while young people identified burglary (34%), violent assault (23%) and street theft (17%). Fear of sexual assault was, not surprisingly, four times greater among females surveyed than among males. Concern about crime has some roots in people's experiences: nearly one in two adults (44%) surveyed reported that they had at some time been victims of burglary, 32% had their car stolen, 12% had been victims of street theft and 10% had been victims of violent assault. One in three youth reported that they had ever been victims of burglary, one in five victims of car theft, 14% victims of street theft. Moreover, 17% of youth surveyed reported that they had been victims of violent assault and 14% (mainly girls) victims of sexual assault. The survey suggests, in contrast to media coverage and political point scoring, that Sydney's NESB inhabitants, like their ESB neighbours, are more likely to be victims of crime than offenders, although they typically appear as criminals in the media and in political debate.

Community safety is the other side of the coin to fear of crime. The research reported here reveals an important paradox in regard to community safety in Sydney. The same people who revealed the extent of their concern about crime also thought that their local area was a safe place to live in. This finding is all the more startling since most of those surveyed lived in Sydney's south-western local government areas (LGAs), the very suburbs that are regularly reported as being at the heart of crime-ridden Sydney. Overall, 71% reported that they felt safe in their own area, a finding roughly comparable with recent research (Tulloch et al. 1998b:18–19). The Australian Bureau of Statistics national crime survey also found that 80% of people felt safe inside their homes during the day, but this dropped to 69% at night (cited in Wainwright 23–24/8/03a:3). In our study, feelings of safety were highest in the Hurstville LGA (80%), and lowest in the Fairfield and Bankstown LGAs, the areas most frequently represented as dangerous in the media, where around 55% of those surveyed felt safe there. Males felt safer in their suburbs (78%) than did females (65%), with youth generally feeling safer in their local area than adults

South-western Sydney's 'unsafe' places are mostly public transport nodes at night: the railway station, the car park and the bus stop. Only three out of every ten surveyed felt safe using Sydney's public transport at any time, with youth feeling safer on public transport than adults. In contrast, an earlier NSW Police survey found that 72% felt safe on public transport during the day (although this drops to 20% when asked about night-time travel (cited in Tulloch 1998a:26). Parks and recreation areas were also felt to be dangerous at night. The local shopping centre can also be a place where adults in particular can feel unsafe: 30% of adults surveyed felt unsafe in the local shopping centre (about the same as the NSW Police survey), compared to 12% of youth surveyed.

There was tension, however, between youth and adults with respect to use of these public spaces. In respect of this tension, the youth ranked conflict with police highest, followed by conflict with adult residents, security guards and shopkeepers. This highlights a critical issue about community safety in Sydney. Other studies have also found that when young people do hang out in groups in Sydney's public spaces such as shopping malls, many are made unwelcome, especially when they are seen to lack a legitimate purpose, such as spending (White 1998; YAPA 1997).

Youth gangs have captured many a media headline in Sydney over the past four years. It is not surprising then that 64% of adults surveyed agreed that there was a problem with youth gangs. Youth seem more ambivalent on this issue, with 55% agreeing that there is a problem with youth gangs in the Sydney area. Given the coverage of 'ethnic crime' in recent years, we investigated the perceived link between ethnicity and youth gangs in the minds of the multicultural public in south-western Sydney. Perhaps surprisingly, the majority (albeit a slight majority only) did not link youth gangs with particular cultural backgrounds. Those that did so were more likely to living in the Canterbury, Rockdale and Hurstville LGAs than in the Fairfield, Auburn, Liverpool and Bankstown LGAs. Those who did link criminal and youth gangs to particular cultural groups most commonly volunteered the categories 'Lebanese', 'Middle Eastern' and 'Arabic' or 'Asian', 'Chinese' and 'Vietnamese'. What emerges strongly here is that crime and criminal gangs have been ideologically reconstituted as an 'ethnic problem', that is, as a non-Anglo-Celtic phenomenon in Sydney, despite crime statistics and histories to the contrary.

The survey found that community attitudes to policing were clearly polarised. About six out of ten adults thought that the police were handling organised crime and youth gangs in Sydney 'very well' or 'well'. Two out of three adults ranked police handling of young people — as distinct from gangs — as 'very good' or 'good'. On the other hand, six out of every ten youth surveyed rated police handling of organised crime and youth gangs in their area as 'poor' or 'very poor', and over half (55%) rated police handling of youth in general as 'poor' or 'very poor'. Almost two in every three youth surveyed (62.8%) thought that police picked on young people because of their cultural background: those from Asia, the Middle East and Lebanon were mentioned most often.

Several conclusions can be drawn from these findings. First, many of those surveyed shared in perception of a 'crime wave' encouraged by some media and politicians, and expressed levels of concern which reflected that perception. Second, many shared the racialised association of ethnicity and crime that was part of media coverage and political debate — a link that also seemed to be accepted by many community leaders discussed earlier. Third, however, there is also a creeping distrust of the police, as representatives of law and order in Sydney, which accords with the second of the two frames that we analysed in Chapter Two.

Most importantly, the discrepancy between the perception of crime as a major social problem and the feelings of safety in these supposedly crime-ridden areas suggests that NESB people, like Australians generally, share in the pervasive social mood exhibiting significant fear of crime, but that this fear is still a relatively abstract concern, not related directly and simply to everyday experience. The often hysterical coverage of crime in south-western Sydney suburbs, not the personal experience of it, has buttressed an exaggerated concern for crime in the minds of many Sydney-siders. This distinction between abstract fears and concrete dangers is a fundamental one to the risk society literature (Furedi 1997:105), and fear of crime studies consistently demonstrate the discrepancy between the 'objective' likelihood of falling victim to crime and the 'subjective' perception of that risk (Tulloch 1998a:8). It suggests that there is more at issue here than a rational assessment of the real threats people face in their daily lives.

It is difficult to compare the findings from this project with those of the (very few) fear of crime studies undertaken in Australia; not just because the sample here is not representative of the nation as a whole, but also because of the variations in the instruments and methodologies used in those few studies, and the subjective nature of the issues at stake. Nevertheless, it is worth repeating here several findings from elsewhere. The first point is that a regular NSW survey of people's perceptions of the problems of crime in their localities shows that while the proportion of people answering that there was a problem has increased over the decade across NSW, there has not been an increase in Sydney itself (although there have been annual fluctuations). In 2001, 55.4% of residents of NSW felt that crime was a problem in their neighbourhood, while the figure in Sydney was 58% (Wainwright 23–24/8/03a:3).

The second point is that these studies echo the oft-repeated finding that fear of crime varies according to gender and age (Tulloch 1998a:16). The conclusions that fear of crime is higher amongst the poor, less educated and ethnic minorities are, however, less clear-cut (Tulloch 1998a:17). These findings on social class and ethnicity contrast with a survey conducted by BOCSAR in 1999, which found that people living on Sydney's north shore (with a higher concentration of residents from wealthier backgrounds) recorded a higher level of fear of crime than those in the outer west. Moreover, they were more likely to be worried about youth gangs and louts, while residents of Fairfield and Liverpool were concerned about drug-related crimes and burglary (*Daily Telegraph* 30/6/99:3). Don Weatherburn concluded that this showed people were more concerned about issues that directly affected them, but while it does confirm a distinction between abstract and concrete fears, it also suggests that there is a class and racial dimension to fear of crime when youth gangs are involved. The fear of such gangs is highest where there is a higher concentration of Anglo Australians of high socio-economic status, and where such gang activity is less likely to occur.

If we conducted our survey today, when September 11, the Bali bombings, asylum seekers, the 'race rape' cases and the law and order election campaign are fresh in the minds of Sydney-siders, it might well reveal different results: and, most notably, perhaps a diminution of perceived community safety in Sydney. Certainly, analysis of media coverage, including letters to the editor, indicates a heightening of social fears and a narrowing of the gap between abstract fears and concrete dangers.

The discrepancy between objective likelihood of falling victim to crime and the subjective perception of risk has its corollary in media and political commentary on the terrorist threat to Australia. We have been told for several years now, and we are still being told, that Australia has become a prime target for terrorist attacks. The *Herald* headed a report of comments by Clive Williams, director of Terrorism Studies at the Australian National University, as 'Australia near top of terrorist list' (Goodsir 22–23/2/03:14). The same journalist wrote a story emphasising the 'traitors within (Goodsir 14/7/03:1). The *Australian* paraphrased remarks by

Attorney-General Daryl Williams as 'We're in reach of Mid-East Terrorists' (Kerin & Stewart 28/5/03:1). The Prime Minister warned that a terrorist attack was a 'grim possibility', even though he had had no reports of such a threat (Allard & Snow 9–10/8/03:16). Against these claims, a much less widely reported assessment of Australia's vulnerability to terrorist attack by a risk assessment analysts listed Australia as 38 out of 168 countries, and lagging well behind the US and Britain (Harris 28/8/03:5). Yet this seems somewhat incidental to rising panic around the possibility of attack: indeed, the threat seems very near. In the current international climate, fear of local crime and distant terrorist threat have merged to become 'the fear outside everyone's door' (Murphy 27–28/4/02:25).

Fear of everything

Fear of crime is not simply a reasonable calculation of falling victim to crime: as we have already seen throughout this book, the social perception of crime is interwoven with a range of ideological frames and assumptions, and is folded in with an array of social events and concerns, which makes the fear of crime more than just a fear of crime. The burgeoning literature on the rise of 'risk society' rightly demonstrates that social anxieties are rarely straightforward manifestations of real threats. We fear some dangers more than others, Furedi (1997:27) points out, not because of the real threat they pose — we are of course much more likely to be injured in a car or a bath than attacked by a gang or killed by a terrorist — but because they embody deeper anxieties about social cohesion, trust, human control, a meaningful life. When moral panics around crime are interlinked with concerns around 'boat people' and terrorists, and articulated with insecurities about sundry minor changes of daily life in Australia, then we have a layered social phenomenon built on a complex of anxieties which 'find their voice' at particular moments in specific objects of concern. The pervasiveness of these anxieties and the chains of association we have mapped in this book result in the rendering of a range of culturally different behaviours as 'deviant', a process of criminalisation which conflates illegality with transgression of the social conventions of the dominant culture. As we suggested in Chapter One, this complex involves anxieties around social and cultural cohesion, economic change and the failure of political order — indeed, it exudes a fear of everything, but is given a racial hue.

This complex of racialised fears was evident in the recent furore over the proposed building of a prayer centre for Muslims (particularly those of Indian origin) in the semi-rural Sydney suburb of Annangrove, in the strongly middle class, Anglo-Celtic Hills district, which is heavily sprinkled with Christian fundamentalists. Baulkham Hills Council rejected the plan after massive, negative community response (with around 5000 objections), claiming it was not compatible with the area and 'not in accordance with the shared beliefs of the community'. One local feared that people would come from 'outside' the area — from 'as far away as Granville and Earlwood', to worship at the centre. The mayor, emphasising that the centre did not fit in with the values and aspirations of the community, said there was a fear of 'what could happen' as a result of the presence of Muslims' (Morris 19/12/02:21).

Yet this claim is spurious. While Baulkham Hills LGA, in which Annangrove is located, is one of the areas least affected by waves of recent migration, it is hardly free of a migrant presence: 37% of males are overseas-born (Millett 5–6/7/03b:30). The oft-stated claim about the area being a distinct and somewhat secluded entity with a strong sense of community is also something of a myth: it is on the edge of the second-fastest growing region in the state and has the highest level of car ownership in Sydney (Richards & Saleh 1/8/03:25).

Nevertheless, there is a real sense of a 'quiet community' under threat. While locals in the Annangrove stressed that they were not being racist, just simply asking to retain their community feel, it is the ethnic nature of this community and what is perceived to threaten it that are explicitly at issue. With what can only be an allusion to the 'ethnic gang rape' incidents, the mayor argued that he was 'concerned about the girls and ladies in the community' (Morris 28/11/02:7). After the Land and Environment Court over-ruled the Council's decision, other locals were more abrupt, claiming that Muslims were 'coming in from the outside', and that they should 'stay in Muslim Areas', 'like Punchbowl'. The site proposed for the prayer centre was vandalised with racist graffiti, saying 'Mosques out' (Saleh & Morris 31/7/03:11). While this belongs to a longer history of (largely Anglo-Australian) resistance to the development of mosques in local government areas based on racist stereotypes of Islamic fanaticism, patriarchy and intolerance (Dunn 2001), the current contexts of 'ethnic rape' and international terrorism have given these responses greater resonance. It is not surprising, then, that a One Nation (2003) election pamphlet should begin by asking 'Is There a Mosque Coming Near You?', and answering that mosques attract 'hordes of men with too much time on their hands'.

Abbas Aly, the man who is proposing to build the Annangrove centre, commented: 'They use the word "fear" — I want them to define what that fear is, then solve it'. The President of the Supreme Islamic Council of NSW, Gabriel Elgafi, responded to objections that the prayer centre, or 'mehfil', would 'be contrary to the shared beliefs, customs and values of the close-knit community' (O'Rourke 13/5/03:3) with the questions, 'what is the belief of the community? What are they? Are we not part of that community?' (Morris 19/12/02:21). It is exactly that vague sense of fear and the equally vague but exclusive sense of what the 'community' is and believes which are at stake here. As Aly suggests, we need to unpack what exactly constitutes this complex of fears.

The first and most obvious theme built into this complex is the fear of the Other. As we illustrated in Chapters One and Two, the construction of an 'Arab Other', which ideologically weaves together groups of disparate people, exhibits a deep-seated anxiety towards the presence of 'exotic strangers' in or near Australia. This 'invasion anxiety' has been a recurring feature of Australian society since the arrival of Europeans — especially fears about Indigenous people and about the 'Yellow Peril' or the 'Asian hordes' (Burke 2001). In many ways the Arab Other has simply assumed the role of the primary threat, both as the 'unpredictable stranger' central to fear of crime (Lupton 1999a) and as the external threat central to our invasion anxiety. But the Other is always a necessary fiction in the construction of modes of national belonging and identity which says more about those modes of belonging and identity than the putative object itself. In identifying and excluding the Other, we project onto this object problems that emanate from within the social formation. An invasion anxiety is fundamentally an anxiety about vulnerability to invasion rather than a fear of the invader. Nevertheless, blaming the Other — the Aborigine, the immigrant, the refugee — is a pervasive operation in contemporary Western societies (Back, Schuster & Solomos 6/5/02:13).

This same move has occurred in Australia, where immigration and the social policies of multiculturalism are ideologically represented as a primary cause of a raft of economic and social problems. This came through very clearly in each of the events discussed in this book. But the issue is not immigrants themselves, rather what they do in and to Australia that causes problems. Many letters to the editor and opinion pieces stress this — that the authors have no problems with people coming to Australia (indeed, many of their best friends are probably foreigners!), it is their failure to assimilate (or integrate) with an Australian way of life and its attendant values and beliefs that is being criticised. We have already cited a number of correspondents and commentators bemoaning the failure of immigrants to assimilate in Chapter One: others repeat this desire for the assimilated migrant in different ways. One letter-writer to the *Telegraph*, attempting to 'defend' people from other cultures and religions in the wake of the furore over the banning of Santa Claus in a Christian school, gave examples from a Hindu gathering of children with a 'broadminded view that makes them tolerant and inclusive': 'Surely these are the sort of new Australians we need. Those who appreciate our traditions and are able to integrate easily into the community with no fuss' (Beckle 13/12/02:31). Here we have not a right-wing diatribe against migrant intolerance and inassimilability, but liberal applause for the migrant who integrates: either way, however, the assumptions about the value of assimilation, and the cohesiveness of the culture migrants are integrating with, are the same. As we saw in the 'lost between two cultures' discourse, the debate turns on shared values that themselves may need interrogation.

But what is the problem here? NESB Australians are still very much in the minority in this country — long-time Australians and ESB migrants (who are usually presumed to share this culture) still dominate numerically and in terms of positions of economic and political power. Can anyone force long-time Australians to adopt foreigners' ways and values? Apparently there is a perception, as we saw earlier, that 'Australians' (that is, white, Anglo-Celtic Australians) are being forced to abandon their own culture and adapt to others' ways. There are two or three interleaving elements here, then: anxiety around cultural dissolution and its consequences for social cohesion, and hence anxiety around social change; and anxiety around the compulsion to change, around political authorities and economic forces intervening in people's lives.

The fear that Australia has become a place of cultural division, not just cultural difference, is a pervasive one. In March 2002, a front-page *Herald* article announced, 'Fears of cultural rift as Sydney's migrant magnet works overtime'. The influx of mainly Asian and Middle Eastern migrants was producing 'two Australias', riven by a 'cultural divide' (Millett 18/3/02:1). This was really about a division between Sydney and Melbourne on one hand, and the rest of the country on the other, partly but not entirely resulting from patterns of migration, yet was presented primarily as an ethnic division. Two months later, the *Australian* ran a series of items over several days under the same title of 'The Cultural Divide'. Though these articles were overwhelmingly positive about migration, cultural diversity and multiculturalism (see, for example, *Australian* 8/5/02:12–13), the title under which they ran sets the tone for the overall debate, repeating the kinds of assumptions about cultures that we saw in Chapter Three. The theme of fragmentation has been an increasingly pervasive one in Australia over the last decade. In the wake of the Federal election in 2001, Mike Seccombe described Australia as a 'fractured nation' (17/2/02:25,30–31). Sydney in particular is seen to exemplify this fragmentation: 'Fractured Sydney' is seen to be riven equally by 'race and wealth' (Millett 5–6/7/2003b:23,30). Based on claims by academic researchers that there were now 'two Sydneys', the media accentuated the divisions around property and wealth and cast them in terms of the 'ethnic map' of the city, or 'The two *faces* of Sydney' (*Sydney Morning Herald* 5–6/7/03:32, our emphasis). This fear of a divided 'home' — be it city or nation — is, of course, what gave purchase to the slogan, 'One Nation'.

Of course, much of the concern that cultural conflict is inevitable with groups such as Muslims, Afghans and Lebanese is ill-founded: the history of Afghan traders and Lebanese hawkers in Australia, and Australian soldiers in the Middle East in World War One spring to mind as examples of amicable relations and demonstrate that there is no essential 'cultural clash'. A similarly problematic assumption is that Australia is being swamped by migrants from exotic cultures and religions. Australia's 'racial make-up' is still predominantly European (Megalogenis 9/5/02:13). A different belief that Sydney is home to a series of 'ethnic ghettoes' is similarly inaccurate (Megalogenis 13–14/7/02:19,22) — but still holds popular sway. Many white Australians feel they are being swamped, excluded, forgotten — as the denizens of Annangrove attest. A One Nation (2003) pamphlet for East Hills asked (of an implicitly Anglo-Australian voter) during the 2003 NSW election: 'Are you sick of multiculturalism — feeling like a stranger in your own country?' As a result, the cause of social division and the dissolution of community is seen to be the presence of cultural difference, as the criticisms of unassimilated migrants suggest. It is only by untangling this web of anxieties that we can begin to see how, for example, a number of rapes by a small number of NESB men come to be seen as evidence of fundamental social fracturing, and of the failure of multicultural social policies. The 'failure' of multiculturalism is an overriding theme in the opinion pieces of the *Telegraph* and elsewhere. One *Telegraph* article explained, amidst the gang rape trials, 'Why the melting pot is ready to boil over' — a metaphor earlier resorted to by the *Australian* (Chulov 18–19/8/01:1,4) — citing a survey that claimed that Parramatta, the heartland of multicultural Australia, was 'bubbling with barely concealed racism' (Morris & Hu! 12/7/02:6). In all these articles and letters the point is made repeatedly that 'they' (ungrateful migrants and intolerant workers) killed social and multicultural harmony, that it is a problem of someone else's doing.

In the weeks leading up to Christmas, 2002, one bizarre furore captured the fever pitch of Australia's anxieties regarding cultural difference and change. The headmaster of a fundamentalist Christian school sent parents a newsletter explaining their policy of disabusing students of the fantasy of Santa Claus, arguing that it was not part of Christian tradition. (This was a *fundamentalist Christian* school, incidentally —a fact lost on many complainants railing about 'fundamentalist' Muslim immigrants!) This unleashed a whirlwind of invective, led by the *Telegraph*, directed at the excesses of multiculturalism. This in itself was bizarre, because the school's policy was based on a strict Christian focus on the birth of Jesus as the central feature of Christmas. Nevertheless, it automatically became a debate about multiculturalism, and in particular the intolerance of Muslims towards Christian traditions (Connolly & Cazzulino 30/11/02:1–2), and the problem of 'divisiveness' arising from 'Australians' having to 'defer to other cultures in fear of causing offence' (*Daily Telegraph* 30/11/02:24). The *Telegraph* ran a 'save Santa' campaign, including posters declaring, 'Santa, We Believe', as though this was a central tenet of white, Western, Christian culture. Anxieties around cultural division were woven into anxieties about cultural change and the end of childhood innocence; unsurprisingly, the Prime Minister stepped in to 'defend' Santa (Connolly & Cazzulino 30/11/02:1–2).

But it is not simply differences in cultural values that are at stake: given the evaluative judgements implicit in the language of barbarism and civility, and perceptions of Christian and non-Christian values, the problem is seen to be that migrants from different cultures have a lesser morality than the dominant Anglo-Celtic one. In this, the criticisms of Islamic terrorism, Lebanese crime and Sharia law, as in the sentence to stoning of a woman in Nigeria for adultery, and the 'attack on Santa', are at one. Explaining danger or threat typically relies on a moral frame, because it allows for the easy attribution to someone, often an outsider, of fault, and hence calls for vengeance. Blame also serves the social function of solidarity (Douglas 1992:5–6). Rejecting the argument that poverty and inequality are the fundamental causes of crime, *Telegraph* columnist Piers Akerman argues that the Great Depression did not produce the same crime waves in Australia: 'Purely and simply, a stricter code of community morality existed'. While Akerman does not make an explicit link to migration, as a well-known critic of multiculturalism and someone who has frequently commented on the problems of 'ethnic crime', his allusion to the different 'communities involved in criminal activities' in Sydney and New York in this article plainly refers to the impact of migration on this dissolution of a clearly defined community morality (Akerman 23/5/02:28).

Part of Australia's problem is that 'we' are so damned decent: 'We are becoming so tolerant and accepting of other cultures that we are losing our cultural identity' (Mulhall 3/12/02:26). In a series of letters compiled under the heading 'Lesson of a society apart', correspondents to the *Telegraph* (20/8/02:19) make it clear that Western and Middle Eastern cultures are incompatible, linking this to the crimes of the 'Lebanese' rapists, the separatism of women-only gyms, and the inability of Lebanese and Muslim migrants to integrate, to 'accept the Australian way of life'. Similarly, it is 'they' who discriminate, such as was perceived in the case of the Muslim women-only gym.

It is not simply cultural difference that is at issue here, or even different moral systems: immigration is increasingly seen as the cause of an array of social problems, especially in a place like Sydney: demographic and urban change, and environmental destruction, as well as crime. The 'cultural rift' discourse referred to above, talked about how the influx of migrants into Sydney was 'skewing the city's demographics'. The resulting 'cultural schism' was 'increasing the economic, political and social pressures on Sydney as it faces people movements unrivalled elsewhere in the country' (Millett 18/3/02:6). The division here was more than between Sydney and Melbourne on one hand, and the rest of Australia on the other. Given Sydney's constant preoccupation with real estate, it was inevitable that the recent events would fuel another call to reduce immigration levels on grounds of urban sprawl. This time, Bob Carr called [again] for reduced intakes, arguing [again] that over-population was adding to Sydney's urban woes, increasing residents' concerns regarding over-development and the erosion of lifestyle, and linked to the environmental impact of high migration (Totaro & Nicholls 30/11/02:25). The 'great Australian dream' of a house with a backyard is becoming an object of nostalgia, as Sydney becomes an 'international-type city' with greater demands for apartments or home units (Connolly 27/11/02:9). Also, of course, immigration has often been seen as a cause of unemployment (Duffy 17/8/02:16); now it is seen as the cause of Sydney's 'splitting' (Millett 5–6/7/03a:1). It is perhaps no coincidence that a furore over a prayer centre should occur in Annangrove, not because it is the centre of Anglo-Australia, but because it is on the fringe of rapid and extensive urban development, suffering from an absence of infrastructure. Concerns about social change and the loss of a sense of local community, therefore, have much deeper roots than the threat posed by a small Indian Muslim prayer centre, but in a context of terrorism and 'ethnic crime', these are projected onto the very visible difference of Islam. As discussed in Chapter Five, in the name of environmental and urban care, Bob Carr has emerged as one of the most outspoken critics of Australian immigration since Pauline Hanson.

Rather than simply see these as bad explanations of social phenomena (which they certainly are), we also need to see these moments as expressing real anxieties around economic change. The articles discussing cultural division mentioned above inevitably refer to the economic dimensions of social division, even if this is initially seen in terms of ethnicity. An article on Hurstville in Sydney's south after several violent crimes occurred there linked the escalation of crime in the area to immigration, but also to high density housing policy and to changes in the local economy of the suburb (Murphy 27–28/4/02:25). Amidst fears of economic downturn in Australia, and in the midst of drought and its economic consequences for farmers and Australia's agricultural exports, it is no wonder that the description of refugee detention centres as 'Five star asylums' (Penberthy 17/12/02:1) renewed the bile which the *Telegraph*'s letter-writers directed at asylum seekers and the costs of supporting them. It is not always easy to tease out these dimensions of the anxieties directed towards migrants, refugees and NESB Australians, but they bubble away underneath, compounding an earlier association. Well before these events, Pauline Hanson tapped into the insecurities resulting from globalisation, economic restructuring, rising unemployment, the casualisation of work and the decline of rural Australia. Her trump card was to link this insecurity to ethnic and Indigenous minorities. As suggested in Chapter Two, the links between social phenomena are often implicit because of the accumulation of cultural representations. Sometimes it is more explicit: Michael Duffy's article on the 'racial reality' of multiculturalism pointed out that many Lebanese migrants were unemployed and drew on welfare, producing ethnic ghettoes. He also argued however that the presence of these migrants caused greatest suffering to working class white Australians, because migrants constituted 'competition for working class jobs' (Duffy 17/8/02:16).

The current fears of globalisation are, however, more implicit than in the rhetoric of One Nation, perhaps partly because the current climate involves vitriolic attacks on left-wing anti-globalisation protesters. Nevertheless, concerns regarding the consequences of globalisation abound in odd ways. Most obviously, the recognition of the global nature of terrorism articulates one set of anxieties about living in a globalised world. The image of Osama bin Laden as an octopus with tentacles around the globe reaching to Australia, apart from echoing the infamous nineteenth-century *Bulletin* cartoon of a 'Chinaman' as an octopus and its white Australian fears of Asian hordes, captures this sense of penetration from the outside (Warren 28/10/02:14) (see Figure 4). The idea of bin Laden as an octopus was a common throughout the west (Bruce 18/9/02). The *Telegraph* headlined 'GLOBAL TERROR' when Chechen rebels occupied a Moscow theatre (Wilson & Harvey 29/10/02:1), linking it to Al Qaeda, and articles on the new global nature of terror included world maps showing this degree of penetration, and the end of Australia's isolation from it (*Time* 28/ 10/02:44–45; Dickins 30/10/10–11). Reference to Australia's innocence was paralleled by talk of Australia no longer being a 'safe haven'; as the *Telegraph* put it, in this 'world fed on hate', 'Terrorism is no longer on our doorstep, it is here' (20/11/02:30). In the midst of this emerged claims that mosques in Australia were being financed by Middle Eastern money (Cameron 25/11/02:1,4).

The anxieties expressed in these examples also convey a sense of the failure of State institutions. In Chapter Two we demonstrated how the war metaphor was also turned against police and political leaders, who were seen to be as much of a problem as violent 'ethnics'. After several years in which the NSW Police Service had become highly politicised and prone to scathing attacks, largely by right-wing media commentators, the undermining and subsequent departure of Commissioner Peter Ryan did little to restore public faith in the leadership of policing in NSW. As analysts at the time argued, the appointment of Michael Costa as the new NSW Police Minister continued to demonstrate that political and media intervention in policing were powerful factors in the management of the force (Wilkinson 7/2/02:4; Poynting 2002:239).

This resulted in what Miranda Devine referred to as 'jaded citizens' (Devine 7/12/02:12). A series of events after Ryan's replacement by Ken Moroney — further restructuring of the force, fears of a handgun epidemic, internet trade in firearms, a series of murders, including the murder of a policemen, and savage fights amongst armed youth, including several based around schools, as well as the release of statistics showing increases in violent crime — did little to diminish the sense of failure. At the same time, various initiatives — increased use of surveillance technologies, the allowing of police to work in their spare time as security officers, random knife searches and the greater use of dogs in searches, the presence of police in schools — raised concerns about increased police powers. While the majority of commentators and letter-writers approved of these new powers and dismissed the spectre of a 'police state' (*Daily Telegraph* 23/4/02:14), others were less sanguine about the 'invasion of our civil liberties' (Clark 24/5/02:25). This wasn't just a NSW issue: Australian police, for example, have been shown to use phone-tapping at 20 times the rate of their US counterparts (Banham 24/9/02:16).

As well as the NSW police, the state government was held accountable for many of these problems, and much venom was also directed, as it was during the rape trials, at a legal system which supposedly failed to punish criminals appropriately, or even at all. Miranda Devine (7/4/02:15) condemned the NSW government, its public service and the courts for 'Turning a blind eye to blood on the streets'. But it was not just police and state political leaders that have been the object of criticisms, and it was not just in relation to gangs and crime — a range of authorities came under fire during many of the media stories we have described here. The Anti-Discrimination Board, and bureaucracy generally, was roundly condemned for 'political correctness' and 'multiculturalism gone mad' during the 'Muslim gym' affair (*Daily Telegraph* 15/8/02:30). David Penberthy, in a particularly crude example of populist demagoguery, lined up 'small-s society' (us), 'a vast and disorganised mass of humanity which judges issues on their merits', against 'Big-S Society' (them), groups which operate on the basis of self-interest or ideology — The Law Society, the Council for Civil Liberties, leftish judges, academics and other organisations (20/9/02:28). A One Nation (2003) state election pamphlet makes comparable elisions by simply listing its gripes as multiculturalism, the health system, criminal justice and policing.

Both the refugee and the terrorist crises have occasioned criticism of wider political authority. Particularly but not only in the wake of the 'children overboard affair', distrust of political leaders has been high, with trenchant criticism from the liberal left. The popular response to the federal government's handling of the asylum seekers has been, on the surface, largely supportive. However, we suspect that in the long run this will only confirm Australians' political cynicism. One regular survey of levels of 'well-being' found that satisfaction with government fell 5 points to 52.2% during 2002 (Kerin & Balogh 10/7/02:3). Other evidence suggests that cynicism is growing. In the midst of the federal government's calls for us to be alert, it was revealed that the 'war on terror' would be cramped by 'cost bungling': 'Australia's defence forces face cuts to vital weapons programs as they prepare for the dangerous new world of terrorism and increased regional instability' (Allard 16/12/02:1). This followed the bizarre standoff between the major parties regarding the anti-terrorism laws, resulting in the failure to pass any legislation for several months. This 'political brinkmanship over Australia's security' which showed the major leaders 'at war' (Banham 14–15/12/02:1) was seen as a case of party politics compromising issues of national security by members of the letter-writing public. While the *Telegraph* Vote-line was probably divided on party lines — 46% of readers felt the government should not be blamed for not allowing enough time for debate, while 54% disagreed with this (*Daily Telegraph* 16/12/02:21), presumably many blaming the Opposition and the Greens for not passing the legislation — this division itself expresses a failure of national unity at a time when political leaders stress that this is what is needed. As Joan Kelly of Miranda put it, under the heading 'An act of irresponsibility':

> I am absolutely appalled that our politicians have not agreed on new anti-terrorism laws and have opted instead to go on holidays ... Our politicians were elected to manage and protect our country. In the interests of the nation, they should return immediately and remain there until an agreement has been reached and legislated (16/12/02:18).

At the same time, there is concern that new anti-terrorist legislation of whatever ilk could usher in the kind of police state that seemed hysterical six months previously. A generally positive front-page article by the *Telegraph* nevertheless alerts 'TERROR POWERS: Police can search first and ask questions later' — feeding upon this anxiety towards increased political intervention (English 19/11/02:1). On the other hand, letter-writers condemn Australian leaders and the various authorities for being unprepared for terrorist attacks, making Australia an 'Open House for terrorists' (*Daily Telegraph* 5/11/02:18). Similarly, the heavy-handed ASIO raids, while generally supported by 'right-thinking' Australians, combined with other examples of the ineptitude of intelligence organisations, confirms a lack of faith in political authority as a whole.

Taking all these things together, there is clearly an extensive *complex* of fears — the loss of social cohesion, the unsettling presence of cultural difference, moral decay, the failure of political leadership and institutional authority, globalisation and economic change — lying underneath the very public reactions to the events discussed in this book. Australia is a very scared place.

Fear of everything, everywhere

These fears congeal around particular events and objects, but they are always about a range of anxieties that are pervasive and ongoing, and not reducible to the presence of exotic migrants per se. What is important is that the anxieties are given materiality — a face ('of evil', whether it be Saddam Hussein, Osama bin Laden, the gang rapists, or an identikit of a young man of Middle Eastern appearance), a place (Gangland, Iraq, Bankstown, Afghanistan), a name (Lebanese, Taliban, Al Qaeda, Punchbowl Boys, Islam), and a 'crime' (rape, discrimination, terror, inassimilability) — a materiality which allows us to identify and at least symbolically control that anxiety. This tangible thing is something to aim for, to avoid, to blame, to capture, to fight, to punish, to imprison, to exclude: it gives us something on which we can act. For, when we are thrown up against events over which we have no control, we turn back onto those things we do (or think we do) — we recuperate a sense of agency and power lost in the immensity of threat, and exacerbated by the self-representation of innocent victimhood resulting from the desire to foreground the moral dimension of crime.

Yet at the same time, the global nature of these fears combines with our increasingly intimate relation to the objects of those fears to undermine the attempts we make to distance ourselves, morally, culturally and physically, from the underlying sources of anxiety, and hence undermines our attempts to recuperate power. The attempts to locate the object of fear somewhere removed from us fail, because, as with our sense of escalating crime, it is 'the fear outside everyone's door'; and, with global terrorism, it is 'no longer on our doorstep'. Not only is the problem here, then; it is everywhere. As Dave Madden, the NSW Deputy Commissioner of Police, said, 'I'm asked "Are shopping centres targets?", "Are night clubs targets?"; anything can be a target' (*Channel 7 News* 20/11/02). Indeed, as the articles kept reminding us, 'TERROR HITS HOME' (Karvelas 30/10/02:8).

This increasing awareness that we are no longer removed from terror is some recognition, however muted, that the problem is not out there, nor someone else, but is part of Australian society. There are hints at this throughout the articles cited above — particularly in regard to economic and political anxieties. But even in relation to concerns regarding cultural dissolution and social cohesion, there are moments that register that immigration is not the only, nor even the major, cause of our anxieties.

Attempts to construct a unified Australian-ness in the wake of Bali in particular — headlines that announce we are 'AUST-RALIANS TOGETHER' (*Daily Telegraph* 18/10/02:72–73), '19 MILLION MATES' (*Daily Telegraph* 19/10/02:1), and so on, come across as somewhat anxious attempts to reassure ourselves that there is no disunity, or that we can recover the unity that was once ours. This is predicated on the mythic belief in a once cohesive Australian community, but Australian society has always had social and cultural divisions — Indigenous and Irish Catholic inhabitants would happily testify to this — as well as significant economic inequalities of class, and political antagonisms.

The 'family' theme of national belonging is interesting here. Piers Akerman criticised the 'Muslim rugby league player' Hazem Al Masri after he had publicly called on Premier Carr to recognise Muslims as Australian to help them 'feel part of one family'. Akerman responded by saying 'Australians' had always been accommodating and happily invite migrants into the national 'family', but, quoting a local, radical Islamic magazine, argued that it was Muslim migrants who 'removed' themselves from this 'family' (Akerman 13/8/02:14). A few months after this, NSW Police Commissioner Ken Moroney admitted that the police could not fix all of Sydney's problems — that parents needed to take more responsibility, and instil respect in their children. The article implicitly compares Moroney's 'strong family' with a Tongan family whose boys were 'running wild' — implicitly associating poor parenting with ethnicity (Cameron 7–8/12/02:3).

On top of criticism of the history of the policy of the removal of Indigenous children from their parents, of the problems with the operations of departments of community and family services in Australia, of the federal government's treatment of refugee children in both the 'children overboard affair' and the detention centres, it seems disingenuous to criticise, as Howard did during the asylum seekers crisis, the bad parenting of NESB migrants. Again, it seems that deeply embedded anxieties regarding our own social fabric are played out through the fragile construction of a fictional bad Other onto whom we can project our own self-doubts.

Despite our attempts to contain our fears through the creation of objects of aggression and immorality, they always overflow that containment; they always exceed the rational. This is evidenced in some of the bizarre associations made in recent years, like that between fire and terrorism. What we can conclude from these associations is that not only do we fear everything, but that the things we fear are everywhere. As one 'expert' was quoted as saying, 'Watch out for danger everywhere' (Morris 22/11/02:4).

The management of fear

The problem for the State and for media organisations is how to handle these fears: the promotion of fear helps sell papers as much as governments, but only if the media, like government, can offer some apparent resolution to these fears, to tame them, to restore some sense of equilibrium. As the 2001 federal election showed, the successful deployment of public concerns around refugees and terror can be coupled with increasing levels of apathy and cynicism: these issues were considered important but overall there were low levels of public engagement (Bean & McAllister 2002:272). In any moment of uncertainty, there are always tendencies to both fundamentalism and cynicism: neither is beneficial to social cohesion or social justice (Hoggett 1989:32); but they are politically useful if they can be managed.

Moral panics, especially when they constitute a broader climate of fear, are not simply cultural affairs, negotiations over representation; they are tied to institutional power and state actions (Goode & Ben-Yehuda 1994:31), as Chapter Five has demonstrated. As we suggested at the beginning of this chapter, the 'politics of fear' is not quite complex enough to capture how governments and media have participated in the escalation of this panic culture. Certainly they have engaged in the cynical manipulation of fears, but they have not produced them in any simple and direct sense; moreover, these fears have to be handled carefully, not just inflamed, because their value lies in balancing fear and reassurance. As Douglas argues, fear tends to strengthen the lines of division in a society, not reduce them (1992:34); but in a society increasingly preoccupied with risks of all sorts, the strategies employed for taming our anxieties may also paradoxically exacerbate them (Lupton 1999b:13). It is perhaps better to say that we have seen processes exemplifying the management of fear, both for the handling of crime and offenders, and also as the handling of the wider population, at federal, state and local levels. The dilemmas of justice and identity, Burke argues, are reduced in Howard's vision to a managerialist task of facing change but providing reassurance. Yet the cause of the resentment may be government policy and the effects of globalisation, rather than imported terror itself (Burke 2001:186–7).

There is a lot of emphasis on reassuring Australians at the moment — at the expense of some serious effective social policy. There is a shift in government strategy at all levels to the cynical management of public mood. NSW Premier Bob Carr, turning his attention from domestic crime to the international crime of terrorism, admitted that 'we are trying to send a message of reassurance to the people of NSW' (*ABC News* 18/12/02); his government needed to show, he claimed, that the 'authorities' were responding to terrorism: 'people need that reassurance' (*Channel 9 News* 17/12/02). Similarly, Police Commissioner Moroney has made it clear that his task is as much about solving 'fear of crime' as it is solving the reality of crime (Cameron 7–8/12/02:3). In August 2003, Moroney, whose work performance was proposed to be judged on social 'perceptions' of crime as well as crime rates, called for the first comprehensive survey of fear of crime, echoing the Premier's comments of eight months earlier: 'People want reassurance'. He added that 'the fear of crime can be as debilitating as the crime itself'. In a telling admission, however, he claimed that: 'I need to know that the strategies and policies we are implementing are working. The best approach would be to survey community attitudes on the fear of crime' (Wainwright 23–24/8/03a:3). As both Akerman (23/5/02:28) and Wainwright (23–24/8/03b:29) suggest, our 'sense of security' regarding crime and policing has been 'shattered' because of the focus on local crimes, national issues such as illegal immigration and international political crises.

To reassure us, however, we need to be anxious. We live in a world where campaigns for public safety (such as 'stranger danger') require the promotion of the fear in the first instance: we promote safety by promoting fear (Furedi 1997:25). The Howard Government's management of fear is well shown in its anti-terrorist campaign. Full-page advertisements in the major papers entitled, 'Protecting the Australian way of life from a possible terrorist threat' — were aimed to reassure us that all will be OK if we stay alert, but they fan the fears they seek to put out by reminding us that we need to be alert, that there is reason to feel threatened (Commonwealth Government 29/12/02:12).

To see how the Federal Government's anti-terrorism campaign is part of a larger genre of fear promotion, it is worth comparing the 'Let's look out for Australia' kit (Commonwealth Government 2003) to 'A kit for protecting your home from intruders', distributed by the Attorney-General's Department (2001) as part of the Commonwealth Government's National Crime Prevention Programme. The anti-terrorism kit is subtitled, 'Protecting our way of life from a possible terrorist threat'. The Intruders kit carries the same discourse of security and threat, safety and protection, with an implicit acknowledgment of a threat from 'outside'. Moreover, the Intruders' kit, while emphasising a discourse of the 'family' as being under threat, also locates this within a frame of national belonging; the anti-terrorism kit, while emphasising the issues around national security, links this to personal security and the need to protect Australian families. The latter begins with 'An important message from the Prime Minister', the former with 'A message from the Minister', Chris Ellison, giving it the imprimatur of national community. Against this overwhelming threat, both kits offer a sense of agency, a chance to do something in the face of near insurmountable fears — the Intruders kit talks about 'taking an active role, the anti-terrorism kit talks of 'playing a part'. The anti-terrorism kit offers a handy checklist of 'Possible signs of terrorism' and 'suspicious activity' (such as cars with low suspension or people videotaping important sites). The Intruders kit similarly provides a checklist 'to reduce the risk' and a practical guide to a 'safety audit'. The anti-terrorism kit offers a fridge magnet with emergency numbers; so does the Intruders kit. The point here is to draw attention to the shared generic features — of content, language and style — to emphasise how this economy of terror has become commonplace over the last decade and is not simply the result of recent international events. Our fears have been managed for some time now; the anti-terrorism campaign feeds upon these anxieties.

Similarly, Premier Carr was foremost in promoting a language of ethnic crime and Lebanese gangs (Collins et al. 2000), and yet also steps in at times to 'defend' the Muslim community and to promote racial harmony (Wainwright 18/10/02:3), and initiate cultural and leadership programs for Arabic youth (Kerr 11/7/01:4). The ASIO raids on the homes of Muslims with vague connections to Indonesian Muslim radicals was clearly a public relations exercise with the (majority Anglo-Celtic) electorate in mind — it was designed to be *seen* to be doing something, like zero tolerance and community policing, as much as, if not more than, achieving real intelligence, especially as one of those raided had previously invited ASIO to discuss his supposed contacts with Jemaah Islamiah (Morris 4/11/02:1). Carr also used this to his advantage, calling for defence force staff to guard Sydney targets, and introducing his own Terrorism Bill as his federal colleagues undermined the plan put forward by Howard (Allard et al. 23–24/11/02:27,34). Carr also used the theme of 'security' in his election campaign in March 2003. Placed just after the *Telegraph*'s regular coverage of the war in Iraq, which spans several pages, and most significantly following the sub-section on the 'War in Iraq: Home Front', the Labor Party placed a full-page advertisement headed 'A Secure Future' featuring a large photo of Carr in front of the national flag (Australian Labor Party 21/3/03:10). Carr is clearly drawing on allusions to the threat of international terrorism although this is not a state issue.

Late capitalist society is marked by what Zedner calls 'the pursuit of security', a preoccupation not just in crime control, but which extends through various levels of State and commercial activity, private and public life. The boom in private security services and technologies exemplify this 'security industry' as much as the growth in intelligence activities, and these both parallel the emergence of vigilantism and community-based crime prevention initiatives (2000:200, 207).

The consequence of this is, however, that in promoting fear to promote safety, governments and media always run the risk of being unable to contain the fears and anxieties they seek to assuage. As Allard et al. (23–24/11/02:27,34) register: 'Making people secure has in some ways enhanced anxiety'. Alongside the anxieties of the dominant culture, of course, are the very real fears of people of Muslim or Middle Eastern ancestry, who are increasingly becoming the target for social exclusion, racial vilification, state surveillance, intensive policing and race-hate campaigns (English & Cazzulino 2/10/02:11); there is a sense that they are 'Under siege and bracing for a war' (English & McDougall 1/10/02:10). Muslims in particular were increasingly 'in fear of growing paranoia' across Australia

(Karvelas 30/10/02:6). Barrie Unsworth, the NSW chairman of the Australia Day Council, has recently suggested that the anti-terrorist ads have contributed to a climate of 'fear and suspicion', and have especially undermined the confidence of the Islamic community (Taylor 23/1/02:28). As the levels of fear and paranoia grow, surveys have shown that Australians' sense of well-being has diminished markedly in the last few years (Horin 9/9/02:4; Morris 23/12/02:4).

Panic culture: the national paranoia

In the late 1980s, in what seemed at the time an example of postmodern hyperbole, Kroker, Kroker and Cook proposed the idea that the West, and especially the United States, embodied a 'panic culture', because panic had become 'the key psychological mood of postmodern culture'. They claimed that panic had become a free-floating reality, that ecstasy and anxiety were entwined, attaching themselves to all events and institutions: we had panic politics, panic sex, panic capitalism, and so on. Panic culture was marked by the disappearance of external standards of conduct, such that the social becomes the transparent field of cynical power, and by the dissolution of internal foundations of identity, such that selfhood becomes attached to the spectacles of a mediatised culture (1989:13–16). Social changes intersected with inner anxiety, producing depressive and persecutory anxieties — despair on the one hand and scapegoating on the other. They also resulted in a deep distrust of political leadership, and a retreat into fantasy, exemplified by the rise of the gated community (122–4,209). Hyperbole aside, and with some shifts of emphasis, Kroker et al. were not that far off the mark: we would say, however, that in the uncertainty, flux and fragmentation of late capitalism, we experience constant low-level fear, like a 'background radiation saturating existence' (Massumi 1993:24; Lupton 1999b:11), but which spikes in moments such as those we call moral panics.

This book has demonstrated that there is clear evidence in Australia of the pervasiveness of panic and its attachment to diverse phenomena exacerbated by media reportage, and of scapegoating, political cynicism and distrust, and that these articulate with the fantasy of a protective national community. The result is that we live in the state of what Hage calls 'paranoid nationalism': a nationalism that rests on an institutionalised culture of worrying which 'is the product of an insecure attachment to a nation that is no longer capable of nurturing its citizen'; instead of being a reality that needs to be protected, the nation becomes 'a fantasy that needs to be protected from reality'. This protection takes the form of an obsessive preoccupation with the threat of disorder (2002:3–4), and hence we must find constant objects of hostility.

Political paranoia, as described by Robins and Post (1997), typically involves delusions of persecution, and the projection of conflict and distrust onto malevolent others to provide an alternative to an unbearable reality. At issue in the complex of fears around terrorism, however, is more than just 'psychic disarray' caused by some vague western malaise of psychological 'emptiness' (Carroll 2002) — such a view neatly sidesteps the material foundations of these anxieties. Anxiety, as Wilkinson (2001) shows, is not just a psychological phenomenon, but a reaction to larger social changes that are experienced in subjective terms. The complex of fears we have described is more than just an arbitrary linkage of diverse anxieties. We are no longer talking about concrete fears in our immediate environments, but abstractions that are felt as present and immediate. Anthony Burke has detailed Australia's obsession with security throughout its history, an imperative shaped by our perilous existence as an outpost of European colonialism in the Asia-Pacific region. He cites an earlier 'refugee crisis' of 1999, which Philip Ruddock called a 'national emergency' and a threat to the nation's integrity, arguing that governmental responses of recent years have been out of all proportion given Australia's long tradition of dealing with illegal migration, and given the relatively minor problem Australia faced compared to other countries. Australia exhibits a desire to be secure from cultural strangeness, asserting a sense of national integrity that reveals more about its vulnerability, and produces a particular perception of security that rests on the exclusion and suffering of others (2001:xxii–xxv). Burke's analysis suggests that there is more at stake here than just policy, but a profound need for an ontological guarantee of existence and of a future, a search for historical, strategic, economic and ontological certitude (xxxvi,184). The power of the idea of security is its promise to secure and enable being, but it is a being that we need to question. It rests on a hegemonic masculinity that perceives politics as disordered, needing force for security, and it rests on the insecurity of others (265). Yet ultimately, Burke suggests, this form of security reproduces the very fear it is meant to contain, revealing the vulnerability of an impoverished sovereignty, Australian democracy and freedom of expression (325,328). There is, as he argues, a profound anxiety underlying the vision of John Howard about the lack of fixity to the Australian identity (187).

The mobilisation of fear amongst populations — and especially fear of the Other, but also fear of the unknown and fear of change — has always been a crucial implement for the maintenance of power. However, the development of organised capitalism and its attendant state complex saw this mobilisation become a more systematic mechanism. In the twentieth century, an increasing number of nation-states marshalled an array of resources in which the promulgation of a popular fear was an increasingly pervasive element. The 'populate or perish' dimension of the White Australia Policy is one such local example. Alongside state-based mechanisms, the twentieth century also saw the mass commodification of fear — popular cinema, for example, especially in the science fiction, war and horror genres, serviced this popular fear. News media — and especially the tabloid press and talkback radio — also operate on the ground of popular fears. The reasons for this need have been well covered elsewhere — the increasingly abstract social relations of organised capitalism, the resulting experiences of alienation and loss of community, globalisation and the increasing intensity of international conflict, technological change, increasing transnational flows, and so on. But it is of significance that we live in a world that is far safer than at any time in history (except for the potential threat arising from the nuclear arms race), and yet we are preoccupied more than ever with risk, danger and insecurity (Furedi 1997:54).

Fundamental to this paradox is the prevailing mood of existential insecurity: the world of late modernity is one in which we are no longer sure who we can trust, whether our identities and communities are meaningful any more, whether we have any agency in a hi-tech, corporate world. In an increasingly individuated world, the social character of human action is lost and we become accommodated to powerlessness (Furedi 1997:171).

As Giddens (1991:38) has argued, we strive for 'ontological security' — the sense of trust we have in the surrounding world. We need a basic confidence in the things and people around us to make it possible to act in the world. In a world of change, of complex social relations, we need constantly to secure our identities and relations to make our lives viable. The similarity between the anti-terrorism and home security kits is not coincidental: the home is the place where we most typically ground that ontological security (Dupuis & Thorns 1998) and the home is the site where the connections between private life and national belonging are forged (Noble 2002). It is no wonder, then, that the suburban home and ordinary mums and dads figure in our deepest anxieties about social conflict, as we saw in Chapter Two, or that Bali — as our 'backyard' — should have such great resonance for Australians and their perception of international terrorism as a direct threat. What seemed so shocking to some Australians about the incidents of group sexual assault, perhaps, was that it was 'RAPE IN THE SUBURBS', right next door (Wockner 12/7/02:1). In September, 2003, a number of incidents led to concerns that there was a spate

of 'gangland-style' hits in Sydney's suburbs: one article characterised these as 'attacks on homes' and, although brief, managed
to refer to 'homes' nine times (although the police raids in response
were noticeably conducted only on 'properties'), and managed to
make reference to the families of four of the victims (Kennedy 3/
9/03). It is clear that these events are seen to strike to the very
heart of Australian family life and suburban community.

Bauman (1999:14,5) suggests that in contemporary society
we desperately we seek a 'community without fears', but in vain,
and that this is really an issue about three things — in/security, un/
safety and un/certainty — which overlap. Looking back over the
coverage of these various incidents in this book we can see these
concerns of security, safety and certainty interweaving through
preoccupations with borders, violence and values. 'Safety', for
example — safe sex, personal and public safety, helplines, home
security — became a fundamental value in the 1990s as we
developed a greater consciousness of risk and a greater fear of
crime (Furedi 1997:1). Now 'security' has become as significant a
value, as Burke shows. Certainty (versus relativism) has been a
central problem in the debates around multiculturalism and a core
Australian culture: the *Sydney Morning Herald* included a feature
on 'Keeping the faith in a world less certain' to mark Australia
Day in 2003 (Morgan & Stephens 25–26/1/03:A2). These different
dimensions of fear feed upon each other.

Bauman argues that we only deal with these in one of two
ways. First, we fashion a sense of unity founded on 'killing an
enemy' (15): the Arab Other functions as this enemy in contemporary Australia, and its murder is both symbolic and increasingly
literal. Second, by turning our existential fears into something smaller
to worry about, some 'practical task' to perform, we find an object
for human action — harsher laws and sentences, tightening border
security and the detention of asylum seekers. But what we really
seek, Bauman suggests, is a more lasting sense of community,
agency and vision (44). Yet these short-term 'solutions' only

exacerbate the impossibility of addressing the real needs. Hage (2002:9) argues that 'hope' is in increasingly short supply in Australia; we cannot show compassion to marginalised people because 'to be able to give hope one has to have it'. US President George W Bush recently argued that 'government can write cheques — but it cannot put hope in people's hearts or a sense of purpose in people's lives' (Zackman 22/1/03:40). Howard's eschewal of 'the vision thing' of the previous Labor Government, and Carr's pragmatism, amount to much the same philosophy of political leadership. Yet, as we have shown, while the State increasingly disavows the task of providing hope, it does so at the same time it increasingly engages in the promotion of fear.

While we have stressed, in line with contemporary media theory, that 'fear of crime' and associated anxieties can't be reduced to or blamed on sensational media reporting (Tulloch 1999:34), the media have fundamental roles in voicing and shaping (often contradictory) perceptions about crime and related social problems: roles that help explain the disparity between escalating fear of crime out of proportion to the personal experience of crime. The media may be the only place we experience some threats, such as terrorism, and it provides a daily catalogue of such hazards (Wilkinson 2001:118). Crucially, the media encode crime, disorder and social hazards as fragmentation made coherent (Tulloch 1999:42). In doing this, they turn social anxieties into narratives of crisis and its containment that are consumable: contemporary media reshape violence and crime as a popular entertainment (Presdee 2000). Alongside the proliferation of police TV dramas and the current affairs reporting of crime and terror is the proliferation of documentaries and dramas around events such as September 11. While it is too simplistic to say that the media produce our anxieties, by offering endless, competing representations of social problems and crisis, especially in the forms of crime and terror, they produce uncertainties and conflicting interpretations that help create the grounds for wider anxieties (Wilkinson 2001:9,129).

The alignment of state policy and commodification of popular fears means that western nations in particular have a peculiar 'economy of terror': the promotion of fear and its appeasement. Governments, like popular media, help produce the anxieties they then seek to ameliorate — in the post-September 11 world, and in Australia after Bali, for example, governments and media 'talk up' the prospect of terrorist attacks, biological warfare, and the threat of nations such as Iraq — in order to reassure us that these threats can and will be dealt with. The same kind of economy of terror operates in the realm of law and order — the threat of ethnic gangs/drugs/rape etc are talked up in order to reassure us they will be overcome. However, this manipulation of fears and anxieties has dire consequences for the trust central to our 'ontological security'.

This economy of terror constantly throws up challenges to our ontological security in order to reassure us: the long-term effect of this is that our ontological security is ultimately undermined — and social anxieties become much more profound and destructive and less amenable to amelioration. The economy of terror described above operates largely as a fear of the Other, of difference, but in constantly throwing up threats it undermines the stability and coherence of our daily lives, revealing the fact that these threats emanate from us, from here, not from them or there. If national belonging is framed in terms of victimhood and persecution, there must ensue a crisis of social responsibility in which agency is given up (Young 1996:53,58). Australian identity and community has increasingly been framed not just in terms of fragmentation, but in terms of a nation *endangered*. The nation is aligned with 'white victimisation' that involves the construction of internal threats from Indigenous and ethnic minority groups (Mackey 1999:109–111).

We have demonstrated that alongside the attempts to depict the threats of crime and social decay as coming from Others, the depiction of threats *within* our social institutions — the police, courts, government, media — makes this process of blaming the Other unstable. Two brief examples will suffice: in July, 2003, a rising rugby league player Kane Mason was killed in an example of what the *Telegraph* admitted was 'a vicious hate crime', in a front-page article which screamed 'HATE KILLING', because the alleged murderer had intended to 'kill some niggers' (Goldner 29/7/03:1). The ethnicity of the alleged offender, Michael Clifford, was not given (nor was the Indigenous background of Mason explicitly stated) — in stark contrast to the 'race rape' coverage — yet it is implicit that this racist crime could not be sheeted home to non-English speaking background migrants. This followed (limited) coverage of Anglo-Australian racism towards Muslims in the wake of September 11 — both from extremist groups such as White Pride who conducted a 'race hate' campaign in Sydney's west (Morris 30/5/03:21) and from 'ordinary' Australians who give voice to the 'MINDLESS HATE IN THE SUBURBS' (Jopson 20–21/ 10/01:18). At the same time, the threat of the Arab Other has become somewhat less exotic: two men linked to Al Qaeda in September, 2003, were unhesitatingly, and repeatedly, identified as 'Australian men' (*Daily Telegraph* 4/9/03:17). The *Herald* was more abrupt and wider in its implications: 'Terror contact: finger points at Australians' (Goodsir et al. 4/9/03:1). Suddenly, the Other is not so Other.

The responses to these deep anxieties — the defence of ordinariness, the recuperation of national agency — can only be temporary, they cannot be sustained, and ultimately 'we' may be recognised as the source of our own fears. These tensions, however, fuel the increasingly 'paranoid nationalism' that constitutes Australia's national belonging and which keeps searching for objects of hostility onto which we can project our anxieties. What we have demonstrated throughout is that these anxieties are not simply remote concerns about some abstract notion of national belonging: this paranoia touches the very suburban heart of Australian national life. Themes of home, suburbia, ordinariness, family and local community resonate throughout the media reports and political rhetoric we have analysed in this book. There are close relationships between localised fear of crime and the feeling of safety in your neighbourhood and the perceptions of the threat of international terrorism. Moreover, the sense of threat destabilises the certainty and security we desire from the local and the familiar.

At the same time, it becomes harder to sustain the idea of the radical difference of Others. Hage (2002:141–2) argues that in the post-September 11 world it is not xenophobia that is the problem (fear of the Other), but a fear of the same. What really terrifies 'us' in the acts of suicide bombing, for example, is not the radical difference of the perpetrators, but their common humanity — the fact that they could be just like 'us'. Certainly, amidst the claims and images discussed here, we can see underneath a concern with the fate of humanity — not just at the hands of others, but in our own as well. Our world has a diminished sense of humanity and its potential, not only of others, as Hage suggests, but also of our own: we have an increasing sense of our passivity and fragility (Furedi 1997:10). The *Daily Telegraph* spoke of 'broken humanity' in the aftermath of the Bali bombings (Lalor 15/10/02:4–5). The shifting of agency onto a violent but mythic Other, in the face of the futility of our institutional responses, only exacerbates this. Our 'paranoid nationalism' rests on a narcissistic culture of worrying, rather than an ethic of care: a worrying that evinces a fragile national belonging premised on an obsessive concern with borders and their trans-gression (2002:3–4). In this environment, our collective and personal ontological security is massively eroded, exacerbating a sense of alienation and fostering a climate in which short-term and desperate responses — like the scapegoating of ethnic groups — becomes increasingly aggressive. What we really need, at this moment, is a different way of thinking community, agency and vision.

Conclusion

Against racist penal populism

This book has shifted a long way from its initial concern with the perceived link between crime and people of Middle Eastern ancestry in a context of increasing international concern regarding terrorism. In asking, 'How does a crime committed by an individual or group of individuals come to be seen as the fault of an entire ethnic group?', we demonstrated that this link involves not just some kind of racist mistake, but complex social perceptions which have at their heart larger issues to do with national belonging, multi-culturalism and international and domestic politics. They also, of course, centrally involve matters of economic disadvantage (Collins et al. 2000). We have shown how there have been in Australia and particularly in Sydney over the last few years, waves of moral panic around 'ethnic crime', youth gangs, 'race rape', asylum seekers and terrorism: a moral panic that sutures together, over time, a number of discrete events around a figure we have called the Arab Other which impacts at various levels of political and social life.

We have argued that the social imagining of the criminal in contemporary Australia increasingly involves the evocation of the Arab Other as a primary folk devil of our times: a figure which conflates Arabs, Muslims and Australians of Middle Eastern ancestry, and is grounded in an Orientalist pathology of crime, violence, barbarism and sexual rapaciousness. This racialised frame rests on the equation, in media reportage and political rhetoric, of the rowdy youth with the gang member, the rapist, the refugee and the terrorist, and their condensation into an aggressive Other. It also entails the criminalisation of cultural difference, set off by the merest examples of 'dog-whistling', as deviance from cultural and not just legal codes becomes the threatening transgression of social and moral order. This mythic figure informs not just the conservative perspectives on crime gangs, rape and terrorism, but also the responses of ethnic community leaders and more progressive attempts to understand 'cultural clash', yet it bears little relation to the lived experiences of (especially young) people of Arab and Muslim backgrounds. It provides, therefore, an ideologically charged 'explanation' of complex problems of crime, terror and cultural difference.

As we have outlined, the fear of crime has less to do with the calculation of real dangers than with a complex of fears that reveal deep and abiding anxieties embedded within contemporary Australian society and with the processes of economic, political and social division which increasingly structure cultural difference. These anxieties reach deep into the heart of Australian national belonging and suburban life. Rather than being ameliorated by social policy and debate, our fears around crime and terror are exploited by the media and by various levels of government. They have helped produce a climate where fear of crime is not just on the increase, but merges with perceptions of terrorist threats to foster a paranoid nationalism. This is not simply a symbolic process, but has substantial effects, as we have seen in various chapters, on policing and intelligence services, the judicial system, legal change, government, immigration and welfare policy.

The 'pursuit of security', and the increasing mobilisation of the rhetoric of security in these areas of social and political life, have culminated in what some commentators, here and overseas, have suggested is tantamount to a burgeoning 'police state' or 'state terrorism' (Ramsey 21–22/6/03:43; Klein 8/9/03:11; McCulloch 2002:54). While this is sometimes exaggerated, western and other countries have certainly seen the expansion of various law enforcement and intelligence powers in the wake of September 11 — in Australia, these include the extensions of powers to detain without charge, including those as young as sixteen, the extension of interrogation powers, the increase in jail terms for failing to cooperate, and so on (Walker 18/6/03:2). This is paralleled by increasing use of surveillance technologies and communications interception in Australia, at various levels of law enforcement (Lowe 12/9/03:10). These changes come on top of changes to policing and the criminal justice system — increasing numbers of police, anti-gang laws, zero tolerance tactics, new powers of search, standard minimum sentences, greater 'accountability' for judges, and so on — and the expansion of the private security industry. A central element across these changes is the associated rhetoric, supposedly responding to community demand, of 'getting tough' on crime and terror. Premier Bob Carr's NSW election campaign of 2003 was centred around this rhetoric (as had been Tony Blair's election in England). This was illustrated by a leaflet used to advertise the Labor government's 'tough decisions' (Australian Labor Party 2003): it featured the word 'TOUGH' spelt out with handcuffs.

A recent study has examined the international rise of this 'penal populism' and its recognition of the electoral benefits in heightening fear of crime. It argues that the law and order auction in state and federal politics is a relatively recent phenomenon, emerging most strongly during the 1990s, and relates directly to 'scaring up the votes' (Roberts et al. 2003; Totaro 27/1/03:). Despite research which shows that harsher punishments have no effect on crime rates, various governments and their oppositions have engaged in this 'penal populism', promising to increase penalties and the length of sentences, build more prisons, and to let murderous criminals, as Bob Carr promised, 'die in jail' (Peterson 5/9/02:5). Sparks (2000) argues that penal populism is linked to wider problems of state legitimacy in a neo-liberal environment of 'crisis management' which too easily uses punishment as a political device in the context of the dismantling of welfare programs and policies. As Roberts et al. (2003) argue, this populism, driven by (often spurious) 'public opinion', has short-term benefits for the parties involved, and sells newspapers, but it has no benefits for a humane and effective system of policing, law and imprisonment; it simply drives the fear of crime which underlies this opinion. The task of deterring crime, they suggest, needs more than bigger jails and longer sentences; and such reform would be aided by enlisting the insights drawn from research into crime, not simply bending to the whim of talkback radio and tabloid journalism.

The 'pursuit of security', realised in this penal populism, comes at some social cost. As Zedner (2000:211) and others have argued, the promise of community safety and solidarity is made at the expense of the social exclusion of marginalised groups, as particular ethnic minorities are identified as potential wrongdoers and sources of disorder. As we have suggested, rather than creating a sustainable sense of national belonging, this eats away at it, producing a paranoid nationalism. At stake, then, is not just the issue of better law enforcement and criminal justice policies, or even culturally sensitive policing (Chan 1997), as important as these are, but the wider issues of citizenship, community and cultural diversity. In this context of social exclusion, multiculturalism, as the set of policies that come to be seen as the source, rather than the response, to cultural difference, comes increasingly under attack. At the same time, effective responses to and insights into the complex causes of the fear of crime and its attendant perception of social disorder are lost in the rush of penal politics.

The death of multiculturalism?

Telegraph columnist Michael Duffy pronounced multiculturalism dead in August 2002 (17/8/02:16). The thrust of Duffy's argument was that the Lebanese Muslim rapists, by making their assaults into racial attacks, asserted their cultural separateness from mainstream Australia. He then detailed the extent of 'their' failure to assimilate, referring to high levels of unemployment, reliance on welfare, ghettoisation and criminal activity, as manifestations of this cultural separateness. He lambasted 'elites' for protecting a failed system on ideological grounds, and on grounds of self-interest (since they apparently benefited through cheap domestic servants) and hence doing a disservice to 'ordinary Australians'. Sundry opinion pieces and letters to the editor echoed the sentiment, as we have seen in the previous chapters. The same writers who are writing on gangs, rape and terrorism have also set their sights on wider issues such as multiculturalism, but at the same time they are attacking what they see as the left-wing elites whose interests it serves.

It wasn't the first time multiculturalism has been pronounced dead, and it wasn't the last. Duffy argued much the same thing the previous year, in the wake of the Tampa incident. He added a swipe at the 'human rights industry' to his customary attack on 'the multicultural industry' as the indulgence of 'elites', which had been a favourite formula of One Nation. This concern was explicitly connected to crime:

> The elite gets all the benefits of refugees and poor immigrants and none of the drawbacks.

> To take an example: areas of western and southwestern Sydney for years have been suffering from criminal ethnic gangs.

> But the elite of Sydney lives far away, in predominantly Anglo-Celtic enclaves, so they are rarely victims of the crime and social problems caused by their continuing advocacy of more poor immigrants from cultures very different to our own (Duffy 8/9/01:23).

This argument was repeated two months later (and two days before the federal election) by Miranda Devine in the same newspaper, railing against inner-city 'wankerati' who do not have to suffer the purported crime wave of western Sydney, which she mentioned alongside 'boat people' (Devine 8/11/01). This criticism of elites is at heart a criticism of liberal and radical intellectuals who not only support the idea of multiculturalism but challenge the conservative line favoured by the government and tabloid and talkback commentators — on crime, immigration, refugees, international politics and social policy — by pointing to more complex roots of these problems than individual or 'ethnic' pathology, and to the complicit role of government policy in practices of social exclusion. The attempts at silencing the critical voice is tantamount to a fear of social explanation which Hage (2002:140–141) believes lies at the heart of the need of the dominant culture to ignore the humanity of the Other.

The failure of multiculturalism has been a constant theme amongst right-wing commentators since the inception of the broad array of social policies ushered in under this rubric in the 1970s. It has reached a crescendo in recent years, piggy-backing on the events we have described here, as evidenced in Chapter Four. In one infamous article, Janet Albrechtsen blamed 'multicultural zealots' for September 11, because 'in awe of Multicultural Man, we tolerated the intolerant for too long' (4/9/02:13). Multiculturalism, Albrechtsen claimed, allowed Muslims to remain culturally separate. Several months earlier, she had again argued for the need to challenge 'the cult of multiculturalism', attacking the left for promoting community fears because of its support for 'unchecked immigration and unquestioned multiculturalism', and she managed to make the link between Islam and crime into the bargain (8/5/02:11). Her criticisms of Islam and her dislike for radical intellectuals are merged more symbolically in a piece in which she describes 'the Left' as 'fanatics', 'fundamentalists' and 'militant mullahs' who are intolerant of alternative opinions (Albrechtsen 30/7/03:11).

Tabloid columnist Mark Day had similarly declared in 2001 that 'Tolerance needs a reality check'. Asserting that gang crime in Sydney was mainly 'an ethnic phenomenon', he argued that: 'Tolerance does not extend to pack rape, home invasions, heroin pushing, extortion, fraud, smuggling, shoot-ups and standover gangs' (Day 8/8/01:27). A raft of replies arrived the very next day, and the heading of the *Telegraph*'s letters column echoed the opinion piece: 'Tolerance wearing thin'.

Piers Akerman's column, entitled 'Opening our doors to a wave of hatred', was accompanied by a drawing of a woman in a chador with a brick wall instead of human eyes showing through the gap.

Akerman began by marshalling the September 11 events for an attack on Australian multiculturalism: 'The terrorist attack on the US should provide a wake-up call to Australia to re-examine its policy of multiculturalism'. He concluded:

> When we look within Australia we find a separatist clique unsure whether it follows religious or cultural practices.
>
> A beard, a scarf, a headdress or the length of a sleeve or dress are all important to some of these people and the supporters of multiculturalism tell other Australians that they are the ones who must exhibit tolerance when they are spat upon or cursed for wearing ordinary clothing in keeping with the dominant culture.
>
> It is the Muslims who must show tolerance to others here and in other Western nations otherwise they will always be separate (Akerman 18/9/01:22).

Across these articles, the same themes are drawn and redrawn, whether the issue be crime gangs, pack rape, terrorism, immigration or refugees. In a remarkable camera obscura, it is the Muslim/ Lebanese/asylum seeker who exemplifies violence and discrimination, while the 'ordinary' (white) Australians are the victims of intolerance. At root is said to be a multiculturalism ideologically supported by 'elites'. The two prongs of the critique are the threat of the Other, which we explored in Chapter One; and the treason of the elites. Hage (1998) has deftly explored the shift in national identity and multiculturalism in terms of class-based forms of symbolic capital, and how the backlash of resentment represented by One Nation involves a conflict over national belonging and the rise of what he calls cosmo-multiculturalism. We need not repeat his powerful argument here, except to say that these journalists exemplified above have taken up the line developed by Pauline Hanson — rather, we want to suggest that the popular rejection of multiculturalism may be somewhat overstated.

There is something of popular concern in the direction multiculturalism has taken in recent years, but the current truism that it is on the nose with the Australian people may be an ideological claim not fully supported by the facts. A recent study commissioned by the Special Broadcasting Service (SBS) focused on the lived experience of Australia's cultural diversity and reached very different conclusions. The report, based on a national sample of over 1400 Australians — including five non-English speaking samples of about 400 each (Filipino, Greek, Lebanese, Somali and Vietnamese), and 56 Indigenous people from six communities — found a more complex, but overwhelmingly positive response to Australia's cultural diversity across all groups (Ang, Brand, Noble & Wilding 2002). The study found, for example, that two-thirds of the national sample (with a much higher figure amongst the NESB groups), believed that immigration had been a benefit to Australia, and 59% felt that cultural diversity was a strength of Australian society. While a smaller majority — 52% — supported multi-culturalism, in the current climate this is a strong showing. The negative responses amounted to only about 10% of the population. Moreover, the study showed a strong civic and social engagement with cultural diversity: the majority of Australians 'lived and breathed' this diversity, fashioning hybrid lives and intercultural relations across their environments (in the way that we discussed in Chapter Three). This 'everyday cosmopolitanism' was in contrast to the assumptions about ethnic ghettoes which dominate tabloid debate. The most insular group was long-time Australians, largely of Anglo-Celtic ancestry, who lived in more culturally homogeneous worlds. The one finding which seemed to stand out as discrepant was that the vast majority of first generation migrants, and most of their children, did not identify as 'Australian', even though they saw Australia as home. It was this factor which was reported by the media. Even the *Herald* emphasised this seeming fragmentation, claiming that 'we're still strangers', even though the report as a whole did not reflect this (Banham 25/11/02:4). The tabloid press and the radio shock jocks complained about migrants not assimilating (Clark 25/11/02), and once again shifted the blame for social disorder onto migrants.

What comes out of this report is that the vitriolic criticisms of multiculturalism in the name of the people distort the accommodating experience of intercultural relations in Australia. Maybe Australians are more comfortable with cultural diversity than they are credited with. Perhaps, as we found with the discrepancy between abstract fear of crime and the sense of safety people experienced in their own neighbourhoods, we fear multiculturalism when it is posed as an abstract system, but live with it happily in our daily lives. Either way, the hysteria associated with the attacks on multiculturalism represents the ideological agendas of conservative politicians and the commercial imperatives of tabloid journalism more than it does popular opinion. Having said that, as multicultural policies are slowly dismantled, along with social welfare policies generally, it may be time to rethink the nature and direction of multiculturalism and national belonging in Australia in the twenty-first century.

Rebirthing multiculturalism

Ironically, perhaps, some members of the left seem to agree with the right-wing ideologues we have discussed in thinking that it is time to abandon at least the word 'multiculturalism' (Bauman 1999:199; Turner 2002). Even some ethnic minority politicians share a discomfort towards the language of multiculturalism. In 2000, on the advice of its powerful Lebanese-Australian minister, Eddie Obeid, the Carr Government of NSW assessed that even the word 'ethnic' was an electoral liability and decided to rename the Ethnic Affairs Commission as the Community Relations Commission, arguing that 'ethnic' was a 'divisive' term (Obeid 2000). This moment reflects the need to move towards a more inclusive multiculturalism; but we must not forget that these terms carry the acknowledgment of economic inequalities and the imperative for the ongoing work of social justice as well as the demand for cultural recognition. Moreover, the positive response found in the SBS study may suggest that the concept of 'multiculturalism' still has a useful role to play in the negotiation of intercultural relations in Australian society — it has a currency that is not yet worthless.

Giddens writes about those significant crossroads when individuals are called on to take decisions that are particularly consequential for our lives, because the 'business as usual' attitude is broken by events. These 'fateful moments' are threatening to our ontological security and so we may feel the need to return to traditional authorities or fundamentalisms or turn to experts; but they are also opportunities to be embraced (1991:112–114,142–3). We may characterise this as a 'fateful moment' in the life of Australian multiculturalism. Perhaps what we need to do is to use this opportunity to rethink the sense of community, agency and vision of multiculturalism and of national belonging. Both rest on the idea of connection and community (despite what the critics of multiculturalism say about its purported divisiveness; in any case, many Indigenous inhabitants see national community as divisive).

The problem with 'community' has always been that it is a useful but flawed concept. It evokes nodes of collectivity and con- nection — determined by geography, class, ethnicity, history, and so on — but such aggregations are always riven by other divisions or other nodes of collectivity. Further, community rests on a changeable relation between symbolic forms of identification and socio-structural forms of relationship. There is a tendency to emphasise connection over division, but this can often be ideological rather than simply utopian. When leaders attempt to fashion their subjects as a community, this is usually a function of some form of subordination. When a group fashions itself as a community, this is often done for some political purpose of representation and protection, or relates to some historical process of change. Therefore we can never take the claim to community for granted.

The modern concern with 'community' emerges in the nineteenth century, alongside the emergence of the discipline of sociology, amidst rapidly shifting relations of class and gender, and mass migrations between country and city and across state borders, as all that had seemed solid melted into air in the face of the inexorably advancing commodity relation. 'Community' takes on an important ideological and political function that works by excluding others. The effect of the ideological retrieval of community in the first half of the twentieth century can be seen most sharply in the attachment of the concept of community (*Gemeinschaft*) with the racially conceived 'people' (*Volk*) of a nation-state or empire in the Nazi ideology of *Volkgemeinschaft*. This ideology of community rested on the blaming of foreigners (or other 'races') for economic woes, loss of national pride and identity, crime, immorality and the rest, in a way that simply set the benchmark for other projects of national and racial belonging, and is echoed in the political strategies we have outlined in this book. Race-based, ideological yearnings for community serve to provide imagined resolutions of real and potentially crisis-inducing contradictions.

Ethnicities are not communities. Collective identities or 'enclaves' designed to keep threatening others out are not communities either. Perhaps, then, we need to think of new models of public connection, a new framework for articulating collective experience that addresses the real problems of social and economic division. Genuine community is a collective practice, a difficult and ongoing shared labour. As Bauman argues, the individuated, privatised worlds we live in increasingly make such labour impossible. We keep looking for occasions of communal motivation (1999:9–10), linking private experiences and public spectacles of solidarity, but the privatisation of public space makes it harder to find spaces for such spectacles. Moreover, the state can no longer guarantee collective safety in a globalised, corporatised world where power is increasingly removed from the political sphere, and where fears are increasingly the source of new forms of commodification (19,40). The only form of togetherness conceivable under these circumstances is community by exclusion, resting on the fears of many and the suffering of others; where we draw strength from providing outlets for pent-up anger from an array of origins, directed at specific targets and through practical tasks which seem to offer a sense of agency (47–8). But, as Bauman argues, individuals cannot be free unless they are free to institute a society which promotes their freedom; that is, unless they institute collectively an agency capable of achieving this (107). He proposes a 'republic' or 'multicommunitarian' model of debate and negotiation, in which critique, not conflict and allegiance, is at the heart of relationships (166–8,197).

The problem with Australian multiculturalism, we might suggest, is twofold. First, it has devalued some of its original principles — of social justice and equity — for a politics of cultural identity (Hage 2002:110). Multiculturalism as it was developed in Australia had as one of its aims a desire to fashion an equitable society in which true diversity was viable, economically and politically as well as culturally. In a world of increasing privatisation and globalisation, cultural difference increasingly comes to be experienced as social, economic and political inequality. There is little multiculturalism as social policy can do about this, but certainly a state with a rein-vigorated sense of social justice can begin to restore the mechanisms of trust and protection that three decades of neo-liberalism have eroded.

Second, a related flaw of Australian multiculturalism — paternalism — was there from the start. What has been called Galbally multiculturalism, named after the key report that ushered in multicultural programs, was predicated on a top-down model of funding which privileged (ethnic) community leadership over the lived work of community, creating singular lines of accountability and internal patronage, and tying 'leaders' into party political forms of allegiance (Jakubowicz, Morrissey & Palser 1984). The result was also a reification of ethnicity as identity, as a badge of membership (or passport control, see Hoffman-Axthelm 1992:196) rather than a resource for living. We now live with essentialised notions of ethnicity which do not conform to the 'living diversity' of Australian society, but rather act as sources of tension and conflict amongst differently identified groups. This model of ethnicity easily becomes a model of anatagonisms. This is not to side with the Albrechtsens and Akermans, but to realise that a more livable form of multiculturalism is one that bends with cultural diversity, rather than caging it. This book has, in some ways, outlined the kind of multiculturalism we have in Australia because of the social, economic and political forces which have shaped it in recent years. This is not to reject multiculturalism as a project, but to critique the uses of racialised discourses embedded in Australian multiculturalism in order to envision a policy and practice more in step with cultural diversity.

The renaming of the Ethnic Affairs Commission in NSW was one moment when such a shift was seemingly possible. When Bob Carr spoke at Government House on the occasion of its rebadging as the NSW Community Relations Commission, he argued that the term 'ethnic' has no salience today in NSW. Yet the day after, and in the many days since, he continued to use the word 'ethnic', but in one context only: in relation to crime. The reification of ethnicity produces the possibility of selective ethnicity; that it belongs only to some, and hence can become a source of social division and an explanatory pathology for social behaviours.

This selective ethnicity is pervasive in Australia and reflects the 'invisibility' of whiteness, its tendency to see itself as normal and non-whiteness as different. Moreover, ethnicity becomes a prison from which one cannot escape: the journalists and shock jocks who bemoan the inability of migrants to assimilate are the same ones who insist on referring to 'Lebanese gangs' and 'Chinese triads'. Australian multiculturalism shares with Australia's racist history an emphasis on ethnicity over citizenship. When migrants arrive in Australia their former nationality becomes an ethnicity they can never shake off in the eyes of white Australia, yet they are criticised for declaring an attachment to this identity. It is no wonder NESB people didn't identify as 'Australian' in the SBS study — they are not allowed to be. Similarly, as Adele Horin points out in relation to the proposed prayer centre in Annangrove, ethnic groups are damned if they stick together, and damned if they leave it and try to live in 'true-blue Christian Australian' communities (21–22/12/02:25).

We must abandon an 'over-defined' or 'ethnic' nationalism for a fluid-state nationalism (Nairn 2002/3:6) which uses the commonalities and differences of social experience as the basis for a dialogic relation to national community: as a reason for welcoming difference rather than as a barricade for protecting us from it. Our notions of both national belonging and cultural identity must be inclusive not exclusive; they must be about possibilities of extension and intermingling, not borders designed to keep others out. They must be mechanisms for acting together, for shaping mechanisms of collective agency, which recognise our shared humanity first and foremost (Hage 2002:139). As Bauman (1993:183) has argued, responsibility is fundamental to the structure of subjectivity. In the claims about multiculturalism, crime, terrorism and cultural difference detailed here, it is always someone else's fault. In abrogating responsibility we lose a sense of social and collective agency.

It is not rejection of multiculturalism being proposed here, and a return to nostalgic forms of national identity or fundamentalism which breed antagonism, and it is certainly not a romantic evocation of some fuzzy one-ness. We need to recreate a multiculturalism that is deeply critical but ethical. It should be critical in challenging the assumptions and essentialisms that pervade multicultural policy as it currently stands, undertaking a constant interrogation of its social, economic and moral bases, the rules of its possibility. What Hage calls the fear of social explanation undermines, for example, effective organisation of the criminal justice system because it silences those who may have greatest insight into these social problems and their relation to cultural diversity. Rather, a critical multiculturalism should embrace the task of seeing things in all their complexity and as articulated with wider economic and political structures. Similarly, sophisticated crime prevention policies and programs need to look more substantively at issues of community regeneration and associative democracy with a stronger pluralist ethos (Hogg & Brown 1998:181).

Such an approach to both multiculturalism and criminal justice needs to be more 'ethical'. Multiculturalism has always been a moral project — it is, at some level, about forms of acceptable behaviour towards others — this is not the same as a moralistic injunction, which is the kind of criticism often levelled at the 'politically correct' multicultural industry. Ang (2001) asks similarly for an ethics of multiculturalism. She argues that Australian multiculturalism has always been deeply ambivalent — it has preached a message of harmony but practiced forms of division; it claimed to be anti-racist but has at its heart a repressed sense of race (143,96,104–5). She suggests we need a new national narrative that can account for change, rather than reify a nostalgic sense of Australian and ethnic pasts (107). An ethics of multiculturalism would acknowledge this ambivalence and ask us to consider again the problem of how to act towards each other in a culturally diverse nation (145–6). Unless we interrogate this ambivalence, we will maintain a multiculturalism that preserves a conservative element of racialisation (111). A positive conception of this ambivalence would provide the basis for a vision of what a multicultural society could be. Hogg and Brown argue similarly that in the hostile climate of law and order debate, we need a 'politics of civility' which challenges the unwritten social codes of incivility and moves towards greater recognition of shared responsibility (1998:16,177).

This would also mean abandoning the macho posture which dominates contemporary politics — against that language of 'getting tough' (on crime, on terrorists), and not being 'soft' or 'weak' or uncertain, we need an ethics of care, reciprocity and responsibility. Such an ethics would rest on the idea of responsibility, not as self-serving and individuated, but rather responsibility *for* the Other (Levinas 1997). This would also allow for the possibility of a multiculturalism which refused to see ethnicities as peripheral adjuncts to mainstream society, as things to be reified (Stratton 1998:16,208–9).

The task then is not *just* to continue to celebrate the differences we rightly value, nor *just* to attack the State whose actions serve to denigrate and discriminate against Arabic-speaking communities, but to problematise the not so easily seen part, the space in between. We need to refashion a national identity which questions the apparent neutrality at the heart of Australian identity, and to refashion a multiculturalism which does not just sit at the edges of the lives of 'ordinary Australians', or allow for the fabrication of 'bin Ladens' in every suburb, but questions what it means to be an 'ordinary Australian'.

References

AAP (Australian Associated Press) (17/1/01) *Boat people a security risk*, 17 September, <http://www.news.com.au>.

AAP (13/9/01) 'Attack on WA mosque', *The Sunday Mail*, 13 September.

AAP/*Weekend Australian* (24–25/3/01) 'Trinity culprits avoid conviction', The *Weekend Australian*, 24–25 March, p 11.

ABC News (18/12/02) 7pm News, ABC, 18 December.

ABC News Online (12/9/01) 'Australian Muslims urge racial tolerance as children attacked', 12 September, <http://abc.net.au/>.

ABC News Online (2/10/01) 'Muslims urge authorities to work with community', 2 October, <http://abc.net.au/news/state/nsw/metnsw-2Oct2001-2.htm>.

ABC News Online (31/10/02) 'ASIO raids slammed as "publicity stunt"', ABC News Online, 31 October, <http://abc.net.au/news/>.

ABC News Online (21/11/02) *Row erupts over Nile comments,* 21 November, <http://www.abc.gov.au/news/2002/11/item2002112120 5810_1.htm>.

ABC Online (24/8/01) 'Carr to meet chief justice over sexual assault sentences', *ABC Online* Local News, New South Wales, 24 August, <http://www.abc.net.au>.

Abdel-Fattah, R (21/10/02) 'Our leaders should mind their tongues', *Age*, 21 October, p 15.

Ackland, R (8/9/01) 'Uninformed stunts leave legal system crying rape', *Sydney Morning Herald*, 8 September, p 10.

Age (1/11/02) 'Muslims Condemn "Heavy-Handed" Tactics', 1 November, <http://www.theage.com.au/articles/2002/10/31/1036026979308.html>.

Ahmed, I (1992) *Postmodernism and Islam*, Routledge, London.

Akerman, P (18/9/01) 'Opening our doors to a wave of hatred' *Daily Telegraph* 18 September, p 22.

Akerman, P (4/10/01) 'Cargo bound by definition', *Daily Telegraph*, 4 October, p 22.

Akerman, P (9/10/01) 'Publicity stunts self-defeating', *Daily Telegraph*, 9 October, p 16.

Akerman, P (14/10/01) 'Pay no mind to paranoid hippies', *Sunday Telegraph*, 14 October, p 95.

Akerman, P (16/12/01) 'Chilling video a sign for mullahs', *Daily Telegraph*, 16 December, p 109.

Akerman, P, (23/5/02) 'No tolerance for law of the jungle', *Daily Telegraph*, 23 May, p 28.

Akerman, P (13/8/02) 'Fraternal claims that ring hollow', *Daily Telegraph*, 13 August, p 14.

Akerman, P (18/8/02) 'Rape judge earns applause', *Sunday Telegraph*, 18 August, p 83.

Akerman, P (22/8/02) 'Merciful message for stone throwers', *Daily Telegraph*, 22 August, p 28.

Akerman, P (1/9/02) 'Barbarism that defies tolerance', *Daily Telegraph*, 1 September, p 97.

Akerman, P (12/9/02) 'Schoolgirl's rant sets alarms ringing', *Daily Telegraph*, 12 September, p 24.

Akerman, P (15/10/02) 'Atrocity must not go unpunished', *Daily Telegraph*, 15 October, p 20.

Akerman, P (17/10/02) 'Sympathy for the devil in disguise', *Daily Telegraph*, 17 October, p 34.

Akerman, P (29/10/02) 'Clean out the snake pit and we'll play ball', *Daily Telegraph*, 29 October, p 16.

Akerman, P (26/1/03a) 'We must stop global firebugs', *Daily Telegraph*, 26 January, p 111.

Akerman, P (29/5/03) 'Exorcising the devils that live among us', *Daily Telegraph*, 29 May, p 23.

Alam, N (27/8/01) 'Labelling Muslims', *Sydney Morning Herald*, 27 August, p 11.

Albrechtsen, J (8/5/02) 'No mincing of words, just sacred cows', *Australian*, 8 May, p 11.

Albrechtsen, J (17/7/02) 'Blind spot allows barbarism to flourish', *Australian*, 17 July, <http://www.theaustralian.news.com.au/common/story_page/0,5744,4718201%255E7583,00.html>.

Albrechtsen, J (4/9/02) 'Defend to the death our western ways', *Australian*, 4 September, p 13

Albrechtsen, J (4/12/02) 'Justices leave the door wide open to killers', *Australian*, 4 December, p 15.

Albrechtsen, J (30/7/03) 'We're all sinners to these fanatics', *Australian*, 30 July, p 11.

Allard, T (14/9/01) 'Reith links boat people, terror fight', *Sydney Morning Herald*, 14 September, p 6.

Allard, T (16/12/02) 'War on terror cramped by cost bungling', *Sydney Morning Herald*, 16 December, p 1.

Allard, T (7/1/03) 'Terrorist alert here to stay after danger period runs out', *Sydney Morning Herald*, 7 January, p 2.

Allard, T & Fray, P (13–14/9/03) 'Australia was told: war will fuel terror', *Sydney Morning Herald*, 13–14 September, p 1.

Allard, T & Snow, D (9–10/8/03) 'PM's grim terrorism warning to Australia', *Sydney Morning Herald*, 9–10 August, p 16.

Allard, T, Cameron, D, Stevenson, A & Wainwright, R (23–24/11/02) 'The party's over', *Sydney Morning Herald*, 23–24 November, pp 27, 34.

AM (31/10/02) 'More ASIO raids expected', radio program, ABC Radio, 31 October, 8.04am.

AM (1/11/02) 'Downer unapologetic over ASIO/ AFP raids', radio program, ABC Radio, 1 November, 8.08am.

AM (21/11/02) 'Fred Nile attacks Muslim women's traditional dress', radio program, ABC Radio, 21 November, .

Ang, I (2001), *On Not Speaking Chinese*, Routledge, London.

Ang, I, Brand, J, Noble, G & Wilding, D (2002) *Living Diversity: Australia's Multicultural Future*, SBS Corporation, Artarmon.

anon (n.d., but September 2002) *The Problem They Tried To Cover Up! Rape Alert! Don't Be A Victim Of Multiculturalism Gone Mad!!*, leaflet distributed in Sydney, possibly by Australia First Party whose address is shown [photocopy in the possession of the authors].

Anti-Discrimination Board of New South Wales (2003) *Race for the Headlines: Racism and media discourse,* Anti-Discrimination Board of NSW, Sydney.

'Atiyah, N (1973) *The Attitude of the Lebanese Sunnis Towards the State of Lebanon,* PhD thesis, submitted for the degree of Doctor of Philosophy, University of London, London.

Attorney-General's Department (2001) *A kit for protecting your home from intruders*, Commonwealth Government, Canberra.

Australian (20/9/01) 'Life for gang rape', 20 September, p 8.

Australian (22/1/02) 'Summer Terror', 22 January, pp 4–6.

Australian Arabic Council (2001) *Increase in Racial Vilification in Light of Terror Attacks: Sep 2001*, [unpublished photocopy], Australian Arabic Council, Melbourne.

Australian Bureau of Statistics (2001) *Census of Population and Housing 2001*, <http://www.abs.gov.au>.

Australian Labor Party National Office (2001) *Fighting Terrorists Today*, [election leaflet distributed in Marrickville, NSW].

Australian Labor Party (21/3/03) 'A Secure Future', *Daily Telegraph*, 21 March, p 10.

Australian Labor Party (2003) *TOUGH*, campaign leaflet, March.

Australian Muslim Public Affairs Committee (2001) *Exposing Janet Albrechtsen's dishonest attack*, published on ABC *Media Watch* website, dated 18 June 2002, <http://www.abc.net.au/mediawatch/>.

Back, L, Schuster, L & Solomos, J (6/5/02) Letters, *The Guardian*, 6 May, p 13.

Baker, M (23–24/11/02) 'Australia now a "prime target"', *Australian*, 23–24 November, p 1.

Banham, C (24/9/02) 'The phone and the Bill', *Sydney Morning Herald*, 24 September, p 16.

Banham, C (1/11/02) 'Raids not done lightly: ASIO chief', *Sydney Morning Herald*, 1 November, pp 1, 7.

Banham, C (1/11/02) 'Executives talk security, right down to fire hydrants', *Sydney Morning Herald*, 1 November, p 7.

Banham, C (25/11/02) 'Ain't life grand in Australia — it's a pity we're still strangers', *Sydney Morning Herald*, 25 November, p 4.

Banham, C (15/12/02) 'Howard, Crean at war over terrorism', *Sydney Morning Herald*, 14–15 December, p 1.

Barak, G (1994) 'Media, Society and Criminology' in Barak, G (ed) *Media Process and the Social Construction of Crime*, Garland Publishing, New York, pp 3–32.

Banham, C (1/11/02) 'Executives talk security, right down to fire hydrants', *Sydney Morning Herald*, 1 November, p 7.

Barkham, P (10/11/01) 'Australia votes on how tightly to close the door', *The Guardian*, 10 November.

Bankstown-Canterbury Torch (22/8/01) 'Barrage of Abuse Ignited', 22 August, p 1.

Bankstown City Council (2001) 'Bankstown — A community under siege', [press release], 21 August.

Barker, M (1981) *The new racism: conservatives and the ideology of the tribe*, Junction Books, London.

Barrass, T (30/11/02) 'JI training camps held in Blue Mountains, ASIO told', *Sydney Morning Herald*, 30 November, p 6.

Bauman, Z (1993) *Postmodern Ethics*, Blackwell, Oxford.

Bauman, Z (1999) *In Search of Politics*, Stanford University Press, Stanford.

Beach, M (11/10/01) 'Sleuths in the sky join the hunt', *Daily Telegraph*, 11 October, p 3.

Beach, M (21/9/01) 'Evil caught on film', *Daily Telegraph*, 21 September, p 5.

Bean, C & McAllister, I (2002) 'From Impossibility to Certainty: Explaining the Coalition's Victory in 2001' in Warhurst, J & Simms, M *2001 The Centenary Election*, University of Queensland Press, Brisbane, pp 271–286.

Bearup, G (21/11/98) 'Fight to restore confidence', *Sydney Morning Herald*, 2 November, p 4.

Bearup, G (7/11/98) 'Under fire', *Sydney Morning Herald*, 7 November, pp 33, 43.

Beckle, R (13/12/02) 'Teaching tolerance', *Daily Telegraph*, 13 December, p 31.

Bessant, J (1995) 'Violence, the Media and the Making of Policy', *Journal of Australian Studies*, vol 43, pp 45–58.

Birch, S (15/8/01) 'Face of a rapist', *Daily Telegraph*, 15 August, p 1.

Board of Imams, Victoria, and the Islamic Councils of Victoria (n.d.), *Press Release from the Board of Imams, Victoria, and the Islamic Councils of Victoria: Muslims express support and concern*, <http://www.icv.org.au/ASIORaids.htm>.

Brenchley, F (24/9/02) 'Target Iraq', *Bulletin*, 24 September, pp 16–19.

Brown, P (12/10/01) 'Arabic festival cancelled for fear of attack by bigots', *Australian*, 12 October, p 2.

Bruce, I (18/9/02) 'Tentacles of terror spread to more than 60 countries', *Herald*, 18 September, <http://www.theherald.co.uk/news/archive/18-9-19101-0-14-10.html>.

Burchell, D (2003) *Western Horizons*, Scribe, Melbourne.

Buckler, I (1/8/03) 'Casualty of culture clash', *Daily Telegraph*, 1 August [letter to the editor], p 26.

Burke, A (2001) *In Fear of Security: Australia's Invasion Anxiety*, Pluto, Annandale.

Burke, K (16/9/01) 'Bigotry stalks the streets as the airwaves prattle', *Sydney Morning Herald*, 15–16 September, p 4.

Burke, K (25/10/02) 'Talkback racists targeting Muslims', *Sydney Morning Herald*, 25 October, p 5.

Burke, K & AAP (14/9/01) 'Muslim women, children targeted', *Sydney Morning Herald*, 14 September, p 8.

Burnside, J (23/1/02) 'Refugees: The Tampa Case', *Web Diary*, 23 January, <http://old.smh.com.au/news/webdiary/2002/01/23/FFXNANTZ RWC.html>.

Byers, B (1999) 'Hate Crimes in the Workplace: Worker-to-Worker Victimisation and Policy Responses', *Security Journal*, vol 12, no 4, pp 47–58.

Callinan, R, Targett, T & Marx, A (2/11/01) 'Is this a terrorist camp in our midst' (sic), *Daily Telegraph*, 2 November, p 3.

Calvert, J (9/3/02) 'Knife torment charge', *Herald Sun*, 9 March, p 9.

Cameron, D (16/10/02) 'Mob drives Muslim leader out of home', *Sydney Morning Herald*, 16 October, p 3.

Cameron, D (28/11/02) 'Hell breaks loose over prayer hall', *Sydney Morning Herald*, 28 November, p 2.

Cameron, D (7–8/12/02) 'Respect the family: Moroney's crime-fighting motto', *Sydney Morning Herald*, 7–8 December, p 3.

Cameron, D et al. (11/11/02) 'As we remember them', *Sydney Morning Herald*, 11 November, p 6.

Carr, B (2001) *Premier announces Partnership Plan to prevent violence and crime among Arabic speaking young people*, Premier of NSW's Media Release, dated 10 July 2001.

Carroll, J (2002) *Terror*, Scribe Publications, Melbourne.

Casey, M & Ogg, M (3/11/98) 'Dial-a-Gun: Gang says it is easier than buying a pizza', *Daily Telegraph*, 3 November, pp 1, 4–5.

Castillo, A & Hirst, M (2000) 'Look Both Ways' in Collins, J & Poynting, S (eds) *The Other Sydney: Communities, Identities and Inequalities in Western Sydney*, Common Ground, Melbourne and New York.

Castles, S, Kalantzis, M, Cope, B & Morrissey, M (1988) *Mistaken Identity: Multiculturalism and the Demise of Nationalism in Australia*, Pluto Press, Sydney.

Centre for Contemporary Cultural Studies (1982) *The Empire Strikes Back*, Hutchinson, London.

Chan, J (1995) 'Systematically Distorted Communication?', *Australian and New Zealand Journal of Criminology*, vol 29, pp 23–30.

Chan, J (1997) *Changing Police Culture: Policing in a Multicultural Society*, Cambridge University Press, Cambridge.

Channel 7 News (20/11/02) 6pm, 20 November.

Channel 9 News (17/11/02) 6pm, 17 December.

Charlton, P, (3/11/98) 'A grim echo of Beirut', *Courier-Mail*, 3 November, p 11.

Crichton, S & Stevenson, A (14–15/9/02) 'Crime and prejudice', *Sydney Morning Herald*, 14–15 September, pp 30–31.

Chulov, M (18–19/8/01) 'Rape menace from the melting pot', *Australian*, 18–19 August, pp 1, 4.

Chulov, M & Payton, I (13–14/7/02) 'Crime against community', *Weekend Australian*, 13–14 July, p 23.

Clark, L (24/5/02) 'Sniffing out invasion of our civil liberties', *Daily Telegraph*, 24 May, p 25.

Clark, Philip (30/7/01), radio program, Radio 2GB, 30 July, 7: 09am.

Clark, Philip (25/11/02), radio program, Radio 2GB, 25 November.

Clark, Pilita (20/9/01) 'Anti-Muslim backlash. Sorry I'm too busy: PM declines invitation to dinner at mosque', *Sydney Morning Herald*, 20 September, p 2.

Clark, Pilita et al. (17–18/11/01) 'Swinging Sydney', *Sydney Morning Herald*, 17–18 November, pp 27, 36.

Clennell, A (9/11/98) 'Tea and snags in the war zone', *Sydney Morning Herald*, 9 November, p 4.

Clennell, A (15/10/01) 'PM stole my boat people policies: Hanson', *Sydney Morning Herald*, 15 October, p 8.

Clennell, A & Kennedy, L (19/10/98) 'Kneecappings may be linked to boy's murder', *Sydney Morning Herald*, 19 October, p 3.

Clifton, B (16/8/02) 'Mother can't accept son is a monster', *Daily Telegraph*, 16 August, pp 4–5.

Cock, A & Fynes-Clinton, M (15/7/02) 'Ethnic crime is linked to language barrier', *Daily Telegraph*, 15 July, p 6.

Cock, A & Williams, N (30/11/02) 'Suburban rocket launcher seized', *Daily Telegraph*, 30 November, p 5.

Cohen, S (1973/1987) *Folk Devils and Moral Panics*, Basil Blackwell, Oxford.

Coleman, P & Tanner, L (1978) *Cartoons of Australian History*, Thomas Nelson, Melbourne.

Collins, J, Noble, G, Poynting, S & Tabar, P (2000) *Kebabs, Kids, Cops and Crime: Youth, Ethnicity and Crime*, Pluto Press, Sydney.

Collins, J, Noble, G, Poynting, S & Tabar, P (2002) *Gangs, Crime and Community Safety*, Centre for Transforming Cultures, University of Technology, Sydney.

Commonwealth Government (29/12/02) 'Protecting the Australian way of life from a possible terrorist threat', *Sun-Herald*, 29 December, p 12.

Commonwealth Government (2003) *'Let's look out for Australia' kit*, Canberra.

Community Relations Commission (CRC) (2002), <http://www.crc.nsw.gov.au>.

Community Relations Commission for a Multicultural NSW (2002) *Plans to Deal with Community Unease* [press release], 18 October, <http://www.crc/nsw.gov.au/press/bali_hotline.htm>.

Connolly, E (21/12/00) 'Trinity boys tied up and raped, court told', *Sydney Morning Herald*, 21 December, p 5.

Connolly, E (6/2/01) 'Culture of rumbling, bullying', *Sydney Morning Herald*, 6 February, p 6.

Connolly, E (7/2/01) 'Trinity head denies culture of abuse', *Sydney Morning Herald*, 7 February, p 3.

Connolly, E (25–26/8/01) 'Mother's plea: give victims a voice', *Sydney Morning Herald*, 25–26 August, p 2.

Connolly, E (3–4/11/01) 'Fury over jail term for rapist', *Sydney Morning Herald*, 3–4 November, p 5.

Connolly, E (10/10/02) 'Guilty your honour. No, you're not.' *Sydney Morning Herald*, 10 October, p 2.

Connolly, E (13/2/03) 'Mother's tears for dead son as killer sentenced over stabbing', *Sydney Morning Herald*, 13 February, p 7.

Connolly, E & Kennedy, L (24/8/01) 'Outrage as gang rapists get cut-down jail terms', *Sydney Morning Herald*, 24 August, p 3

Connolly, F (27/11/02) 'Throwing out the Victa for a balcony', *Daily Telegraph*, 27 November, p 9.

Connolly, F & Cazzulino, M (30/11/02) 'Save Santa', *Daily Telegraph*, 30 November, pp 1–2.

Cope, B & Kalantzis, M (2000) *A Place in the Sun: Re-creating the Australian way of Life*, Harper Collins, Sydney.

Cornford, P (30/12/02) 'We're all going to die. It's true, my hairdresser told me', *Sydney Morning Herald*, 30 December, pp 1, 6.

Couldry, N (2000) *The Place of Media Power*, Routledge, London.

Crawford, B, (2/11/98) 'Terror Australis: police in the firing line', *Australian*, 2 November, p 1.

Crichton, S & Stevenson, A (14–15/9/02) 'Crime and prejudice', *Sydney Morning Herald*, 14–15 September, pp 30–31.

Critcher, C (2003) *Moral Panics and the Media*, Open University Press, Buckingham.

Crittenden, S (19–20/7/03) 'Clash of the Century', *Sydney Morning Herald: Spectrum*, 19–20 July, pp 4–5.

Crosweiler, A (4/11/98) 'Blast Rocks Police Station: Arrests after new attack', *Daily Telegraph*, 4 November, pp 1–2.

Cunneen, C (2001) *Conflict, politics and crime: Aboriginal communities and the police*, Allen and Unwin, Sydney.

Cunneen, C, Findlay, M, Lynch, R & Tupper, V (1989) *Dynamics of Collective Conflict: Riots at the Bathurst Bike Races*, The Law Book Company, Sydney.

Daily Telegraph (2/11/98) Anarchy pulls the trigger', 2 November, p 10.

Daily Telegraph (3/11/98) 'The lost boys: caught between cultures in Lakemba', 3 November, p 1.

Daily Telegraph (6/11/98) 'Lebanese leaders attack Carr', 6 November, p 4.

Daily Telegraph (30/6/99) 'What we fear most', 30 June, p 3.

Daily Telegraph (6/11/00) 'Community fighting for our children', editorial, 6 November, p 20.

Daily Telegraph (13/7/01) 'All rapists' names must be released', editorial, 13 July, p 20.

Daily Telegraph (6/8/01) 'Having the courage to face reality', editorial, 6 August, p 20.

Daily Telegraph (9/8/01) 'Tolerance wearing thin', letters page, 9 August, p 30.

Daily Telegraph (17/8/01) 'The illegal armada keeps coming', 17 August, p 7.

Daily Telegraph (18/8/01) 'Commissioner warns on rapes', 18 August, p 11.

Daily Telegraph (22/8/01) 'Ethnic Rape Debate. Brutal Truth: While ethnic leaders argue, four attackers will be sentenced for the crime that sparked a crisis. This is what happened', 22 August, p 1.

Daily Telegraph (22/8/01) 'Comments insult all Australians', editorial, 22 August, p 30.

Daily Telegraph (23/8/01) 'As Sydney battles gang crime, these images are targetting young people', 23 August, p 1.

Daily Telegraph (24/8/01) 'A judicial minefield', 24 August, p 10.

Daily Telegraph (24/8/01) 'Astray in a judicial minefield', editorial, 24 August, p 26.

Daily Telegraph (25/8/01) 'Community must face crime issue', editorial, 25 August, p 16.

Daily Telegraph (31/8/01) 'Judges get sentencing manuals', 31 August, p 6.

Daily Telegraph (1/9/01) 'Cautionary tale of legal hypocrisy', editorial, 1 September, p 22.

Daily Telegraph (5/9/01) 'Naysayers must face ugly truths', editorial, 5 September, p 30.

Daily Telegraph (12/9/01) 'World Terror', 12 September, pp 1–12.

Daily Telegraph (12/9/01) 'Act of War', 12 September, p 1.

Daily Telegraph (14/9/01) 'Carr warns against ethnic hate attacks', 14 September, p 8.

Daily Telegraph (15/9/01) 'Act of War: Islam backlash continues', 15 September, p 10.

Daily Telegraph (16/9/01) 'Muslim backlash', 16 September, p 9.

Daily Telegraph (5/10/01) 'Raid on "jihad group"', 5 October, p 9.

Daily Telegraph (9/10/01) 'Muslims protest at uninsured mosques', 9 October, p 7.

Daily Telegraph (12/10/01) 'Entry is a privilege not a right', editorial, 12 October, p 20.

Daily Telegraph (13/10/01) 'Vindication of our line in the sand', editorial, 13 October, p 24.

Daily Telegraph (26/11/01) 'More abuse for Muslims', 26 November, p 13.

Daily Telegraph (23/4/02) 'A random approach to crime', 23 April, p 14.

Daily Telegraph (17/7/02) 'Recognising loathsome racist acts', 17 July, p 28.

Daily Telegraph (15/8/02) 'Muslim gym ruling unfit', 15 August, p 30.

Daily Telegraph (16/8/02) 'Courage is rewarded with justice', 16 August, p 22.

Daily Telegraph (16/8/02) 'Vote-line', 16 August, p 25.

Daily Telegraph (19/8/02) 'PM's tacit approval of rape sentence', 19 August, p 4.

Daily Telegraph (20/8/02) 'Lesson of a society apart', 20 August, p 19.

Daily Telegraph (23/8/02) 'Demolish the barriers to sharing', editorial, 23 August, p 22.

Daily Telegraph (11/9/02) 'vote-line', 11 September, p 33.

Daily Telegraph (14/10/02) 'VICTIMS OF WAR', 14 October, p 1.

Daily Telegraph (14/10/02) 'Terrorism won't take a holiday', 14 October, p 20.

Daily Telegraph (15/10/02) 'Harness anger to best effect', 15 October, p 20.

Daily Telegraph (17/10/02) 'The loss of innocence', 17 October, pp 4–5.

Daily Telegraph (17/10/02) 'Muslims live in fear — TERROR'S TOLL', 17 October, p 11.

Daily Telegraph (18/10/02) 'AUSTRALIANS TOGETHER', 18 October, pp 72–73.

Daily Telegraph (19/10/02) '19 MILLION MATES', 19 October, p 1.

Daily Telegraph (28/10/02) 'Ordinary people in their sights', 28 October, p 14.

Daily Telegraph (31/10/02) 'Like scenes from a movie', 31 October, p 7.

Daily Telegraph (5/11/02) 'Open House for terrorists', 5 November, p 18.

Daily Telegraph (14/11/02) 'Evil speaks', 14 November, p 1.

Daily Telegraph (20/11/02) 'Facing up to a world fed on hate', 20 November, p 30.

Daily Telegraph (26/11/02) 'Carr in call for slower immigration', 26 November, p 2.

Daily Telegraph (30/11/02) 'Whatever became of good will', 30 November, p 24.

Daily Telegraph (10/12/02) 'Judge accepts Lee case plea', 10 December.

Daily Telegraph (16/12/02) 'Vote-line', 16 December, p 21.

Daily Telegraph (31/12/02) 'Hotline may be target for hoaxers', 31 December, p 4.

Daily Telegraph (4/2/03) 'Vote-line', 4 February, p 16.

Daily Telegraph (7/5/03) 'Girl, 13, driven to park and raped', 7 May, p 5.

Daily Telegraph (31/7/03) 'Visiting Muslims "a threat"', 31 July, p 4.

Daily Telegraph (4/9/03) 'Australian men linked to al-Qaeda', 4 September, p 17.

Dawson, J (15/10/02) 'Attack on Western values', letter to the editor, *Daily Telegraph*, 15 October, p 22.

Day, M (8/8/01) 'Tolerance needs a reality check', *Daily Telegraph*, 8 August, p 27.

Day, M (5/9/01) 'Beware bias in talkback', *Daily Telegraph*, 5 September, p 31.

Department of Immigration and Indigenous Affairs (DIMEA) (2002), <http://www.immi.gov.au/grants>.

Devine, A & Skelsey, M (10/7/03) 'Justice Revolt', *Daily Telegraph*, 10 July, pp 1–2.

Devine, M (3/11/98) 'A community's heart beats strong', *Daily Telegraph*, 3 November, p 10.

Devine, M (12/8/01) 'Rape, hatred and racism', *Sun-Herald*, 12 August, p 15.

Devine, M (19/8/01) 'Across the grating divide', *Sun-Herald*, 19 August, p 15.

Devine, M (26/8/01) 'Sorry, but the rapists mentioned race first', *Sun-Herald*, 26 August, p 15.

Devine, M (30/8/01) 'Revolving doors at the courthouse', *Sydney Morning Herald*, 30 August, p 12.

Devine, M (8/11/01) 'Victims are screaming but no-one hears', *Sydney Morning Herald*, 8 November, p 14.

Devine, M (11/11/01) 'Triumph of evil in dancing on American graves', *Sun-Herald*, 11 November, p 28.

Devine, M (7/4/02) 'Turning a blind eye to blood on the streets', *Daily Telegraph*, 7 April, p 15.

Devine, M (14/7/02) 'Racist rapes: Finally the truth comes out', *Sun-Herald*, 14 July, p 15.

Devine, M (18/8/02) 'Sentence to smile about', *Sun-Herald*, 18 August, p 15.

Devine, M (11/11/02) 'Where security counts, tolerance goes two ways', *Sun Herald*, 11 November, p 27.

Devine, M (28/11/02) 'Tough measures are our rights', *Sydney Morning Herald*, 28 November, p 13.

Devine, M (7/12/02) 'Let police fight crime, not each other', *Sydney Morning Herald*, 7 December, p 12.

Dickins, J (30/11/02) '121 nations are not safe', *Daily Telegraph*, 30 October, pp 10–11.

Dickins, J & Farr, M (20/11/02) 'DIRECT THREAT', *Daily Telegraph*, 20 November, p 1.

Dixon, D (2003) 'From Service to Force?: Policing New South Wales', *Current Issues in Criminal Justice*, vol 15, no 2, p 193.

Doherty, L & Jacobsen, G (23/8/01) 'Spray at Muslims, call for floggings, Hanson back on radar', *Sydney Morning Herald*, 23 August, p 7.

Douglas, M (1992) *Risk and Blame*, Routledge, London.

Downie, S (2001) 'Gang attacks on women spread', *Daily Telegraph*, August 29: 3.

Duff, E (14/7/02) 'They have heaped shame on Islam', *Sun-Herald*, 14 July, p 4

Duff, E (21/7/02) 'Hounded out of House and home', *Sun-Herald*, 21 July, pp 11–12

Duffy, M (17/8/02) 'When the racial reality hits home', *Daily Telegraph*, 17 August, p 16.

Bin Laden in the suburbs

Duffy, M (8/9/01) 'Outraged elite all lost at sea', *Daily Telegraph*, 8 September, p 23.

Dunn, K (2001) 'Representations of Islam in the Politics of Mosque Development in Sydney', *Tijdschrift voor Economische en Sociale Geografie*, vol 92, iss 3, pp 291–308.

Dunn, M, McPhedran, I & Dickins, J (1/11/02) 'Rambo-style tactics alleged; ASIO terror hunt hits Melbourne', *Herald Sun*, 1 November, p 4.

Dupuis, A & Thorns, D (1998) 'Home, home ownership and the search for ontological security', *Sociological Review*, vol 46, iss 1, pp 24–47.

Eckert, R (2002) 'Hostility and Violence Against Immigrants in Germany since 1992' in Freilich, JD, Newman, G, Shoham, SG & Addad, M (eds) *Migration, Culture Conflict and Crime*, Ashgate, Dartmouth, pp 211–222.

English, B (11/11/98) 'Peter's power: New laws for police to search cars', *Daily Telegraph*, 11 November, p 2.

English, B (4/10/02) 'Searching for the Middle Muslim Road', *Daily Telegraph*, 4 October, p 17.

English, B (19/11/02) 'Terror powers: Police can search first and ask questions later', *Daily Telegraph*, 19 November, p 1.

English, B & Cazzulino, M (2/10/02) 'Campaign of racial hate goes regional', *Daily Telegraph*, 2 October, p 11.

English, B & McDougall, B (1/10/02) 'Under siege and bracing for a war', *Daily Telegraph*, 1 October, pp 10–11.

English, B & Morris, R, (20/11/02) 'Carr: now's the time for suspicious minds', *Daily Telegraph*, 20 November, p 5.

English, B & Walsh, P (3/11/98) 'Carr links ethnic gang to crime', *Daily Telegraph*, 3 November, p 4–5.

Ericson, R, Baranek, P & Chan, J (1989) *Negotiating Control*, University of Toronto Press, Toronto.

Ericson, RV, Baranek, P & Chan, J (1991) *Representing Order: Crime, Law and Justice in the News Media*, University of Toronto Press, Toronto.

Ethnic Affairs Commission of New South Wales (1994) *Police and Ethnic Communities*, Ethnic Affairs Commission of NSW, Sydney.

Express (13/9/01) 'Local MPs back new rape law', 13 September, p 19.

Farr, J (24/8/01) 'Women take second place', letter to the editor, *Daily Telegraph*, 24 August, p 28.

Farr, M (14/9/01) 'Terrorist link with boat people: Reith', *Daily Telegraph*, 14 September, p 8.

Ferrie, M (17/10/02) 'Beware Whose Face You Slap, It May Be Yours', letter to the editor, *Sydney Morning Herald*, 17 October, p 16.

Field, S (13/11/98) 'Coorey calls for curfew', *Canterbury-Bankstown Express*, 13 November, p 6

Fickling, D (23/9/02) 'Racially motivated crime and punishment', *Guardian Unlimited*, 23 September, <http://www.guardian.co.uk/australia/story/0,12070,797464,00.html>.

Finch, L (1993) 'On the streets: Working class youth culture in the nineteenth century' in White, R (ed) *Youth Subcultures: Theory, History and the Australian Experience*, National Clearinghouse for Youth Studies, Hobart, pp 75–79.

Fisk, R (2001) 'Operation Selective Justice by any other name', *Sydney Morning Herald*, 29-30 September, p 35.

Flahault, F (2003) *Malice,* Heron, L (trans.), Verso, London.

Ford, P (11/10/01) 'Terrorism on the seas', letter to the editor, *Daily Telegraph*, 11 October, p 27.

Four Corners (15/4/02) 'To Deter or Deny', reporter Debbie Whitmont, television program, ABC Television, 15 April, <http://www.abc.net.au/4corners/archives/2002a_Monday15April2002.htm>.

Four Corners (6/5/02) 'Jonestown', reporter Chris Masters, television program, ABC Television, 6 May, <http://www.abc.net.au/4corners/archives/2002a_Monday6May2002.htm>.

Francis, S (26/8/01) 'Racial Gang Rape: Another Diversity Disaster', 26 August, <http://www.theneworder.org/news/rape.26.08.01.htm>.

Freitas, N (15/10/02) 'Attack on Western values', letter to the editor, *Daily Telegraph*, 15 October, p 22.

Furedi, F (1997) *Culture of Fear*, Cassell, London.

Fyfe, M (25/8/01) 'Ethnic crime debate rages out of control on Sydney airwaves', *Age*, 25 August, p 4.

Gartside, M (26/8/01) 'Respect all cultures, not just your own', *Daily Telegraph*, 26 August, p 90.

Gee, S (9/8/01) 'Women told to beware', *Daily Telegraph*, 9 August, p 1.

Gee, S (10/8/01) 'Gang Force: 240 police to fight crime', *Daily Telegraph*, 10 August, p 1.

Gerard, I (10–11/8/02) 'Gang rapist handed 18-year jail sentence', *Weekend Australian*, 10–11 August, p 5.

Gerard, I (4/12/02) 'Protection for more children', *Australian*, 4 December, p 5.

Giddens, A (1991) *Modernity and Self-Identity*, Polity Press, Cambridge.

Gilmore, H (6/11/00) 'No-go zones to protect schoolkids', *Daily Telegraph*, 6 November, pp 5, 20.

Glendinning, L & Connolly, E (19/12/02) 'Light sentences fall on a boy's lonely grave', *Sydney Morning Herald,* 19 December, pp 1, 2.

Goldner, V (29/7/00) 'HATE KILLING', *Daily Telegraph*, 29 July, pp 1, 4.

Goode, E & Ben-Yehuda, N (1994) *Moral Panics: the Social Construction of Deviance*, Blackwell, Oxford.

Goodsir, D (23–23/2/03) 'Australia near top of terrorist list', *Sydney Morning Herald*, 22–23 February, p 14.

Goodsir, D (14/7/03) 'The traitors within: Australian network ready to support terrorists', *Sydney Morning Herald*, 14 July, p 1.

Goodsir, D et al. (4/9/03) 'Terror contact: finger points at Australians', *Sydney Morning Herald*, 4 September, p 1.

Goot, M (30/8/02) 'Despite alarm bells and whistles, the tide is turning on immigration', *Sydney Morning Herald*, 30 August, p 11.

Goldberg, D (1993) *Racist Culture: philosophy and the politics of meaning*, Blackwell, Oxford.

Gordon, G (7/12/02) 'Gang wrongly jailed for rape', *Daily Telegraph*, 7 December, p 28.

Gordon, M (7/9/02), 'So, are we all right Jack?', *Age*, 7 September, <http://www.theage.com.au/articles/2002/09/06/1031115938038.html>.

Gordon, S (10/9/02) 'A beef with halal burgers', letter to the editor, *Daily Telegraph*, 10 September, p 16.

Gramsci, A (1971) *Selections from the Prison Notebooks of Antonio Gramsci*, (ed and trans Hoare, Q & Nowell-Smith, G) International Publishers, New York.

Grattan, M (14/9/01) 'Standing by. The US has only to ask for our help: PM', *Sydney Morning Herald*, 14 September, p 6.

Grattan, M (10–11/11/01) 'Campaign that leaves nation tarnished', *Sydney Morning Herald*, 10–11 November, p 13.

Green, A (6–7/10/01) 'Small swing now seems like a huge gap for Labor', *Sydney Morning Herald*, 6 October, p 33.

Guardian Unlimited (13/9/01) 'Anti-Islamic violence breaks out around world', 13 September.

Hage, G (1991) 'Racism, Multiculturalism and the Gulf War', *Arena*, no 96, pp 8–13.

Hage, G (1998) *White Nation: Fantasies of white supremacy in a multicultural society*, Pluto Press, Sydney.

Hage, G (2001) 'Postscript: Arab-Australian belonging after "September 11"' in Hage, G (ed) *Arab-Australians Today: Citizenship and Belonging*, Melbourne University Press, Melbourne, pp 241–8.

Hage, G (31/1/02) 'A contagious mix of fear and paranoia', *Canberra Times*, 31 January, p 11.

Hage, G (2002) *Against Paranoid Nationalism: Searching For Hope in a Shrinking Society*, Pluto Press, Sydney.

Haig, P (8/10/02) 'Bulldog Hazem-Atazz', *Canterbury-Bankstown Express*, 8 October, p 1.

Hall, Stuart (1993) 'Encoding, Decoding' in During, S (ed) *The Cultural Studies Reader*, Routledge, London, pp 90–103.

Hall, S, Critcher, C, Jefferson, T, Clarke, J & Roberts, B (1978) *Policing the Crisis: Mugging, the State, and Law and Order*, Macmillan, London.

Hanson, P (10/12/96) [speech in the House of Representatives] Hansard, 10 December.

Hanson, P (21/2/01) *A Letter from Pauline Hanson*, 21 February, <http://www.onenation.com.au>.

Harris, P (3/6/01) 'Far Right plot to provoke race riots', *Observer*, 3 June, <http://observer.guardian.co.uk/politics/story/0,6903,500605,00.html>.

Harris, S (26/3/00) 'Battle for Bankstown', *Sunday Telegraph*, 26 March, pp 91–93.

Harris, T (20/8/03) 'No 38 on terror list', *Australian*, 20 August, p 5.

Hartley, J & McKee, A (2000) *The Indigenous Public Sphere*, Oxford University Press, Oxford.

Harvey, D (2000) 'Protecting Normal: No loitering laws in Port Kembla, New South Wales', *On the Record 50*, April/May/June, pp 1–4.

Head, M (23/11/99) 'Australian anti-refugee measures flout international law', 23 November, <http://www.wsws.org>.

Heinzmann, S, Farr, M & McDougall, B (15/10/02) 'Desperate search for a mother and sister as Australia mourns its fallen', *Daily Telegraph*, 15 October, p 2.

Helal, M (16/10/02) 'Letters to the editor', *Sydney Morning Herald*, 16 October, p 16.

Hewett, J (19–20/10/02) 'Leave Bali now, Howard advises', *Sydney Morning Herald*, October 19-20, p3.

Hilderbrande, J & Morris, R (16/7/02) 'Racism a factor in gang rapes: Cowdery', *Daily Telegraph*, 16 July, p 4.

Hoffman-Axthelm, D (1992) 'Identity and Reality: the end of the philosophical immigration officer' in Lash, S & Friedman, J (eds) *Modernity and Identity*, Blackwell, Oxford, pp 196–217.

Hogg, R (2002) 'The Khaki Election' in Scraton, P *Beyond September 11: An Anthology of Dissent*, Pluto Press, London, pp 135–143.

Hogg, R & Brown, D (1998) *Rethinking Law and Order*, Pluto Press, Sydney.

Hoggett, P, (1989) 'The Culture of Uncertainty' in Richards, B (ed) *Crises of the Self*, Free Association Books, London, pp 27–35.

Holland, M (15/10/02) 'Blasts wreck symbolic centre of Australian holiday culture, October 15, pp 6–7.

Hollway, W & Jefferson, T (2000) 'The Role of Anxiety in Fear of Crime' in Hope, T & Sparks, R (eds) *Crime, Risk and Insecurity*, Routledge, London, pp 31–49.

Horan, M (26/12/99) 'Officers caught in blitz', *Sunday Telegraph*, 26 December, p 19.

Horan, M (11/8/02) 'Emotional Carr meets rape victim', *Sunday Telegraph*, 11 August, p 2.

Horin, A (9/9/02) 'September marks year of living unhappily', *Sydney Morning Herald*, 9 September, p 4.

Horin, A (21–22/12/02) 'Learning to dance in the new suburbia', *Sydney Morning Herald*, 21–22 December, p 25.

Hornery, A & Wyld, B (25/11/02) 'When you're living on the edge, veiled women can be scary', *Sydney Morning Herald*, 25 November, p 18.

Howard, J (21/11/02) 'Transcript of the Prime Minister The Hon John Howard MP interview with John Laws Radio 2UE', 21 November, <http://www.pm.gov.au>.

Howard, J, & Hardgrave, G, (2002), <http://www.minister.immi.gov.au/minister2/index.htm>.

Human Rights and Equal Opportunity Commission (HREOC) (1991) *Racist Violence: Report of the National Inquiry into Racist Violence in Australia*, Australian Government Publishing Service, Canberra.

Humphries, D (29/3/97) 'Three's-a-crowd law targets street gang', *Sydney Morning Herald*, 29 March, p 1.

Humphries, D (4/11/98) 'Lebanese youths and police to meet', *Sydney Morning Herald*, 4 November, p 5.

Humphries, D, & Marsh, J (3/11/98) 'Lakemba's verdict: this attack was un-Australian', *Sydney Morning Herald*, 3 November, p 1.

Huntington, S (1997) *The Clash of Civilizations and the Remaking of World Order*, Simon and Schuster, London.

Insight (23/8/01) Interview with Pauline Hanson [interviewer Jenny Brockie], television program, SBS Television, 23 August.

Irwin, J (2000) 'Youth — Is it a crime?', paper presented at the Community Legal Centres Conference, *Searching for Justice*, University of Technology, Sydney, 28 June.

Islamic Council of Victoria (2002) 'Media Release', 6 November, <http://www/icv.org.au>.

Jackman, C (4/9/01) 'Don't sigh too soon Australia, it's not over yet', *Daily Telegraph*, 4 September, p 17.

Jackman, C (29/8/01) 'Turning light on the dark side of life', *Daily Telegraph*, 29 August, p 31.

Jackson, S (3/11/98) 'Families cower under lock, key', *Australian*, 3 November, p 5.

Jackson, S, Harris, T & Nason, D, (3/11/98) 'Call to community on shooting', *Australian*, 3 November, p 5.

Jacobsen, G (26/3/01) 'Premier throws light in drug changes', *Sydney Morning Herald*, 26 March, p 6.

Jacobsen, G, Burke, K & Connolly, E (25–26/8/01) 'Carr to question top judge as DPP ponders appeal over rape sentences', *Sydney Morning Herald*, 25–26 August, p 2.

Jakubowicz, A (27/9/01) Interview with Nadya Stani on 'Reporting Race 2, Media scrum in Pakistan', radio program, *Media Report*, Radio National, 27 September, (presenter & executive producer, Mick O'Regan), <http://www.abc.net.au/rn/talks/8.30/mediarpt/stories/s377056.htm>.

Jakubowicz, A, Morrissey, M & Palser, J (1984) *Ethnicity, Class and Social Policy in Australia*, Social Welfare Research Centre Report No. 46, The University of New South Wales, Sydney.

Johnston, D (5/11/01) 'Terror video censored', *Daily Telegraph*, 5 November, p 9.

Jopson, D, (20–21/10/01), 'Muslims harassed, and it is women who bear the brunt', *Sydney Morning Herald*, 20–21 October, p 18.

Kamper, A (8/1/03) 'They're wearing guns like jewellery', *Daily Telegraph*, 8 January, pp 1, 4.

Kamper, A (4/9/03) 'After a single raid on a Sydney warehouse this many handguns are destined for the black market', *Daily Telegraph*, 4 September, p 5.

Karvelas, P (30/10/02) 'Muslims in fear of growing paranoia', *Australian*, 30 October, p 6.

Karvelas, P (31/10/02) 'Raid man denies link to Bashir's network', *Australian*, 31 October, p 7.

Karvelas, P & Chulov, M (30/10/02) 'Officers raid home of suspected JI member', *Australian*, 30 October, p 1.

Kelly, J (16/12/02) 'An act of irresponsibility', *Daily Telegraph*, 16 December, p 18.

Kennedy, L (22/10/98) 'Armed escorts for officers after radio threats', *Sydney Morning Herald*, 22 October, p 3.

Kennedy, L (17/8/01) 'Muslim girls spat at in street', *Sydney Morning Herald*, 17 August, <http://old.smh.com.au/news/0108/17/text/national8.html>.

Kennedy, L (3/9/03) 'Murder and attacks on homes prompt strike force response', *Sydney Morning Herald*, 3 September, <http://www.smh.com.au/articles/2003/09/02/1062403517893.html>.

Kennedy, L, & O'Malley, N (25/11/00) 'Ambushed: Pregnant woman dies, man critical', *Sydney Morning Herald*, 25 November, p 9.

Kent, P (24/8/01) 'They don't realise they're stupid — TAUNTS OF THE RAPISTS', *Daily Telegraph*, 24 August, p 6.

Kerin, J & Balogh, S (10/7/02) 'Gender gap puts smile on women', *Australian*, 10 July, p 3.

Kerin, J & Stewart, C (28/5/03) 'We're in reach of Mid-East Terrorists', *Australian*, 28 May, p 1.

Kerr, J (11/7/01) 'Arab gangs targeted by $2.2m plan', *Sydney Morning Herald*, 11 July, p 4.

Kidman, J (29/7/01) '70 girls attacked by rape gangs', *Sun-Herald*, 29 July, p 1.

Kidman, J (29/7/01) 'Brutal sex assaults linked to race gangs', *Sun-Herald*, 29 July, pp 4–5.

Kidman, J (30/9/01) 'ASIO swoop in hunt for BinLaden link: Muslim woman claims gunpoint interrogation', *Sun-Herald*, 30 September, pp 4–5.

Kidman, J (18/5/03) 'Rapists team up in latest assaults', *Sun-Herald*, 18 May, p 34.

Kitney, G (22/11/02) 'The new language of Mr Untouchable', *Sydney Morning Herald*, 22 November, p 13.

Kitney, G (23–24/11/02) 'Free speech has a price', *Sydney Morning Herald*, 23–24 November, p 10.

Klein, N (8/11/03) 'Abuses packaged for an easy sale', *Sydney Morning Herald*, 8 September, p 11.

Knowles, L & Casella, N (5/10/02) 'Cricket bat thug "got off too lightly" — Brain damaged boy angry at sentence', *Daily Telegraph*, 5 October, p 6.

Kremmer, C (20–21/4/02) 'Spy chief calls for police investigation into secret service raid', *Sydney Morning Herald*, 20–21 April, p 10.

Kroker, A, Kroker, M & Cook, D (1989) *Panic Encyclopedia: the definitive guide to the postmodern scene*, Macmillan, Basingstoke.

Labi, S (1/10/01) 'ASIO raids "revenge" by Muslim groups in conflict', *Daily Telegraph*, 1 October, p 3.

Lagan, B (10/3/01)'Mean streets', *Sydney Morning Herald*, 10 March, p 27.

Lagan, B et al. (29/3/01) '"Nazi-style" drug laws may be open to abuse', *Sydney Morning Herald*, 29 March, p 4.

Lakoff, G (1991) 'Metaphor and War', <http://lists.village.virginia.edu/sixties/HTML_docs/Texts/ScholarlyLakoff_Gulf_Metaphor_1.html>.

Lalor, P (15/10/02) 'Hardened professionals cry in the face of broken humanity', *Daily Telegraph*, 15 October, pp 4–5.

Lateline (27/2/02) 'Downer speaks from people-smuggling conference', television program, reporter Tony Jones, broadcast 27 February, transcript at <http://www.abc.net.au/lateline/s492712.htm>.

Lateline (26/11/02a) 'Dowd and Brandis on anti-terror legislation', television program, 26 November, transcript at <http://www.abc.net.au/lateline/s735539.htm>.

Lateline (26/11/02b) 'Proposal to boost ASIO powers has judges worried', television program, 26 November, transcript at < http://www.abc.net.au/lateline/s735537.htm>.

Lawrence, K (27/11/00) 'Murder Street: Police charge two over killings', *Daily Telegraph*, 27 November, p 7.

Lawrence, K (3/8/00) 'Police raid tames a street of silent fear', *Sydney Morning Herald*, 3 August, p 3.

Lawrence, K (21/3/03) 'Rape leader "sent white powder" to prison boss', *Daily Telegraph*, 21 March, p 27.

Lawrence, K (27/3/03) 'Hijacked by hatred', *Daily Telegraph*, 27 March, pp 1–2.

Lawrence, K & McDougall, B (14/10/02) 'Young mates killed as dream tourist resort is torn to shreds', *Daily Telegraph*, 14 October, p 2.

Lawson, V (10/2/01) 'Private school, public disgrace', *Sydney Morning Herald*, 10 February, p 29.

Lebanese Muslim Association (3/11/02) 'Mufty Alhilali and Muslims to meet Christians, Jews, Buddhists and Sikh', media release, 3 November.

Lebanese Muslim Association (18/11/02) media release, 18 November, <http://www.Islamicsydney.com>.

Legal Information Access Centre (1997) *Hot Topic: Juvenile Justice*, Legal Informaton Access Centre, reproduced in Department of Social Communication and Journalism, *Communication and Journalism Archive*, <http://www.uts.edu.au/fac/hss/SCJ/archive/lakemba/lak_timeline.html>.

Lesley, I (24/8/01) 'Women take second place', *Daily Telegraph*, letter to the editor, 24 August, p 28.

Leunig, M (24–25/11/01) 'The Warlords of Suburbia', *Sydney Morning Herald: Spectrum*, 24–25 November, p 2.

Levinas, E (1997) *Otherwise Than Being*, Duchesne University Press, Pittsburgh.

Lewis, J (18/8/03) 'Meanest streets in town that put fear on the map, *Sydney Morning Herald*, 18 August, p 5.

Lipari, K (24/6/02) '10 years'prison for rapists: Brogden', *Daily Telegraph*, 24 June, p 2.

Lipari, K (28/10/02) 'Bali bombs spark 40 attacks on Muslims', *Daily Telegraph*, 28 October, p 6.

Lipari, K (6/1/03) 'Bail Watch', *Daily Telegraph*, 6 January, pp 1, 6.

Lipari, K & Skelsey, M (26/2/02) 'Bob Carr doesn't want a population boom...', *Daily Telegraph*, 26 February, p 8.

Livingston, E (1987) *Making Sense of Ethnomethodology*, Routledge and Kegan Paul, London.

Loader, I, Girling, E, & Sparks, R (2000) 'After Success?' in Hope, T & Sparks, R (eds) *Crime, Risk and Insecurity*, Routledge, London, pp65–82.

Lowe, S (12/9/03) 'Personal privacy being destroyed in the name of public safety', *Sydney Morning Herald*, 12 September, p 10.

Lupton, D (1999a) 'Dangerous Places and the Unpredictable Stranger', *The Australian and New Zealand Journal of Criminology*, vol 32, no 1, pp 1–15.

Lupton, D (1999b) *Risk*, Routledge, London.

MacCallum, M (2002) 'Girt by Sea: Australia, the refugees and the politics of fear', *Quarterly Essay*, no 5, pp 1–73.

Mackay, H (26–27/10/02) 'Anxiety is keeping Howard on top', *Sydney Morning Herald*, 26–27 October, p 30.

Mackay, H (16–17/2/02) 'Numbed voters take spin doctors' orders', *Sydney Morning Herald*, 16–17 February, p 31.

Mackey, E (1999) 'Constructing an Endangered Nation' in Lupton, D (ed) *Risk and Sociocultural Theory*, Cambridge University Press, Cambridge, pp 108–130.

Mackie, V (2002) 'Afghan Nights: media representations and the power of discourse', paper presented at the Cultural Studies Association of Australia annual conference, University of Melbourne, Melbourne, December 5–7.

Maher, L, Dixon, D, Swift, W & Nguyen, T (1997) *Anh Hai: Young Asian Background People's Perceptions and Experiences of Policing*, University of New South Wales Faculty of Law Research Monograph Series, Sydney.

Manne, R, (29/10/01) 'Voting for Labor but with a heavy heart', *Sydney Morning Herald*, 29 October, p 16.

Manne, R, (12/11/01), 'How a single-issue party held on to power', *Sydney Morning Herald*, 12 November, p 10.

Manne, R, (10/6/02) 'Oh, for a show of mercy, sincerity', *Sydney Morning Herald*, 10 June, p 15.

Marr, D & Wilkinson, M (20–21/10/01) 'They shall not land', *Sydney Morning Herald*, 20–21 October, pp 29, 40–41.

Martin, B (10/11/98) 'Urban Warfare', *Bulletin*, 10 November, pp 26–27.

Massumi, B (ed) (1993) *The Politics of Everyday Fear*, University of Minnesota Press, Minneapolis.

Mayberry, J (15/10/02) 'Attack on Western values', letter to the editor, *Daily Telegraph*, 15 October, p 22.

McCulloch, J (2002) 'Either you are with us, or you are with the terrorists' in Scraton, P (ed) *Beyond September 11*, Pluto Press, London, pp 54–59.

McDougall, B, Lawrence, K, Morris, R & Miranda, C (6/8/01) 'Gangland: the crisis Sydney's community leaders are too timid to confront', *Daily Telegraph*, 6 August, p 1.

McDougall, B & Miranda, C (6/8/01) 'Alarm as numbers keep growing', *Daily Telegraph*, 6 August, pp 4–5.

McGeough, P (10/9/01) 'The face of fear hidden behind a veil of tyranny', *Sydney Morning Herald*, 10 September, p 10.

McGuinness, PP (23/7/02) 'No One Gang Has The Monopoly On Rape', *Sydney Morning Herald*, 23 July, p 11.

McLachlan, B & Reid, I (1994) *Framing and Interpretation*, Melbourne University Press, Carlton, Victoria.

McNamara, D (10/10/02) 'Judge rejects plea in Lee case', *Daily Telegraph*, 10 October, p 21.

McPhedran, I (2/11/01) 'Jihad declared on Australia', *Daily Telegraph*, 2 November, p 1.

McRobbie, A (1994) *Postmodernism and Popular Culture*, Routledge, London.

Media Report (7/11/02) 'Measuring the Mood of the Community', radio program, ABC Radio National, 7 November, <http://www.abc.net.au/rn/talks/8.30/mediarpt/stories/s719210.htm>.

Media Watch (9/9/02) television program, ABC Television, <http://www.abc.net.au/mediawatch/stories/default.htm>.

Megalogenis, G (9/5/02) 'Census reveals whiter shade of pale', *Australian*, 9 May, p 13.

Megalogenis, G (13–14/7/02) 'New faces, old frictions', *Australian*, 13–14 July, pp 19, 22.

Mehboob, A (14/11/02) Australian Federation of Islamic Councils (AFIC) Media Release, 14 November, <http://www.icv.org.au/baliafic.htm>.

Mercer, N (12/5/01) 'Police chief hits out at ethnic gang violence', *Sydney Morning Herald*, 12 March, p 1.

Mercer, N (16–17/2/02) 'Ryan's reckoning', *Sydney Morning Herald*, 16–17 February, p 25.

Messerschmidt, JW (1993) *Masculinities and crime: critique and reconceptualization of theory*, Rowman & Littlefield, Lanham, MD.

Middap, C (21/8/01) 'Same story across the world', *Daily Telegraph*, 21 August, p 6.

Miles, R (1982) *Racism and Migrant Labour*, Routledge and Kegan Paul, Boston.

Miller, L (13/2/03) 'Son's killer may go free in three years', *Daily Telegraph*, 13 February, p 17.

Millett, M (18/5/02) 'Fears of cultural rift as Sydney's migrant magnet works overtime', *Sydney Morning Herald*, 18 March, pp 1, 6.

Millett, M (5–6/7/03a) 'Bulging Sydney's splitting image', *Sydney Morning Herald*, 5–6 July, p 1.

Millett, M (5–6/7/03b) 'Fractured Sydney', *Sydney Morning Herald*, 5–6 July, pp 23, 30.

Miranda, C (13/9/00) 'Schoolgirls in fear after sex attacks', *Daily Telegraph*, 13 September, p 14.

Miranda, C (24/10/00) 'Rogue police hunt in a pack', *Daily Telegraph*, 24 October, p 7.

Miranda, C (8/1/01) '40 gangs battle for control of our streets', *Daily Telegraph*, 8 January, p 4.

Miranda, C (24/2/01) 'Criminal warfare "to rip this city apart"', *Daily Telegraph*, 24 February, p 4.

Miranda, C (16/8/01) 'Guns for Hire: Red Army soldiers recruited to city gangs', *Daily Telegraph*, 16 August, p 1.

Miranda, C (17/8/01) 'Gangs acknowledged as unit's target', *Daily Telegraph*, 17 August, p 8.

Miranda, C (12/10/01a) 'Bin Laden groups in Sydney suburbs', *Daily Telegraph*, 12 October, p 5.

Miranda, C (12/10/01b) 'TERROR AUSTRALIS: "Bin Laden groups in our suburbs"', *Daily Telegraph*, 12 October, pp 1, 4.

Miranda, C (28/4/03) 'Boys are back in town', *Daily Telegraph*, 28 April, p 5.

Mitchell, A (12/8/01) 'Libs push life terms for gang rapists', *Sun-Herald*, 12 August, p 31.

Moir (8/3/01) 'Gang wars at the coppers' club', *Sydney Morning Herald*, 8 March, p 13.

Morgan, G (1997) '*The Bulletin* and the Larrikin Moral Panic in Late Nineteenth Century Sydney', *Media International Australia*, no 85, pp 17–24.

Morgan, A & Stephens, T (25–26/1/03) 'Keeping the faith in a world less certain', *Sydney Morning Herald*, 25–26 January, p A2.

Morley, D (2000) *Home Territories*, Routledge, London.

Morris, L (4/11/02) 'An offer of help — but ASIO preferred to raid', *Sydney Morning Herald*, 4 November, p 1.

Morris, L (22/11/02) 'Watch out for danger everywhere, expert urges', *Sydney Morning Herald*, 22 November, p 4.

Morris, L (27/11/02) 'Backlash building over security laws', *Sydney Morning Herald*, 27 November, p 9.

Morris, L (19/12/02) 'Council faces court after rejecting Muslim centre', *Sydney Morning Herald*, 19 December, p 4.

Morris, L (23/12/02) 'September 11 made us sadder than the Bali attack — survey', *Sydney Morning Herald*, 23 December, p 4.

Morris, L (21–22/6/03) 'Struggles inside Islam', *Sydney Morning Herald*, 21–22 June, p 36.

Morris, L & Cameron, D (31/10/02) 'World rocked for a Muslim family living the quiet life', *Sydney Morning Herald*, 31 October, pp 1,8.

Morris, L, Cameron, D & Cornford, P (1/11/02) 'Police told man: you are one of JI', *Sydney Morning Herald*, 1 November, p 7.

Morris, L & Thompson, M, (5/11/02) 'Belmore newsflash: Bin Laden, icon of the holy struggle', *Sydney Morning Herald*, 5 November, pp 1, 7.

Morris, R (9/7/01) 'Shame of the gang', *Daily Telegraph*, 9 July, p 7.

Morris, R (11/7/01) '$2.2m to calm gang violence', *Daily Telegraph*, 11 July, p 3.

Morris, R (17/8/01) 'Migrants to declare military experience', *Daily Telegraph*, 17 August, p 8.

Morris, R (22/8/01) 'Premier rejects hatred claims', *Daily Telegraph*, 22 August, p 4.

Morris, R (23/8/01) 'Ethnic opinions split over sheik', *Daily Telegraph*, 23 August, p 10.

Morris, R (5/9/01) 'Gang tackle ... But Islamic leader demands Carr apology', *Daily Telegraph*, 5 September, p 1, 6.

Morris, R (7/9/01) 'DPP to appeal on rape penalties', *Daily Telegraph*, 7 September, p 4.

Morris, R (22/5/02) 'Australia ranks poorly in violent crime survey', *Daily Telegraph*, 22 May, p 9.

Morris, R (8/8/02) 'League star's emotional plea on behalf of Sydney Muslims', *Daily Telegraph*, 8 August, p 7.

Morris, R (28/11/02) 'Cultural clash over prayer', *Daily Telegraph*, 28 November, p 7.

Morris, R (19/12/02) 'Prayer centre snub divides community', *Daily Telegraph*, 19 December, p 21.

Morris, R (30/5/03) 'Hate campaign group exposed', *Daily Telegraph*, 30 May, p 21.

Morris, R & English, B (7/1/03) 'MUFTI CHARGED: Muslim leader collapses after police clash', *Daily Telegraph*, 7 January, pp 1, 4.

Morris, R & Hu!, J (12/7/02) 'Why the melting pot is ready to boil over', *Daily Telegraph*, 12 July, p 6.

Morris, R & Murray, K (10/1/03) 'Trading on Fear', *Daily Telegraph*, 10 January, pp 1, 5.

Morris, R & Rowlands, L (31/10/02) 'Father denies link to feared group', *Daily Telegraph*, 31 October, p 7

Morris, S & Stewart, C (11/12/02) 'No evidence specifying Bali as target', *Australian*, 11 December, p 10.

Moses, A (27/12/02) 'Fear brings flock back to churches', *Sydney Morning Herald*, 27 December, p 5

Moussa, H (23/10/02) 'News faces so easy on the eye', letter to the editor, *Daily Telegraph*, 23 October, p 34.

Mulhall, D (3/12/02) 'Losing cultural identity', *Daily Telegraph*, 3 December, p 26.

Murphy, D (27–28/4/02) 'Good times, bad times', *Sydney Morning Herald*, 27–28 April, p 25.

Murphy, P (10/3/01) letter to the editor, *Sydney Morning Herald*, 10 March, p 35.

Murray, K (22/8/02) 'There's just no room left at the gym', *Daily Telegraph*, 22 August, p 21.

Murray, K & Morris, R (13/8/02) 'Women exercise right to work out', *Daily Telegraph*, 13 August, p 10.

Mydans, S (9/11/01) 'Which Australian Candidate Has the Harder Heart?', *New York Times*, 9 November.

Nairn, T (2002/3) 'On the Modesty of Australia', *Arena Magazine*, iss 62, pp 5–6.

Needham, T (20/9/01) 'Online Offline: Race hate ends Web discussions', *Sydney Morning Herald*, 20 September, p 3.

Newell, P (1990) *Migrant Experience of Racist Violence: A Study of Households in Campbelltown and Marrickville*, Human Rights and Equal Opportunities Commission, Sydney.

Newman, G (18/12/02) 'Politics of fear fuels fires', *Australian*, 18 December, p 36.

News Online (12/3/03) 'Appeal urged on killer sentence',12 February, <http://www.news.com.au/common/story_page/0,4057,5974156%255E1702,00.html>.

Nixon, S (10/10/02) 'All work no pray makes Kamal an angry employee', *Sydney Morning Herald*, 10 October.

Nixon, S (11/10/02) 'Worker relies on God to settle dispute', *Sydney Morning Herald*, 11 October.

Noble, G (2002) 'Comfortable and Relaxed: Furnishing the Home and Nation', *Continuum*, vol 16, no 1, pp 53–66.

Noble, G, Poynting, S & Tabar, P (1999) 'Youth, Ethnicity and the Mapping of Identities: Strategic essentialism and hybridity among male Arabic-speaking youth in South-western Sydney', *Communal/Plural*, vol 7, no 1, pp 29–44.

Oakes, L (3/11/01) 'A sly-dog race card', *Bulletin*, 3 November, p 18.

Obeid, E (2000) 'Speech', May 23, LC Hansard Articles, 52nd Parliament, <http://www.parliament.nsw.gov.au>.

O'Bourne, J (14/7/02) 'Your sons are rapists, says Muslim leader', *Sun-Herald*, 14 July, p 4.

Ogg, M & Casey, M (2/11/98a) 'An Act of War', *Daily Telegraph*, 2 November, pp 1, 4–5.

Ogg, M & Casey, M (2/11/98b) 'Police dig in against gang attacks', *Courier-Mail*, 2 November p 1.

Oloman, EC (9/12/02) 'A curse on stupid smokers', *Daily Telegraph*, 9 December, p 20.

One Nation (2003) *One Nation*, East Hills election pamphlet.

O'Malley, N, Jacobsen, G & Kennedy, L (17/8/01) 'Military past may keep out migrants', *Sydney Morning Herald*, 17 August, p 3.

O'Rourke, C (13/5/03) 'Muslim centre won't fit in, court told', *Sydney Morning Herald*, 13 May, p 3.

O'Rourke, C (14/5/03) 'Jihad declared on residents opposed to prayer centre, court told', *Sydney Morning Herald*, 14 May, p 9.

Overington, C (4/2/01) 'School goes on trial in unholy Trinity case: Dormitory of shame', *Sunday Age*, 4 February, p 1.

Owens, W (11/3/01) 'Teenagers accused of sex attacks', *Sunday Telegraph*, 11 March, p 19.

Pauline Hanson's One Nation (2001) *Pauline Hanson's One Nation Policy Document: Immigration, Population and Social Cohesion*, <http://www.gwb.com.au/onenation/policy/immig.html#8>.

Pearson, G (1983) *Hooligan: A History of Respectable Fears*, Macmillan, London.

Pemberton, A (22/8/01) 'A degrading crime as old as antiquity', *Daily Telegraph*, 22 August, p 4.

Penberthy, D (4/9/01) 'Making sense of the irreconcilable', *Daily Telegraph*, 14 September, p 27.

Penberthy, D (20/9/02) 'Us and them, and they've got no idea', *Daily Telegraph*, 20 September, p 28.

Penberthy, D (17/12/02) 'Five star asylums', *Daily Telegraph*, 17 December, pp 1, 4.

Peterson, A, McDougall, B & Gee, S (17/4/02) 'Click-on crime', *Daily Telegraph*, 17 April, p 1, 4.

Peterson, A (5/9/02) 'Die in jail: Carr's new sentences', *Daily Telegraph*, 5 September, p 5.

Phillips, R (20/9/01) 'Escalating attacks on Muslims and Arabs in Australia', World Socialist Website, 20 September, <http://www.wsws.org>.

Piccoli, A (23/8/01) 'Defeating the enemy within', *Daily Telegraph*, 23 August, p 24.

Pickering, S & Lambert, C (2002) 'Deterrence: Australia's Refugee Policy', *Current Issues in Criminal Justice*, vol 14, no 1, pp 65–86.

PM (24/8/01) 'Ethnic vote tipped to payback Carr in Auburn by-election', radio program, ABC Radio, 24 August, 6.23pm.

PM (14/9/01) 'Australia's Islamic Community Victims of Racial Tension', reporter Lachlan Parker, radio program, ABC local radio, 14 September.

PM (17/10/01) 'Opposition backs Howards deployment of troops', radio program, ABC Radio, 17 October, 6.11pm, <http://www.abc.net.au/pm/s393423.htm>.

PM (21/11/02) 'Nile faces backlash over comments', radio program, ABC Radio, 21 November, 6.20pm, <http://www.abc.net.au/pm/s732087.htm>.

PM (25/11/02) 'Carr seeks solution to Sydney population problem', radio program, ABC Radio, 25 November, 6.40pm <http://www.abc.net.au/pm/s734295.htm>.

Powell, S & Chulov, M (31/10/02) 'ASIO raids target JI sleeper cell', *Australian*, 31 October, p 1.

Poynting, S (1999) 'When "Zero Tolerance" Looks Like Racial Intolerance: "Lebanese youth gangs", discrimination and resistance', *Current Issues in Criminal Justice*, vol 11, no 1, pp 74–78.

Poynting, S (2001) 'Appearances and "Ethnic Crime"', *Current Issues in Criminal Justice*, vol 13, no 1, pp 110–112.

Poynting, S (2002a) 'Racism and Community Safety', *Current Issues in Criminal Justice*, vol 13, no 3, pp 328–332.

Poynting, S (2002b) 'Bin Laden in the Suburbs: Attacks on Arab and Muslim Australians before and after 11 September', *Current Issues in Criminal Justice*, vol 14, no 1.

Poynting, S & Donaldson, M (2002) 'Snakes and Lads: What does the ruling class do when it schools?' in Kalantzis, M, Varnava-Skoura, G & Cope, B (eds) *Learning for the Future: New Worlds, New Literacies, New Learning, New People*, Common Ground, Altona, Victoria, pp 85–108.

Poynting, S, Noble, G & Tabar, P (1998) '"If anyone called me a wog, they wouldn't be speaking to me alone": Protest masculinity and Lebanese youth in Western Sydney', *Journal of Interdisciplinary Gender Studies*, vol 3, no 2, Special Issue on Australian Masculinity, December, pp 76–94.

Poynting, S, Noble, G & Tabar, P (1999) 'Intersections of Masculinity and Ethnicity: A study of male Lebanese immigrant youth in Western Sydney', *Race, Ethnicity and Education*, vol 2, no 1, pp 59–77.

Poynting, S, Noble, G & Tabar, P (2001) 'Caught between Two Cultures?: Second generation Lebanese immigrant youth in Sydney and the rhetoric of rescue', paper presented at the *Lebanese Diaspora Conference*, Lebanese American University, Beirut, 29 June.

Poynting, S, Noble, G & Tabar, P (2001) 'Middle Eastern Appearances: "Ethnic Gangs", moral panic and media framing', *The Australian and New Zealand Journal of Criminology*, vol 34, no 1, pp 67–90.

Presdee, M (2000) *Cultural Criminology and the Carnival of Crime*, Routledge, London.

Pryor, L & Totaro, P (16/8/02) 'Sentence "won't help rape victims"', *Sydney Morning Herald*, 16 August, p 2.

Puplick, C (22/8/02) 'What's all the fuss about?', *Daily Telegraph*, 22 August, p 21.

Ramsey, A (27–28/10/01) 'Forget the rest of the pack, it's the race card', *Sydney Morning Herald*, 27–28 October, p 40.

Ramsey, A (16–17/2/02) 'How the boat people's plans were sunk', *Sydney Morning Herald*, 16–17 February, p 35.

Ramsey, A (22/6/03) 'Stepping back from secret police state' *Sydney Morning Herald*, 21–22 June, p 43.

Rath, T (15/9/01) 'Arabs around world face backlash: Racial attacks spread across the globe', *The Daily Star*, Beirut, 15 September.

Ratnesar, R (23/9/02) 'Confessions of an Al-Qaeda Terrorist', *TIME*, 23 September, pp 28–35.

Reardon, D (20/11/99) 'The shipping news', *Sydney Morning Herald*, 20 November, p 39.

Reed, W (14/4/03) 'Conspiracy of silence has turned us into a soft target for turncoats', *Sydney Morning Herald*, 14 April, p 15.

Rehn, A (28/9/02) 'Force will be with Central Coast as officer numbers boosted', *Daily Telegraph*, 28 September, p 4

Reston, N (24–25/9/02) 'Wrong race card', *Sydney Morning Herald*, 24–25 August, p 21.

Richards, S & Saleh, L (1/8/03) 'The Hills are alive', *Daily Telegraph*, 1 August, p 25.

Riley, M (10–11/11/01), 'Fears over racial hue of FBI mosaic', *Sydney Morning Herald*, 10–11 November, p 18.

Riley, M (23–24/11/02) 'PM rejects chador ban after backlash', *Sydney Morning Herald*, 23–24 November, p 10.

Riley, M & Burke, K (22/11/02) 'PM's veiled comments on how Muslim Woman dress', *Sydney Morning Herald*, 22 November, p 1.

Roberts, G & L. Glendinning, L (2001) 'Muslims try to quell anger after mosque destroyed', *Sydney Morning Herald*, 24 September 24. p 9.

Roberts, J et al. (2003) *Penal Populism and Public Opinion*, Oxford University Press, Oxford.

Robins, B (21–22/12/02) 'Global economy optimism offset by worry about war', *Sydney Morning Herald*, 21–22 December, p 4.

Robins, R & Post, J (1997) *Political Paranoia*, Yale University Press, New Haven.

Rowlands, L & Ogg, M (30/10/98) '24 arrests as police swoop to reclaim "their patch"', *Daily Telegraph*, 30 October, p 9.

Said, E (1991) *Orientalism*, Penguin, London.

Saleh, L & Morris, R (31/7/03) 'Protest without a prayer', *Daily Telegraph*, 31 July, p 11.

Sanders, J (2000) 'Which public, whose space?', paper presented at the Community Legal Centres Conference, *Searching for Justice*, University of Technology, Sydney, 28 June.

Sauiny, S (21–22/12/02) 'After 13 years jailed five cleared of park rape', *Sydney Morning Herald*, 21–22 December, p 13.

Saunders, M (2002) 'Bashir made many visits to Australia, *Australian*, 16 October, p 7.

Saxby, M (12/10/02) 'Cultures collide in prayer', letter to the editor, *Daily Telegraph*, 12 October , p 22.

SBS Radio (1998), Arabic program, radio program, n.d.

Schwartz, L (3/11/02) 'Muslim damn fanatics', *Age*, 3 November, <http://www.theage.com.au/articles/2002/11/02/1036027087623.html>.

Scraton, P (2002) 'Images of terror', paper presented at the University of Western Sydney, Hawkesbury campus, 11 November.

Scott, L (31/10/01) 'Hanson unfazed by turnouts', *Sydney Morning Herald*, 31 October, p 10.

Seccombe, M (17/2/01)'Fractured Nation', *Sydney Morning Herald*, 17 February, pp 25, 30–31.

Senate Select Committee on a Certain Maritime Incident (2002), Hansard, 25–26 March, 4–5, 11–12, 16, 17, 18 April, 1, 2 May, <http://www.aph.gov/au/senate/committee/s-maritInc.htm>.

7.30 Report (13/9/01) television program, ABCTV, 13 September.

7:30 Report (15/7/02) 'Ethnicity linked to brutal gang rapes', television program, ABCTV, 15 July, <http://www.abc.net.au/7.30/s607757.htm>.

Sheehan, P (12/5/01) 'Pitch battles', *Sydney Morning Herald*, 12 May.

Sheehan, P (29/8/01) 'Tolerant, multicultural Sydney can face this difficult truth', *Sydney Morning Herald*, 29 August, p 20.

Sheehan, P (7–8/12/02) 'The great water crisis', *Sydney Morning Herald: Spectrum*, 7–8 December, pp 4–5.

Shepherd, N (17/12/02) 'We are worried about terrorism', *Daily Telegraph*, 17 December, p 12.

Signy, H (9/1/03) 'We're alert for a top day out, but not alarmed', *Sydney Morning Herald*, 9 January, p 1.

Simms, M (2002) 'The media and the 2001 election: Afghans, asylum seekers and anthrax', in Warhurst, J & Simms, M (eds) *2001: The Centenary Election*, University of Queensland Press, St Lucia, pp 93–103.

Skelsey, M (2/3/01) 'Shopping in the Beirut of Bondi', *Daily Telegraph*, 2 March, p 13.

Smith, R (4/9/02) letter to the editor, *Daily Telegraph*, 4 September, p 26.

Sofios, S (22/8/01) 'Discipline lacking', *Daily Telegraph*, 22 August, p 4.

Sofios, S & Skelsey, M (18/2/03) 'Crime and fear still rule our streets', *Daily Telegraph*, 18 February, p 10.

Sparks, R (1992) *Television and the Drama of Crime*, Open University Press, Buckingham.

Sparks, R (2000) 'Perspective on Risk and Penal Politics' in Hope, T & Sparks, R (eds) *Crime, Risk and Insecurity*, Routledge, London, pp 129–45.

Staff reporters (21/8/01) 'Lebanese culture not to blame, Islamic chief: Attacks "reflect Aussie society"', *Daily Telegraph*, 21 August, p 5.

Stani, N (27/1/00) 'How the Media Treats Ethnic Diversity', *Media Report*, radio program, ABC Radio National, 27 January, <http://www.abc.net.au/rn/talks/8.30/mediarpt/stories/s97348.htm>.

Stanko, E (2000) 'Victims R Us' in Hope, T & Sparks, R (eds) *Crime, Risk and Insecurity*, Routledge, London pp 13–30.

Stenson, K (2000) 'Some Day Our Prince Will Come' in Hope, T & Sparks, R (eds) *Crime, Risk and Insecurity*, Routledge, London, pp 215–237.

Stevenson, A (13–14/7/02) 'Open eyes to ethnic crime: DPP', *Sydney Morning Herald*, 13–14 July p 7.

Stephens, T (7–8/8/02) 'A standard of excellence', *Sydney Morning Herald*, 7–8 August p 47.

Stevenson, A (7/11/98) 'Cultural crossfire', *Daily Telegraph*, 7 November pp 32–33.

Stratton, J (1998) *Race Daze*, Pluto Press, Annandale, Sydney.

Sunday Telegraph (26/8/01) 'Our community demands justice', editorial, 26 August, p 87.

Sunday Telegraph (16/9/01) 'Muslim backlash', 16 September, p 9.

Sunday Telegraph (25/11/01) 'Prince's gesture', 25 November, p 89.

Sun-Herald (29/6/01) '70 girls attacked by rape gangs', 29 July, p 1.

Sun-Herald (30/9/01) 'Sydney raid: Suburban home searched as ASIO and police hunt Bin Laden connections', 30 September, p 1.

Sun-Herald (14/7/02) 'Our shame', 14 July, p 1.

Sun-Herald (11/8/02) 'Carr meets gang rape victim, then rails at race claim', 11 August, p 7.

Sun-Herald (29/12/02) 'TERROR THREAT GRIPS A NATION', 29 December p 1.

Sutton, C (25/2/01) 'Boys in the hood', *Sun-Herald*, 25 February, pp 10–11.

Sydney Morning Herald (2/11/98) 'Scene is from Northern Ireland, says shocked Ryan', 2 November, p 5.

Sydney Morning Herald (10/2/01) 'Bullies and cowards', editorial, 10 February, p 40.

Sydney Morning Herald (24/2/01) 'Trinity charge reduced', 24 February, p 2.

Sydney Morning Herald (17/8/01) 'Authorities brace for more arrivals as ailing asylum seekers end horror voyage', 17 August, p 3.

Sydney Morning Herald (21/11/01) 'Carr unveils new cabinet with Costa in police job', 21 November.

Sydney Morning Herald (24–25/8/02) letters to the editor, 24–25 August, p 36.

Sydney Morning Herald (17/10/02) 'Tragedy brings out good and bad', editorial, 17 October, p 16.

Sydney Morning Herald (1/11/02) 'ASIO raids a test of purpose', editorial, 1 November, p 10.

Sydney Morning Herald (11/11/02) 'Deadly slide to assassination', editorial, 11 November, p 14.

Sydney Morning Herald (15/11/02) 'Obscene picture destroys last trace of good relations', letters to the editor, 15 November, p 14.

Sydney Morning Herald (28/11/02) 'Other threats to freedom', editorial, 28 November, p 12.

Sydney Morning Herald (14–15/12/02) 'Bali questions unanswered', editorial, 14–15 December, p 32.

Sydney Morning Herald (27/12/02) 'Australia's role in a war about oil', editorial, 27 December, p 12.

Sydney Morning Herald (5–6/7/03) 'The two faces of Sydney', editorial, 5–6 July, p 32.

Sygall, D (6/10/02) 'Middle East to middle stump', *Sun-Herald*, 6 October, p 93.

Taylor, Z (23/1/03) 'Ads creating climate of fear', *Daily Telegraph*, 23 January, p 28.

Temple, W & Trute, P (20/10/98) 'Across the divide', *Daily Telegraph*, 20 October, p 5.

Temple, W (11/8/01) 'Gang admits to sex attack at knifepoint', *Daily Telegraph*, 11 August, p 3.

Time (28/10/00) 'Terror's new wave', 28 October, pp 44–45.

Time (29/10/01) 'Search and Destroy', 29 October, pp 30–31.

Today (18/11/02) television program, Channel Nine, 18 November.

Torch (27/7/02) 'One Nation call for ban', 27 July.

Totaro, P (27/1/03) 'Time to end rampant "penal populism", MPs warned', *Sydney Morning Herald*, 27 January, p 1.

Totaro, P (16/8/02) 'Carr, Brogden welcome sentence', *Sydney Morning Herald*, 16 August, p 3.

Totaro, P. (9/9/02) 'Luring Carr to a strange lapse in form', *Sydney Morning Herald*, 9 September, p 11.

Totaro, P (27/1/03) 'Scaring up the votes', *Sydney Morning Herald*, 27 January, p 15.

Totaro, P & Nicholls, S (30/11/02) 'The big squeeze', *Sydney Morning Herald*, 30 November, pp 25, 34–5.

Toy, N & Knowles, L (24/8/01) 'Victim tells how rapists taunted her: "You deserve it because you're an Australian"', *Daily Telegraph*, 24 August, pp 1–4, 5.

Trad, K (2001) *The ASIO raids on Muslims: Statements on behalf of victims*, unpublished, Lebanese Muslim Association, Sydney.

Tremain, J (16/8/01) 'Ethnic outrage at rapes', *Bankstown Express*, 16 August, p 1.

Tsavdaridi, N (18/7/02) 'Muslims want to be understood, leaders defend their faith', *Daily Telegraph*, 18 July, p 2.

Tulloch, J (1999) 'Fear of Crime and the Media' in Lupton, D (ed) *Risk and Sociocultural Theory*, Cambridge University Press, Cambridge, pp 34–58.

Tulloch, J et al. (1998a) *Fear of Crime Volume 1: Audit of the Literature and Community Programs*, National Campaign Against Violence and Crime Unit, Attorney-General's Department, Barton, ACT.

Tulloch, J et al (1998b) *Fear of Crime Volume 2: The Fieldwork Research*, National Campaign Against Violence and Crime Unit, Attorney-General's Department, Barton, ACT.

Turner, G (2002) 'After Hybridity: Muslim Australians and the imagined community', paper presented at *Ute Culture*, the Cultural Studies Association of Australia annual conference, University of Melbourne, December 5–7.

Usman Lewis, I (17/11/02) 'Beware Whose Face You Slap, It May Be Yours', letter to the editor, *Sydney Morning Herald*, 17 November, p 16.

van Dijk, T (1991) *Racism and the Press*, Routledge, London.

Vass, N (26/8/01) 'True Justice: Lifetime in prison for gang rapists', *Sunday Telegraph*, 26 August, pp 1–2.

Videnieks, M & Leech, G (25–26/8/01) 'Rape terms not lenient: judiciary', *Weekend Australian*, 25–26 August, p 4.

Wainwright, R (7/8/01) 'We import gangsters, says Premier', *Sydney Morning Herald*, 7 August, p 2.

Wainwright, R (31/8/01) '"Lenient" sentences lead Carr to issue manual for judges', *Sydney Morning Herald*, 31 August, p 9.

Wainwright, R (18/10/02) 'Carr warns against attacks on Muslims', *Sydney Morning Herald*, 18 October, p 3.

Wainwright, R (26/11/02) 'Carr's crush cure: cut immigration by a third', *Sydney Morning Herald*, 26 November, p 4.

Wainwright, R (23–24/8/03a) 'Police chief out to collar the fear factor', *Sydney Morning Herald*, 23–24 August, p 3.

Wainwright, R (23–24/8/03b) 'Fear and the ripple effect', *Sydney Morning Herald*, 23–24 August, p 29.

Walker, F (11/2/01) 'Trinity Victim: "We were all bullied"', *Sun-Herald*, 11 February, p 6.

Walker, F (8/4/01) 'Revealed: our new gangland', *Sun-Herald*, 8 April, pp 1, 6–7.

Walker, F (26/8/01a) 'Don't harm Muslim women', *Sun-Herald*, 26 August, p 10.

Walker, F (26/8/01b) 'Furious Carr rushes new laws to raise maximum penalty', *Sun-Herald*, 26 August, p 10.

Walker, F (26/8/01c) 'Angry young men vow to protect all', *Sun-Herald*, 26 August, p 11.

Walker, V (18/6/03) 'ASIO granted "power to kidnap"', *Australian*, 18 June, p 2.

Walsh, K-A (20/9/94) 'Ethnic gangs easy targets', *Bulletin*, 20 September, p 26.

Warren, B (12/9/01) 'I'm sorry dear — I told them it was okay to stay', *Daily Telegraph*, 12 September, p 33.

Warren, B (22/8/01) 'Danger: Cultural Minefield', *Daily Telegraph*, 22 August, p 33.

Warren, B (16/8/01) 'Complaints', *Daily Telegraph*, 16 August, p 23.

Warren, B (28/10/02) 'Warren's View' cartoon, *Daily Telegraph*, 28 October, p 14.

Watson, R (30/9/01) 'ASIO raids home', *Sunday Telegraph*, 30 September, p 15.

Weatherburn, D (2001) *Media Release: the facts on sexual assault in Bankstown*, 22 August, <http://www.lawlink.nsw.gov.au/boscar1.nsf/pages/media220801_2>.

Weatherburn, D (2002) 'Does Australia have a law and order problem?', public lecture, University of New South Wales, 21 May.

Weber, L (2002) 'The Detention of Asylum Seekers: 20 Reasons Why Criminologists Should Care', *Current Issues in Criminal Justice*, vol 14, no 1, pp 9–30.

Weekend Australian (7–8/12/02) 'DNA test may set park rape gang free', 7–8 December.

West, A (18/11/01) 'Meet Mr Westie, the man who put Howard in power', *Sun-Herald*, 18 November.

West, A & Walker, F (29/12/02) 'Paranoia in the lucky country', *Sun-Herald*, 29 December, p 4.

Westwood, S (24/11/00) 'Mum gunned down: Woman shot dead in front of son', *Daily Telegraph*, 24 November, p 3.

Whaite, J (24/8/01) 'Women take second place', letter to the editor, *Daily Telegraph*, 24 August, p 28.

White, R (1996) 'Racism, Policing and Ethnic Youth Gangs', *Current Issues in Criminal Justice*, vol 7, no 3, pp 302–313.

White, R (1990) *No Space of their Own: Young people and social control in Australia*, Cambridge, Cambridge University Press.

White, R (1998) *Public Spaces for Young People*, Commonwealth Attorney-General's Department, Canberra.

White, R & Perrone, S (2001) 'Racism, Ethnicity and Hate Crime', *Communal/Plural*, vol 9, no 2, pp 161–181.

Wilkinson, I (2001) *Anxiety in a Risk Society*, Routledge, London.

Wilkinson, M (21/11/01) 'Constable Costa clears the air with the gang of three', *Sydney Morning Herald*, 21 November.

Wilkinson, M (24/11/01) 'On the Beat', *Sydney Morning Herald*, 24 November, p 25.

Wilkinson, M (7/2/02) 'Yes, but whose thin blue line is it anyway?', *Sydney Morning Herald*, 7 February, p 4.

Wilkinson, M (16–17/2/02) 'Tampering with the evidence', *Sydney Morning Herald*, 16–17 February, pp 23, 28.

Williams, V (2002) 'Mosque opens doors to honour victims', *Herald Sun*, 21 October, p 8, <http://www.heraldsun.news.com.au/printage/0,5481,5326>.

Williams, M & Moore, M (1–2/9/01) 'Ethnic time-bomb is a slow-burning fuse', *Sydney Morning Herald*, 1–2 September, pp 14–15.

Wilson, B (28/3/03) 'EVIL PROOF', *Daily Telegraph*, 28 March, p 1.

Wilson, D (19/8/02) 'Rapist got what he deserves', *Daily Telegraph*, letter to the editor, 19 August, p 20.

Wockner, C (25/9/01) 'How the allegations were watered down: Clinical exercise in plea bargaining', *Daily Telegraph*, 25 September, p 4.

Wockner, C (9/8/01) 'Gang rapes a form of torture: Judge', *Daily Telegraph*, 9 August, p 2.

Wockner, C (25/8/01) 'How the allegations were watered down', *Daily Telegraph*, 25 August, pp 4–5.

Wockner, C (14/3/02) 'Gang rape sentences are doubled', *Daily Telegraph*, 14 March, p 3.

Wockner, C (31/5/02) 'How a woman's evidence became her only weapon', *Daily Telegraph*, 31 May, p 6.

Wockner, C (12/7/02) 'MAGNIFICENT SEVEN', *Daily Telegraph*, 12 July, p 3.

Wockner, C (6/8/03) 'EVIL STRIKES AGAIN', *Daily Telegraph*, 6 August, p 1.

Wood, M (19/8/01) 'Gangs steal kids' future', *Sun-Herald*, 19 August, p 1.

The World Today (27/8/01) 'NSW Premier proposes tougher rape laws', radio program, ABC Radio, 27 August, transcript accessed at ABC News Online, <http://www/abc.net.au/worldtoday/default.htm>.

Wynhausen, E (10/7/94) 'The politics of gang warfare', *Sun-Herald*, 10 July, p 29.

Wynhausen, E (20/1/03) 'Random path of suburban destroyer — CAPITAL CRISIS', *Australian*, 20 January, p 4.

Wynhausen, E & Safe, G (7–8/11/98) 'Gunshots that broke our peace', *Weekend Australian*, 7–8 November, p 13.

Yamine, E (26/9/02) 'Youths rampage through suburb', *Daily Telegraph*, September 26, p 18.

Young, A (1996) *Imagining Crime*, Sage, London.

Youth Action and Policy Association (YAPA) NSW (1997) *No Standing: Young People and Community Space Project Research Report*, YAPA, Sydney.

Zackman, J (22/1/03) 'Bush gives King a salute but not black rights', *Daily Telegraph*, 22 January, p 40.

Zamir, M (1985) *The Formation of Modern Lebanon*, Routledge, London.

Zedner, L (2000) 'The Pursuit of Security' in Hope, T & Sparks, R (eds) *Crime, Risk and Insecurity*, Routledge, London, pp 200–214.

Index

This is an index to journalists and other authors quoted in the text, as well as to topics that are discussed. Newspapers are indexed by name only for editorials and similar content.

Index

Islam, *see also* Muslims
aggression condemned by 200–202
crime linked to 256
in construction of 'Arab other' 33
inhumanity identified with 42–44
Oldfield on 124
prayer centre application 4, 163–164, 222–223, 229–230, 263–264
terrorists identified with 28–32, 206
Islamic Council of NSW 119
Islamic Council of Victoria (ICV) 194, 200–201
Islamic Egyptian Society (IES) 200–201, 205
Islamic Youth Movment (Lakemba) 31, 60, 209

Jackman, C 24, 142
Jackson, S 65, 93
Jacobsen, G 20, 59, 70, 131–132, 155
Jakubowicz, A 127, 202, 262
Jefferson, T 214
Jemaah Islamiah (JI) 30–31, 61, 71, 172–177, 241
jihad declared on Australia 167–171
Johnson, S 143
Johnston, D 28, 58
Jones, A
Howard on children overboard 27

Mitre on Lebanese parenting 93
on gang rapes 119–120, 122, 124
on Muslim sports facilities 156
Jopson, D 66, 160, 161, 249
journalism, *see* media
judges 233, *see also* criminal justice system; sentencing
'inviting terrorists' into Australia 71
leniency of 125, 129–132, 134, 139–140, 185–189
reflect public opinion 131

Kalantzis, M 82
Kamper, A 55, 211
Karam, D 63
Karouche, H 137
Karvelas, P 31, 158, 171, 173, 235, 242
Kattan, R 192
Kebabs, Kids, Cops and Crime, *see* Collins, J
Keegan, D 47
Kelly, J 234
Kennedy, L 16, 56, 59, 68, 72, 137, 155, 187, 246
Kennedy, M 115
Kent, P 187, 191
Kerin, J 221, 233
Kerr, J 16, 240
Kidman, J 17, 169, 170
on gang rapes 18–19, 58, 118
Kitney, G 27, 166
Klein, N 252
Knowles, L 16, 39–40, 51, 130,

zero nett migration policy
165–167
ontological security 244–245,
248, 250, 260
'Orientalism' 34–35, 40, 150,
250
O'Rourke, C 5, 223
O'Shane, P 144
the 'Other' 34–36, 224, 237, *see
also* 'Arab other'
construction of 179–180
fear and blaming 223–224, 244,
248–250
'other of the body' vii–viii, ix–
x
'other of the will' vii, ix–x
Overington, C 138
Owens, W 117, 126

pack rapes, *see* gang rapes
Palser, J 262
panic culture, *see* moral panics
paranoid nationalism 78, 214,
242–250, 252, 254
parenting 186–188, 236–237
Parramatta 227
Partnership Plan to Prevent
Violence and Crime Among
Arabic Speaking Young People
192, 207
Payton, I 149, 200
Pearson, G 110
Pemberton, A 150
'penal populism' 125, 250–254
Penberthy, D 37–38, 230, 233
Penrith City Star 122
Penshurst Mosque, *see* Chami,
Sheikh K
people smuggling 23–25, 27
Perrone, S 127

Peterson, A 135, 253
Phillips, R 60, 162
Piccoli, A 58
Pickering, S 47
police 67–69, 72–73, 90–91,
113, *see also* Australian
Federal Police
attitudes to 218
expansion of powers 253–254
failure of State institutions
231–232
gangs and 133–134
images 57, 73
survey 217
war metaphors 56–57, 79
Police Association (NSW) 130
Police Powers (Vehicles) Act 86
police state 252
'political correctness' 20, 154,
233, 265
political necrophilia viii–ix
political paranoia, *see* paranoid
nationalism
politicians 69–71, 185-186,
232–233, 247
dog-whistle politics 153–178
on racial aspects of gang rapes
124, 132
populism 71, 74–75, 111
politics of civility 265
politics of culture 89, 102–103
politics of fear 213, 238
Post, J 243
Powell, S 171–172
Poynting, S 57, 63, 79, 90–91,
94, 96, 109, 111, 114, 126,
133, 155, 158, 161, 232
Hage on xi
prayer at work, sacking for 157–
158